LOVE, SEX, and 4-H

MADE IN MICHIGAN WRITERS SERIES

General Editors

Michael Delp, *Interlochen Center for the Arts*
M. L. Liebler, *Wayne State University*

Advisory Editors

Melba Joyce Boyd
Wayne State University

Stuart Dybek
Western Michigan University

Kathleen Glynn

Jerry Herron
Wayne State University

Laura Kasischke
University of Michigan

Thomas Lynch

Frank Rashid
Marygrove College

Doug Stanton

Keith Taylor
University of Michigan

A complete listing of the books in this series can be found
online at wsupress.wayne.edu

LOVE

SEX

AND

4-H

a memoir by

ANNE-MARIE OOMEN

Wayne State University Press

Detroit

19 18 17 16 15   5 4 3 2 1

ISBN 978–0-8143-4078-3 (paperback)
ISBN 978–0-8143-4079-0 (e-book)

Library of Congress Control Number: 2014951469

Publication of this book was made possible by a generous gift from
The Meijer Foundation. Additional support provided by Michigan Council for Arts
and Cultural Affairs and National Endowment for the Arts.

Designed and typeset by Bryce Schimanski
Composed in Chapparral Pro

Needle without thread.
Point without purpose.

Thread without needle.
Back with no bone.

What is more unlike
the one that pierces
than the one that binds?

From *After That*, "Fastenings" by Kathleen Aguero

To all of my 4-H leaders and, most particularly,
my mother, Ruth Jean Oomen

CONTENTS

AUTHOR'S NOTE

Memory is a slippery creature. The least thing happens, and it shifts. You and I may experience the same thing, but we will remember differently, and in the art of telling, memory shifts yet again. And then there's all that stuff about the brain making copies of a memory, and none of the copies are exactly alike. So let's just agree that memory is kind of a mess and different from history or facts, no matter how much they overlap. These are my memories, not a history, and they have been shaped for story. And yet, the book is as true to the real things as I can make it. Because of that, resemblances to actual people may be unavoidable, and so, except for my immediate family, I have changed names to avoid—as much as possible—offense, and the order of events, particularly of the 4-H projects, may have been reshuffled for sense—sensible order being another thing memory defies. So, some inaccuracies may exist, but I have tried to be respectful, and though a few people may be softly lit, most of them come off looking pretty good as they are—except my brother Tom, who takes a couple of hits, for which I hope he will forgive me.

4-H Emblem

The emblem of the four-leaf clover with the letter *H* on each leaflet—
symbolizing the four-fold development of head, heart, hands, and health—
is protected under federal law.

4-H Pledge

I pledge my head to clearer thinking,
my heart to greater loyalty,
my hands to larger service and
my health to better living
for my club, my community, my country, and my world.

4-H Motto

To make the best better

4-H Colors

green and white

PROLOGUE: THE SIXTIES

Our family, that straightforward, plainspoken, clean-faced (for the most part) farm family, lived on the eve of great change, the brink of a national upheaval, the cusp of free love. We had no idea. I had no idea. We lived near a small town in the heart of the Great Lakes, a town named Hart—the pun delighted me—near the coast of Lake Michigan, one of the freshwater seas, in a rural Michigan that had yet to feel anything more than the mildest tremors of turmoil. We might have seen the cracks and quaverings in our cities—Detroit, Milwaukee—if we had not been so insular. There was trouble of course, as there always was in small communities, but that trouble was in other families, separate enough from the Oomens' acreage that we felt our safety as the norm.

Yet, even in our isolation, change seeped to the surface: assassinations, demonstrations turned to riots, a war that scarred us for a half-century. The deaths that became legendary—John, Martin, Robert, and even Janis, Jimi, and Jim—are the edges of my experience, the critical periphery. These famed names and their narratives are common parlance even now, but I was not part of it. That said, because the sixties were so big, those years became the all-important and formative backdrop of my small life. And love and sex insisted on coming, too, dressed in psychedelic colors and higher than kites: rainbow and rain.

For a long time—surrounded by the bandanas, tie-dyed T-shirts, and the black-lit signatures of our youth—I held those quiet vows created by home, church, and 4-H. Home represented my loyalty to my parents and our farm, church represented my loyalty to God, but 4-H—head, heart, hands, health for my club, my community, my country—represented an oath to the larger world. These oaths became a ragged and slowly disintegrating armor. They might have lasted a lifetime if not for those other two, love and sex, those vagabonds and vanguards that broke the forces holding me in place. If they couldn't be brazen, as they couldn't be in Hart, they would be subtle in their purpose. Here were sex and love dressed in church clothes, shirt collar just starting to unbutton—utterly seductive, surreptitious as snakes. Except for the fierce familial love of my people, I had no authentic understanding of either of those lunatics, love and sex, as they were expressed in that time. But I had 4-H, and, because of that, I knew this much: I knew how love and sex would be dressed.

PART I: 4-H

Each time the buttonhole opens its mouth
A back door history escapes.

Kathleen Aguero

DECENT CLOTHES, 1959

The first lesson is the dish towel.

Or an apron.

These are beginning sewing lessons in 4-H, regular as a linen rectangle 15 inches by 30 inches, traditional as a yard of gingham check or a plain waistband. If the ties that loop like long roads at the back of the apron seem like extravagance, they are merely a small feminine extravagance. The lessons—a dish towel and an apron—at first appear logical and clear, and no one questions them; no one considers them deeply at all, certainly not a child of eight.

In the fall of 1959, no whiff of feminism or cultural unrest, let alone uprising, has yet driven down those gravel roads to the farms of Oceana County and my mother's domain. In our farmhouse, the simple majority of four females to three males means only that my mother must be more watchful of the dangers to her three daughters. My mother knows this, especially knows my weaknesses, and wants me focused on *good behavior*. She wants me to have practical skills and someday be a fine *wife and mother*. Perhaps most of all, I need to learn to be *efficient and self-sacrificing*. She knows already these qualities are not housed anywhere in my nature. Sometimes she says things to me as though I am someone older. But most of the time, I am either too young for something or too big for my britches. My mother has a sharp eye on me: on the part of me that talks too loudly to strangers or plays alone for hours, has too many imaginary friends, lies in the grass and stares—the part of me that stares at everything, doesn't listen, and doesn't like to work.

She worries about all five of us because she wants us to *have it better*. Sometimes she tells me stories about going to school when she was my age, about other children who picked on her. When I ask why they did that, she goes quiet, then says, "Well, I didn't have decent clothes." And after a long pause, I hear the shadow in the silence.

The shadow is from her childhood. It is her family's barn burning and horses perishing in flames and then all the insurance transferred to the barn and then the house burning without any insurance and them living in a tiny house with no indoor plumbing. It is a brother dying. It is Grandpa drinking a little too much in order to get through it all. It is the shadow of little money. She doesn't want me to know about any of that. She makes a point of telling us how good Grandpa is, how he came all alone from Belgium to our country when he was twelve, the youngest of twelve, and how he went back to the "old country" to fight in the first World War—there were two?—then returned as a hired hand to win the hand of the farmer's daughter, my grandma Julia. It's only later that I learn that Grandpa Joe's mother died giving birth to him, that his oldest sister was his wet nurse, that there was no place, no land for him in the old country. That even here in this country, with hard work and land, they lost almost everything and had to struggle. She never wants that again; her fear is her secret shadow, except it's not secret.

Mom always invites Grandma and Grandpa to Sunday dinner, and my brothers love to play in the smoke of his cigarettes, the wreath of gray encircling him as he tells stories or jokes with my dad. Grandpa and Grandma look happy then, after the ham or chicken dinner, visiting, their faces like apples just going soft, still sweet but tough.

But sometimes the shadow comes into our rooms with my mother, and that is when her voice is sharp as vinegar. The word *shame* is undefined, unknowable, and more powerful than all the other words of that time. The shadow is made of that word. She has to keep us from being touched by it, from joining it. It is up to her alone: even my father, good as he is, cannot fight this. We all have to be better. Better than anyone imagined possible. So other words, hardworking words, fill up the house, but still they connect like threads to that unknown word, the one still in my future but always in her past.

This shadow word is behind all the other words, the good lesson words, though she isn't at all sure I have any talent for good. Still, it may be done. *Might as well get started now.* There's church, of course, but that's about the soul. She is more worried about keeping my hands busy with constructive work. Practical things are good things. *And so we'll just begin with that dish towel*, because maybe I am *a little young for the apron. We'll see how it goes. Maybe the apron next.*

Depends on how fast I catch on.

Eventually, *decent clothes.*

I look at our hand-me-downs, our church-box sweaters, and wonder how that will happen. But my mother has a plan: my mother has figured out a way to keep all the shadows at bay. It's called 4-H.

I am thrilled that a 4-H club is starting. On a farm where I am the first born of five, I have learned this already: even though I am not yet nine, I am separated from the others by the fact of being the oldest. I know already there are many kinds of loneliness, and being oldest is mine. But in 4-H, there will be a whole clan near my own age covering up the familiar scent of loneliness, of oldest-ness. There will be a *club*, with other boys and girls but mostly girls, and we will do things together.

And there is more news.

I will be guided by my own mother, another reason I can start learning to sew even though I am so young—so I will always have decent clothes, so I will know how to take care of myself. This is part of her plan, as straight as a line of stitching, as square as the grid of a township, as comforting as an old hymn. No one speaks of how the looping ties of the apron can catch in the wind and fly loose. Now one speaks of the shadows, the silent knowings.

Here are the knowings that come to me from the stories she tells us after supper or while she and Grandma peel the peaches for canning.

She was not always our mother.

What? Because we have always all been here, haven't we, in this old farmhouse in Crystal Valley Township? Certainly my brothers, Tommy and Ricky, and I have been here. I can remember a time when there weren't little sisters, Marijo and Patti, but that doesn't really mean we weren't all here in this old farmhouse, does it? They were just someplace else. They are here now. I have thought of this other time but not in the way I am about to learn.

Mom tells us there was a time when she was very young. As young as we are. *When could that have been?* We sit around the scattered peach peelings, shoving the halves, round side up, into the jars. Yes, there was a time when she went to a one-room schoolhouse and washed the boards for the teacher, which meant she was the favorite, but she was lonely because she couldn't walk home with the other kids. I nod; I understand this. She loved school, she tells us pointedly, but before she finished high school, she left her parents' house, left it all suddenly. She does not tell us why, because it's almost time to *put those peaches into the canner.*

Where did you go?

She carries a case of jars to the kitchen.

Chicago. She says this over her shoulder.

Where is Chicago?

She's busy.

Another time: ice cream on a Sunday night. The sweet cream makes her tongue happy, and she talks. She tells us about the train to Chicago: how long it took, how it stopped at every town, how noisy it was. The man who meets her wears a red carnation. She had never seen a red carnation.

She tells us she went to work as a nanny.

She took care of other children. First one family, then another.

Stunning news. We look at each other and giggle but not because we think it's funny.

Were they good? Of course, Tom wants to know.

Well, they were little, but, yes, they were very good.

In a big house.

In a very big house.

Were they farmers?

No, they were bankers.

What on Earth are bankers?

Marijo is pounding on her high chair and making little songs.

Another time we learn how Mom came home. Grandma called her back after Grandpa had a terrible car accident. He was hurt so badly that she left that banker's children and took the train back to the farm to help.

When Grandpa finally got better, she worked in the fruit orchards near Walkerville, saved all her cherry-picking money, and took the test to become a nurse, even though she hadn't finished high school.

We mull this over for a while, licking our spoons. This is the answer to another word that lives in our house, the word *education*. She never wants us to have to *pretend* like she did to take the nursing test. She tells us she passed all the tests, but it was hard, because she didn't have her algebra like the others. She passed and took nursing training in Manistee during the war, the second one. She worked in the hospitals. Sometimes she took care of soldiers who were coming home from the battles. Sometimes she took care of new babies.

Her face is happy.

Another time, late one stormy winter night when school has been called off for the next day and we are eating popcorn, dropping kernels all over the freshly swept floor and playing with the salt, which she asks us not to do, we ask her about the "olden days." She doesn't seem to mind. She tells us that she and Dad knew each other from childhood, that the two families were friends from church. *All those Dutch and Belgian families knew each other from the old country,* she tells us. She's Belgian; he's Dutch. So the families went back and forth, keeping company in the new country.

Here's the best one. The first time Mom and Dad went to the fair together, he asked her to marry him. She said they walked down the midway, and he said, "Well, Toots, let's just get married." And they laughed their heads off. And we do, too, sitting around the table. We don't know what's funnier: that he called her *Toots*—we hoot the word around the table—or that he asked her to marry him when then they were just goofing off.

They were *just kids*.

Dad wanders into the dining room, listening to our giggles. He puts his hand on her shoulder, and she lifts her hand to touch his. I remember he still calls her Toots sometimes.

He went into the army to serve two tours, and she forgot about him.

When I ask about how they got together again, they both get quiet. They smile at each other, but then Dad usually has to go to the barns or fix a machine in the shop. There is always a pause, and then she talks of something else: how they rented our old farmhouse from Grandpa Henry,

Dad's father, who had bought it for the land, so the house was falling apart, and how finally, when they were fed up with renting, they bought it from him. Or how they never borrowed money. Or how everything is made from something else: machines, barns, clothes.

What I figure out is that she keeps secrets. How they got back together is one. It makes me want to know this story above all other stories. I want to know if my parents are like people in the stories I have learned to read or the TV shows I watch: *Walt Disney Presents* or *The Shirley Temple Fairy Tale Hour*. If there was a time when she was not our mother, when she was a nanny and a nurse, was she ever a princess to my father? Did she get wakened with a kiss? Does she ever still?

When I think about it, I don't believe it. My mother is wakened by laundry early in the morning, by my little sister crying in the night with a diaper rash, by the green beans not being picked on time, and by mumps, measles, chicken pox, and croup. Not a kiss. Not love. She doesn't have time. Or not much. She loves us when we are good: when we take our boots off before coming into the house, when we pick up our dirty clothes, when we somehow manage to get through church without crawling under the pews or getting into a tussle with each other. This applies to me particularly—not because I cause trouble but because I am not a good worker. I don't do much that is bad; I just don't do much that is *helpful*. I don't really believe I am good at anything much, but especially not the helpful part. But now, I wonder, is it possible, with this club, with luck, that I will learn to be useful?

Could I learn to make decent clothes?

THE KISS, THE SINGER

At night I hear my parents. The insomnia that will plague me as an adult, that I inherit straight from my mother, from the long line of women for whom the night is not simple, is already beginning to open the darkness for me.

I wake in the upstairs bedroom with the blue-and-pink wallpaper. Even though my sister Marijo sleeps in a crib in that room (baby Patti is downstairs in a bassinet), I am too aware of being alone. I need to pee, so I creep down the open staircase—my hand in the dark holding tight to the beaded railing—cross the living room, and slip into the bathroom.

The bathroom has two doors: the one I enter and another that leads to my parents' room. A large closet, also with two doors, separates the rooms. This closet is a tangle of hangers lumpy with Sunday clothes and woolen sweaters, all scented with old shoes. Usually the closet doors are closed to keep the two rooms and their functions separate—but not always. Sometimes the closet door on the bedroom side gets left open, and sometimes the bathroom door near where I stand by the sink is ajar. I stand in the silence that is not silence, and I can hear them.

Kissing.

It is a soft sound, a small almost-like-eating-taking-in sound, a pucker and bumble, lips and squish, a forwarding, a closing, a pressing, an opening—I know all this because we have been taught to kiss them good-night, and they kiss us good-night. We have seen others kiss, brides and couples in paintings, and, just lately, we have seen kissing at movies—though not yet on TV, which is new for us.

11

But here is something else. The quick is sometimes not—sometimes longer before and after the quickness, a lengthening of quiet. Then the quick sound again, followed by a wait. Do kisses get long? Just one of my questions. This kissing holds questions so hard I cannot shape them, though I am already noted by my teachers as the "most questioning-est girl." I stand in the dark near the door, listening to them. What is this thing that has night sky in it but also a bending of shadow, a sparkling wet, a flash of yellow? What is this secret of stars and bright spit they are keeping in each other's arms?

No words for this, no answer.

Sometimes they are asleep, and I hear my dad snoring and my mother's breathy sighs, and when I pee or flush the toilet, she will wake and call hoarsely, "Anne? What's wrong?" This is always her first question, straight from her innate worry. Something will always go wrong; it is to be expected. This, too, is part of the shadow. And because I already know she will not believe the word *nothing*, I say, "I'm okay." Then we will both be awake for a while in those rooms that are separated by the boxy closet.

But if I catch them—even then it has the cast of *catching*; even then it is like something I should not know even though I want to—if I come into the bathroom and hear the kissing sounds, if I stand in the dark and imagine their room, a sacred room, one we are invited into or may enter, frightened in the night, but which we do not have the run of as we do the house, if I imagine the bed, the square mirror over the scratched blonde dresser, their bodies under the old quilts, the mound and roundness, the hilliness of them, I feel the kissing as a dazzling curiosity so large that it makes me want to cry. Or run away from them. Or toward them. To know. This is the essence: I want to know, and I know I cannot.

What does it mean that they do this in the night? They are my father and mother. Why do they kiss? They are not princess and prince as in the fairy tales. They are married. They are who they are, busy and strong and doing the work and talking and fighting and making food and plowing fields and fixing the tractor and trimming the spirea and picking beans in the garden, always picking some growing thing—tomatoes or crabapples or cucumbers—and always, always looking at the weather and rarely, except at suppertime when we practice listening to each other, looking at each other, so why do they kiss like this, in the cool of the night, in the rounded shadows?

It is the world I cannot enter.

But listen: here is another small knowing. Past the puzzles and shadows, she does love me. I know this because if I stand in the bathroom and she hears me and she asks, *What's wrong*, and I tell her I am sick, she will rise from the warm shadows and come through the closet into the light. She will touch my forehead, and if it is indeed hot, she will draw a glass of cold water and sit on the chair next to the diaper bucket and hold me. So if I cannot know this thing of the dark, I can still call her into the light. But there's the question: in that place of light, can I learn the things she believes I need to know? Can I learn, in order that she will keep loving me, to sew?

Just as there was never a time before the farm, there was never a time before the sewing machine. It has lived here in our farmhouse since time began. But it is mysterious; it appears and disappears. At my mother's will, it lives for days in our presence, then suddenly is gone, turned in on itself, a different thing disguised as a piece of furniture.

On what Sunday of what year do I understand that if the grandmas and grandpas are coming to dinner, there is a bustle of transformation? All the pincushions are swept into sewing baskets, buttons drop into tin boxes, and spools slip onto a narrow tray of spindles hung like a secret inside the case of the machine. Then the machine that now looks like a pert dog is tucked inside its box, and the long foldout top is lifted and folded over to make a small table, a piece of furniture with a furniture's silence. My mother covers it with a starched doily, and if it is spring before the fields are too demanding for the indulgence of flowers, she sets on this crocheted field a green vase filled with mock orange blossoms or peonies or lilacs.

Then she puts on her apron, tying it behind her back as she hurries to the kitchen.

The sewing machine sits obediently silent, careful of its manners, impeccably dressed in its prim lace until the wheat pattern dishes are cleared and the talk crumbles into small gossip and the great aunts and uncles, lost cousins from Detroit, friends from Muskegon and beyond rouse from their chairs and wander, hugging and good-bye-ing, through the doors to the wide yard and climb into their old Buicks and drive the dusty roads to faraway places. All through this, the sewing machine sits to the side of that dining room, light from the porch door with the cracked, frosted window falling quietly on its lilacs. It sits longer still, there on the cool side of the room, away from the busy gestures of the kitchen in its contained squareness, a sentry awaiting a great return.

It is my mother who returns, removing her dirty apron as she does.

There are some hours, not many, when she could be working on the dirty floors, unpicked beans, unhoed cucumbers, but she comes here, stands in the cool light, slips off the lace doily, lays it aside. She lifts the lid that houses the machine, swings open the door to reveal again the spools on silver spindles, scissors, a tape measure. Her rough hands open like book covers the wooden lids that hide the inner creature. She reaches into the box, lifting the sewing machine as you might lift a fawn—it is about that size—by its torso, then drops the lid into place so that as she lowers the machine, it rests on its own tabletop, now alert and waiting.

Its name is Singer.

Its metal is brushed brown, its single ear is a wheel powering a small but mighty motor, and its levers finger the tension of threads. A silvery needle pierces a foot with two toes then slips into the secret place beneath the foot, another tiny compartment, a womb. She slides the silver plate aside, and there the spiraling thing called a bobbin gives up its single thread to the needle. The slim metallic bone reaches down and catches the bobbin thread, and the two threads come together in a small violence called a stitch. And all those stitches hold together pieces of color or one fabric to another or even a thing to itself.

She looks at it like she is hungry. I stay near her now.

She sits. She sets the spool of flashing thread to match the dotted swiss. She pushes the wheel to make it turn, because—she speaks to me now—*you know, Anne, it sticks a little*; the *machine is old* and must *be coaxed to start*. She slips the fabric under the foot, and the foot tongues the taffeta; the needle lifts and lowers, pierces the flannel. The motor hums its Singer song over the banging cupboards of that house, and in that light that is hers alone, her face clears, her lips open a little, and her eyes are intent, like the paintings at church, on the tumble and fold of fabric, on the soft print of cotton remnant. Here her long fingers feel the hum of good, of one thing moving smoothly under her fingertips, one thing that she can trust.

Is this what I am to know, to learn, because I cannot know the yellow kissing?

Is this the secret to warding off the shadow?

I don't ask what she is making there at the machine, what she is shaping from scraps and nothing. I don't question why she is not scolding because I have not done the dishes or asking that the floor be swept or talking to my father about fixing the screen door that will never be fixed or phoning the ladies of the Altar Society about the funeral lunch they must prepare. I don't wonder why she is here when the soup needs to be stirred. She attends the machine as closely as she does her babies.

I watch.

She goes there in the middle of the day.

She sets the spool again, lowers the foot, spins the wheel.

She does not like to be called away. If we come into that dining room crying about some slight or stumble, she will sigh and ask, *What's wrong now?* If the hurt is demanding enough, she lifts us into her arms, but while her arms take us in and our heads may tuck under her chin, her face looks back to the needle and its kin, back to the whirling ear and twirling bobbin with such longing that I can feel it in my skin—we all can—and we know something is being done that, for the moment, is more important than we are.

I stand in the dining room in that worn-out farmhouse and watch. I see. With this machine, she fights the shadow. With this machine, love grows.

She goes there at night, turns on the low light.

Sitting there, she sometimes makes a tiny sound, like the yellow star I hear them make late in the bedroom.

Does her face look like this just before a kiss?

THE CLUB, 1959

The first 4-H meeting is held at St. Joseph's Hall, our parish church hall. The high fluorescents pour gray light over a noisy bunch of kids sitting on folding chairs. I sit in the front row, a bit away from my cousins so my mother can *keep an eye on me*, so I am still lonely.

The Oceana County extension agent who is in charge of all the clubs stands in front and tells us about the projects. This is the big thing. We are to do projects, which will be judged, and if they are good, we can win a blue ribbon. We can win a prize. This floors me. Prizes. We are not the kind of people who win prizes. But the agent insists there are prizes for raising animals: cows and pigs and chickens, and even sheep, which my father refuses because they are too much trouble. And I can't figure out how kids can win prizes for doing something they already do; we already raise these animals. But then she explains that those kids who do the livestock project will *show their animals* at the county fair. The animals must be very clean, without any manure, and must take a lead and obey basic commands. I think to myself that the bull my dad is actually afraid of takes commands from no one.

I'm not much of an animal person, but there are other projects—the sewing projects, the jam and jelly projects, the home decor projects—and I am interested in these projects because though I like our cows, I am a little afraid of them. And these are the projects my mother wants me to do.

After the projects are completed, they *are judged*. I think of the Bible story of the last judgment, and I feel the shadow in the room. But when I look at my mother, she is smiling. She is not worried about this judging.

My mother stands in the too-warm gathering room with the ever-cool linoleum floor in front of the crooked rows of chairs, my mother with her auburn-and-gray hair coiled in a smooth roll around her face. Now the agent lady is introducing my mother to the room of people. The kids don't notice her much—this is boring and they squirm in their chairs—but the other leaders nod, and my mother nods back, and the woman who is the agent talks to my mother in a way that I have not seen before, not like neighbors or relatives, but more like she might be someone I do not know. I look at the other mothers like my mother who are also being introduced. They are leaders. So, why is my mother . . . oh, my mother is a leader. This is a whole different kind of judgment.

My mother as a leader will keep me separate. My mother as leader means that I will be the leader's daughter. No one will talk to me. I will be expected to do things perfectly. Suddenly I don't want anything to do with the 4-H club. I want my mother to go home where she will be impatient and fast-moving through the house and will get supper on the table and drink her coffee all day long, leaving cups half empty in every room where she works. I kick the metal braces on the chair. I untie and tie my shoes. I do not want her to be a leader and certainly not my leader.

What brings me back is the pledge. It sounds like a poem:

> I pledge my head to clearer thinking,
> my heart to greater loyalty,
> my hands to larger service,
> and my health to better living,
> for my club, my community, my country.

I like the sounds of the 4-H pledge better than the pledge of allegiance that we say for our country. It is easier because of the *H*'s, and how they look on the clover helps me keep track—one *H* in each petal. Together we practice saying it aloud. We all pledge *head, heart, hands, health*, and there is all that breathiness in the room, though one boy says *hell* instead of *health*. Everyone gasps, but the agent laughs, and then we all laugh. She says that the *H*'s all stand for good things: *see how each* H *fits into the four-leaf clover—one* H *for each lucky leaf*. As I mouth them into the light, I wonder, What is loyalty? What is clearer thinking? I get a dirty look from my mother when I ask what *larger service* is.

The agent tells us that the *clearer, greater, larger, better* things lead to good fortune, good lives, *good luck*. Then I want to join the club again, because luck is something I know everyone wants more of, and my dad will only nail the old horseshoes on the barn walls with the open end up because if you nail it with the curved end up, all the luck runs out. So in the clover, 4-H is not separate after all, joined as the *H*'s are joined by the breath of their sound, by the stem at the center. They are not alone. I forgive my mother for being a leader.

My dish towel. The first thing I will make.

What is about to happen is the imposition of order, though I don't know it.

Until then, my world has been multiple, manifold as stars. The farm and life around it consist of one point of unconnected light after another: kissing, butchering, calves learning to suck, and running the hand through a wisp of candle flame to discover that the skin puckers. It is bean seeds spilled from the hand planter too many at a time, the fever of measles, sunshine on grass, ice cream on Sundays, and cousins born blue. It is learning prayers, being good in church and bad in school, holding new baby chicks or drowned kittens. It is First Communion in the white lace dress and burying Uncle John at Christmastime.

It is listening to kisses.

All these experiences float in my mind, islands of being—day after day more of them—and I swim among them, and I have no idea that there is an Earth beneath that connects everything. And if there is a moment when, in the middle of a dead run, I am struck by the thought that one island, one point is connected to another in these dark seas and bright skies of girlness, I am moving too fast to stop and absorb it.

Then, on a Saturday morning, the change begins. I am about to encounter the universe of the dish towel.

"We'll go to Gambles and get the material." She is staring at her grocery list and *tsk*-ing into her cupboards and banging the refrigerator door shut and rustling the newspaper for coupons and folding laundry in the back room and stirring soup for the men at lunch.

"What's Gambles?"

"You know, the dry goods store." She claps the cupboard door shut.

"Dry goods? What are . . ." and I stop because I have been told that I ask too many questions. I think about goods. Goods are . . . good. It's good to say your prayers, clean your room, love even your brothers. But then it eludes me. Dry goods? Are there wet goods?

But she says, "You know, right next to the dime store, where we get material, remnants from the bolts, patterns for your dresses, thread and . . ."

And I *do* remember the store set back from the street with big hanging lights, though I prefer the dime store next door with its shining glass bins, one filled with coconut macaroons, which I love, though we can only get hard candy because macaroons are too expensive. The dry goods store is less interesting, less in every way, narrower and crowded, but I don't remember with what.

So we will go to Hart to get the groceries, and we will stop at Gambles and buy the fabric to make the dish towel. And all the long miles, following the roads through the fields of the county to Hart, the real town we come to once a week for the things we can't provide ourselves, I think about these words my mother has begun to say to me: patterns, bolts, cloth—it is called material in our house—for my first 4-H project.

Is this the first time, parking the old Nash on the side street, walking briskly because we *haven't got all day*, coming out of the brightness of Main Street and into the store, that I understand abundance? When I pull open the heavy door and the bell tings its sharp call to attention, it is color I see first, so much of it that I am silenced, me of the questions, by the onslaught. And because of that, I am at first blind to the way that color is ordered, the rank and file of these dry goods.

Imagine you walk into print palisades the color of every harvest you have ever known. You follow your mother through columned walls of rainbow checks and cottons of more colors than the largest Crayola box you have ever seen, which contained thirty-six crayons. You stop when she stops to linger over the new synthetics, the pink chiffon in its gauzy layers. Here is every bloom, from daffodil to mum, wound in intensity, spiraled and stacked, lined up and tucked side by side, one after another, with a single yard left free to drift off the bolt, a skirt of sorts, a length you can touch and lift and hold to your face if you don't get caught, because God knows your nose might be running, and then you'd have to buy it because you dirtied it.

There is order here, but you can't see it yet. You don't yet see how the fabrics are separated by type on each table and, within each color, how the palette ranges from light to night. Over time, you will learn that the tables are islands holding various weights of cotton, wool, rayons, fancy silks, chiffons, satins for wedding dresses. You will come to know the where and why of spools of thread, zippers, patterns. The material will be unfolded, measured, squared into yards. The patterns will answer the puzzle of how to make it, whatever it is—folded in tissue, waiting to be opened in order to make something of order and—you almost know this—beauty.

This place is the raw material for all that.

I do not yet feel order doing its quiet work because all I know is abundance and desire. There is so much here, lined up and ready. I want it. I want it all, this material green as bean leaves or the yellow of squash, plum of plum, and—what is that?—that rainbow of striped cherry and chocolate. And here, cool prints of dogs playing and umbrellas floating. And here is the world set in rows, aisles and narrow canyons of spiraling fabric.

I finger fabric after fabric, despite my mother's scolding—*stop touching! You've got grimy hands.* I want to touch it all. I can see it, this dish towel, the first one I will make, but there will be more, many. I know this now because there is enough material here for a million dish towels. And I know that one of these spiraling bolts is to be mine. *Oh, let it be the yellow!* Let it be the one with the suns spinning wildly.

DISH TOWEL, 1960

Not yellow. Plain cream-colored cotton (*off-white*, she says) with tiny lines of green that go both ways, up and down and side to side, to shape one-inch squares so it is easy to know where to cut. Just follow the lines. There is no pattern—just count the squares, one inch to a square. Easy. She says, "This fabric should be easy to cut, easy to sew." I am not sure what I am more frightened of, the cutting or the sewing.

It is not yellow.

Is this the winter my aunt Barbara's baby is born blue, the winter my cousin drowns, another cousin dies, my Grandpa Joe has a stroke? One of the Illinois cousins dies of something called *lookemea*—no, that was summer. It was hot when we drove away from their farm, and my mother said, "It won't be long."

All those deaths happened in such close seasons so that when I think of the dish towel, I think of those deaths, the way they accumulated step by step, like making something.

After my mother teaches me to use the scissors, I practice on scraps, cutting slowly, first a single layer, then two. Even though they are pinned together, they slip. I cut through layers of old sheets to make rags because it doesn't matter if I mess up. I must learn because this is how it will be when I get to use a pattern, the brown tissue. I practice and practice, but the first time I try to follow the lines on the dish towel's fabric, the scissors angle off; the little green strand running through the linen won't stay between the blades. For the next step, Mom takes a ruler, lays it over the green lines, and draws a line with an ink pen over the green line. It stands out. I start cutting again. The blade still wobbles off course. My mother walks over to look, shakes her head. "Don't you understand that you have to hold everything tight? The scissors, the cloth—all of it?"

I cut strip after strip of the plain linen with the green lines, holding the scissors so tight, my hands cramp. What I have left are rows of little empty squares, like the strips that movies are made on, but the movie is of snow.

It is a cold morning when we hear the baby has died. A *blue baby* my mother says when she brings the news into our house, when she comes home from visiting the hospital.

In my head, the color of the baby's skin.

"Blue as the sky?" I ask

"Dirty snow." She pulls off her scarf and coat, drops them in a chair. "A blue baby has a bad heart, so his skin turns dull. He never had enough air."

Marijo hears the word, walks around singing, "Boobay, boobay," until my mother makes her stop. My mother does laundry and doesn't speak for hours.

My uncle Joe comes to the house to ask my dad to help even though the coffin is small. At the graveside, there is no snow, but a cold, fast wind blows. My aunt Barbara stands near the small coffin as the priest says the long prayers. She is wearing a black coat buttoned all the way up, but the buttons stretch taut over her chest, and the wind catches her hair and blows it wild. She looks down and shakes her head over and over. I want her to speak, but she does not. Maybe she can't.

After days of the scissors making their small scolding sound, I am able to cut a rectangular piece of the proper size. I look at it as she steams the edge flat and wish I was done with this dish towel, this first hard lesson. She says, "Now we pin the edges over and stitch them." I fold the edges a quarter inch and pin them perpendicular to the edge, putting the pins where the green lines are. Then we iron it down so it stays in place. The ends of the cloth look like a silver fence line on the edge of a snow-covered field—as if I were looking at it from a long way away.

To stitch it, I am to use, for the first time, the Singer.

The machine is a small god with a finicky heart. My mother knows what appeases it, but I do not. I shove a cushion onto the chair in front of it and sit as I have seen my mother do. Step by step, we come closer to the rituals that will make it love me. Or not. First, it must be fed with thread, top and bobbin, fabric, and sometimes oil. But sometimes blood—the needle is so strong, it can pierce a nail. "Don't stitch yourself to the towel," she warns. "You'll get blood on it." But I wonder how I would get my finger free.

Or is it the winter that Grandpa Joe dies of a stroke only a few years after he stopped drinking and she had finally gotten to know him better? February is the time when our old people die. Maybe it is February when my grandpa Joe has his stroke.

When my mother comes home from the hospital this time, she calls us into her and my father's bedroom. When we are called to their bedroom, we know something is wrong. That room is the one room in the house to which we are forbidden free entry. We gather on the bed, messing up the covers, but she does not scold us. That too is a warning. The branches of the maple tree make crooked shadows on the window. She looks at the shadows as she tells us Grandpa has gone to the hospital, and *it's very bad*. My brothers want to know what's very bad, and she finally says, "He had a stroke."

They grow quiet. Tom asks what we are all wondering: "What's a stroke?"

It takes a long time, but finally she says, "Something in your head starts to bleed, and the blood can't get out so it gets in the way of everything else. Sometimes you can't move or talk."

We take this in. Something in your head starts to bleed.

When we visit him, he makes an odd noise, raises his arms, calls without our names, snow in his voice. My mother leads us out quickly and sends us home with Mable, our neighbor.

The sewing machine sits in front of me, poised. There is so much to learn, I can't bear it. Too many parts, too many steps. It mixes up in my head, and I am scared of it all. I sit at the machine, pointing and saying the names of parts: spool cap, bobbin winder, thread guide. It growls when I touch it.

He dies a week later. With a wild awe, my brother Tom says, "His head bled to death." My mother is so tired, she does not say a word, even to that. She just walks to the next thing.

On a rainy day, Grandpa is buried. The funeral is held at the old church in Elbridge, the one with a cemetery for Indians and a cemetery for everyone else. After the long prayers, everyone follows the coffin down the church aisle and out into the cold air. I try not to cry, but my head feels like it's full of hard bread, so I make little gasps. I keep trying to stop so my head won't bleed. But then, as we follow the coffin down the cement stairs, breaths come that I cannot keep down. Then she is walking next to me, and for the first time in a long time she puts her arm on my shoulder, and I reach around her waist—like I was already grown-up. I think this will help me stop, but as we walk out of the church, I feel her body shake like leaves in the wind. She is half leaning into me, taking deep gulps of air, and we are together in this, and we cannot stop all along the path to the hearse where the men slide in the coffin all smooth as ice.

I love crying with her. I don't want her to stop. Ever.

It is raining by the time we get to the cemetery.

When men in old military uniforms shoot guns because he was a soldier in World War I, she steps away from me, as though to say, *We're done with that now.* Where they have cleared the snow, the cemetery is muddy, and her shoes are slick with clay. She stands very straight in the rain. Her shoulders darken with rain, and the hem of her skirt flaps in the wind. She doesn't cry anymore, and the sounds of the gunshots are loud cracks of loneliness. No one has an umbrella.

Finally, I sit at the sewing machine with her next to me. She shows me how to put the spool on the spool pin, how to bring the thread through thread guides and down through the tension regulator. After all these weeks, the words that name the parts are delicious and strong. When we are ready, she raises the foot lifter, places the practice fabric, and I snap down the foot. She places my hands on the wheel, places her hand over mine, and we give it a little push. The motor starts to turn, catches, hums its steady hum. I feel it through my body. I am so scared that it makes me want to pee, so happy that it makes me want to laugh. Then she puts my other hand on the cloth and shows me how to steer the fabric under the foot, but it goes so fast, the needle up and down, that after the first inch or two, I cannot see it. It hurts my eyes, and I sew the line crookedly because I am watching the stitches after they pass under the foot, always looking behind.

During thaw time, my five-year-old cousin Sally drowns. She falls through the ice and drowns in the little pond near their house in Fremont. I take the call from my aunt Janet that night, cheerfully asking how she is and not understanding when she says, "Not so good."

It is the time when there are still humps of snow on the ground, pockets of silvery gray, and of course ice still floats on the lakes but has gone soft. Sally had been too little to know that. She was small and very blonde, too young for me to play with, but we all thought she was beautiful.

After that first call, many calls interrupt the night with their sad and repeated ringing. My mother tells my father in whispers that Uncle Neil, my gentle godfather, was okay until he tried to shave in the morning; that was when Sally usually came to him, to watch him shave. I hear my mother say, "How will we get through?" and then she sees me and *tsks*, asks my father if he wants another coffee.

After the ceremony by the graveside, dozens of people walk away from the long prayers, all turning toward the line of cars in the muddy road. My uncle is ahead of me in his gray suit, but suddenly, like someone pulled a string, he turns back toward the grave. I see him almost stumble, his face twisting. And then, just as suddenly, two men come along beside him, right up close, just come up to him and take him up by the elbows and hold him in place. His face is not his real face, not gentle but torn. The men never speak but bend toward him, and then another steps in front, blocking my view, and they surround him, turn him toward the car. He leans against the fender. The men open the rear door and lead him in as though he were blind. I watch, standing still, feeling what the tear must be. Everything tearing. My mother is suddenly there, tugging my hand.

She whispers, "Don't stare." But when I look at her, her eyes look squishy, tight and small. I take a breath to speak. "Don't," she says.

After that, I never see my mother cry at another funeral—and there are many. And we don't speak much of this thing, this death thing. We go on working.

When I can sew a straight line, I put the edge of the hem under the foot, drop it to clasp the fabric, and watch as inch by inch it grabs the material and stiches down the edge. It must be straight; it cannot stray. I hold tight, pray a little.

When I am done, I snap up the foot, snip off the thread. I lift the towel up and look at its perfectly plain regularity. My mother is near, and I hear her put her coffee cup to the side. She lifts the edge, studies the clean line, sees something useful I have sewn on the machine. I hold the other end, stupid with wonder that I have made this thing. At last she nods. The sadness she holds, a sadness that I will always hold the opposite end of, is for the moment clean and plain as this pattern of squares—empty, silent, but ready for use.

MESS

This is about me making a mess. This is about me making a mess without even trying. This about the mess that I think is my mother being a 4-H group leader. This is about me making a mess, something more than the usual messes.

"Okay, help me get ready." My mother is looking at the sewing machine where all my pieces of practice fabric are scattered, where threads are hanging like cobwebs off random scraps, and the machine is stacked with patchworks.

"Why?" I ask, lifting my head from the machine where I am trying to perfect a straight seam.

"Because the girls are coming. They need the sewing machine."

The girls. This is why. I yank the fabric pieces and stuff them into the top of the sewing basket, gather spools and roll thread into place and slip them on the spool rack with small sharp bangs.

"Make sure you leave out the things they will need." She looks at me.

I think about leaving the scissors in the remnant box. That would fix her.

"All of the things," she says pointedly. How does she know these things?

My mother leads the 4-H club, but she is also a group leader, which means she teaches a few other girls separately. When this happens, the entire family is like a bad clock. Dinner is late, the boys get to run wild, and I have to do homework and watch my little sisters. This time it is the Barnes girls who are coming. The Barneses live on one of the back roads.

My mother says they don't have their own sewing machine, so they come here to sew. The bus drops them off from public school long after my bus drops me off from St. Joseph's. When they come, it means I have to do homework. Or watch my little sisters. Stay out of the way.

The girls are older. My mother is teaching them to make dresses, and I am still learning to make dish towels.

I don't want them here.

But come they do, with their paper sacks of half-done projects. I stand in the living room, my homework tossed on the couch, my sisters' toys scattered at my feet. My mother brings the girls to the table and tells them to take out their projects and sit at the table while she looks at what must be done. When their projects have replaced ours on the table, I sneak a look. I'm pretty sure the older girl has made a skirt with a waistband. I chip paint off the doorframe with a dirty fingernail. One of my sisters is crying. I turn back to the living room and spill the entire collection of Lincoln Logs in a pile on the rug.

That should keep them busy.

I watch my mother moving quickly, firmly, showing the girls how to do things I don't know how to do. I watch them as they listen. The one with the perfect waistband begins to hem. She seems uncertain with the needle and thread. My mother guides her hand. The other girl is working on a fancy apron on which she will cross-stitch a design later at home. My mother helps her cut the ties. She speaks in a voice like milk. My mother is in motion, like she always is, but moving smoothly from the table to the sewing machine and back, gliding almost, slowing to look at each thing and touching it, then moving to the other girl. At one point she pulls the 4-H bulletin out of the desk drawer, checks it, and tells the taller girl, "You keep up like this, and next year, you can make a bodice dress." The girl beams.

A bodice dress. I want to kick something.

I ignore my sister Marijo, who is using a Lincoln Log for a drumstick on a good lampshade.

Suddenly there's a taste in my mouth, sour and strange. It is a messy taste, a taste in many directions, like scattered toys on the floor.

This all goes on for an hour. Finally, they pull on their coats, smile, and thank her. My mother smiles back and touches both of them lightly on a shoulder. She says, "See you next time."

When the door is closed after them she says, "Well, they needed that. They just don't have those chances."

Then she sees the mess.

"What have you done?"

I turn. Is she referring to the logs or the broken lampshade?

"I want to make a bodice dress." My voice is, even to me, whining.

She looks at me. She looks at the floor. I think she is seeing something I am not seeing. She says slowly, "I don't think you're ready."

"Why not?" I expect her to say that I can't sew a straight seam, that I can barely cut a piece of fabric, that I'm sloppy with the tape measure, so how do I expect to make a bodice dress?

But she says, "You don't pay attention."

And she stares at the room. I do, too. Together, as though we are looking at a picture of a new planet, we study the scattered toys, broken lampshade, my little sisters who have taken every book from our two shelves and scattered them on the floor. Patti needs a diaper change.

I feel a giggle start to rise, foam on milk. I look up at her to share the joke. Her eyes are red; her face looks squashy. Her shoulders round as though she is lifting something heavy even though she isn't, and, for a minute, she cannot seem to speak. But then she says in a voice so soft that it is worse than if she were mad, "Clean up this mess. Please. Just do this one thing for me." She picks up Patti, takes Marijo by the hand, and pulls them toward the bathroom.

Why is this room not funny?

Suddenly, I feel as tired as she does.

SKIRT, 1961

As if some border is crossed that I could not see, I am ready. And as if all things are coordinated, the club is ready for me. This club, 4-H, is nothing if not sequential. The large group meetings open with the Pledge of Allegiance and then the 4-H pledge. *Head, heart, hands, health. Club, community, country.* Announcements (boring) follow and then activities (mostly boring). After that they gather us farm kids back at the tables, and the extension agent hands out the program books. With our group leader's help, we paw through them, looking for the *area of interest*. There are all kinds of projects. Each year our projects grow more complicated, which means harder. The older girls are flipping to the end; they know what they are doing. The boys are looking at the animal section. I find the section about *domestic arts*. I know mine will be a sewing project because this is what my mother teaches. I flip the pages.

Second year, the year of the skirt. *The skirt, the skirt, the skirt.*

I am happy for the first time in days.

My mother and I go to Gambles to choose the fabric for my skirt. She gives in to polished cotton, which is a little shiny, so it catches the light. The print is pale blue with white flowers so small that they don't make sense until you are up close. It is to have gathers, whatever those are. I ask my mother, "Will it be a full skirt?" I want it to be full, so full I can twirl.

She looks at me and says, "Don't get any ideas."

About what?

The 4-H bulletin is not the first book of its kind in my life. This is also the year I am learning the Baltimore Catechism, which is boring but has all the rules of the church in it. I ask my mother if all souls are the same. What I really want to know is if my soul is like her soul. When I ask this question, she wants to know where I get such ridiculous questions.

I guess that answers my question.

We start on the skirt by cutting out the big pieces and stitching them together. It looks like a huge and shiny towel stitched in a circle. How will it become a skirt? This is when I learn to gather. Gathering is a miracle. Mom sets the sewing machine to its longest stitch, and then she loosens the tension on the bobbin. I run that long stitch straight along the entire waistline of the skirt. Then I take the bottom thread and gently pull it, holding it and pulling. This is what happens: the fabric gathers up into itself, into tiny puckers, little pleats and creases, all tight together, so that what will become the waist gets smaller, exactly the waist size I need. As long as the thread doesn't break and I shift the gathers so that no place along the thread has too many gathers, the skirt puffs bigger than I thought possible, bigger than I dreamed.

Gathers for twirling.

I love to twirl. When I twirl I wonder if I feel my soul. Some pictures in religion class show a turning wisp of cloud leaving the body. Twirling is like that, isn't it?

But the skirt has a waistband. About the waistband there is much pain, sorrow, and ripping out. I cry in frustration when she shows me how my stitches are too crooked on the waistband. I cry when the thread breaks and the gathers unravel. I cry when she tells me that I have to make a placket, the opening that lets you pull the skirt on and off, the little flap that hides your underwear. And hooks and eyes (because buttonholes are too hard) were invented by the devil. But after the long weeks, a hard lesson each week, the skirt is nearly complete.

Achievement Day is only a week away. This year I will model for the judges. Yes, we model our projects. But I'm not thinking about that; I don't care much about that or Achievement Day or winning a ribbon, only that I will twirl. I just want to feel the skirt spread out around my knees. I put the full slip on, pull the skirt over it, stand in front of the mirror, and turn front and back. The blue polished cotton catches the light, and when I look over my shoulder like the women do in the pictures in the magazines, I look like an upside down flower. I curtsy to myself, something I have just learned from watching *The Shirley Temple Fairy Tale Hour* on our new-to-us but used TV. In the *Fairy Tale Hour*, grown-up Shirley Temple has a gown on, one that sparkles, and I imagine that my polished cotton skirt is sparkling satin. I imagine I am a princess, a fairy queen, something even beyond that to an angel.

That spring Saturday my mother bathes the little girls early in the afternoon, so that the small water heater can refill and heat water again for us older kids' baths later on. This is done in preparation to take us all to church on Sunday. While she is doing that, I am left in charge of my brothers, Tom and Rick. We are to stay out of her hair, but what she says to me is, *Don't let them break any windows.* What this really means goes well beyond windows to include the following: don't let them dig any holes in the yard (or any more than they already have), don't let them cut down any trees with saws stolen from Dad's workshop, don't let them drive their pedal tractors through the newly planted garden pretending to plow, and don't let them pull clean sheets off the line to play ghost. Though she doesn't say it, I know she also means, *Don't let them hurt themselves.* Unfortunately, this has proven impossible for anyone in the family to prevent. Around the boys shines a halo of trouble that consists of everything from anaphylactic shock because they harassed a bee's nest to ruptured spleens from a toboggan accident. But they are invincible and they know it. Being in charge of my brothers consists of me telling them to stop in a bossy voice and them doing what they want. Do they even have souls?

But I don't think they will hurt me.

Today's boy project is backyard catapulting. They set up the catapult between the clothesline and the back wall of the house, near the little porch. Catapulting consists of using the old brown foundation bricks, which once had been stacked neatly along the wall of the house, a big cement block from the workshop, and a plank from the barn. They balance the plank on the cinder block, put a brick on one end of the plank, take turns jumping on the other end of the plank, and watch as the brick flies into the air. This is a progressive experiment. At first they just want to see how high it will go and watch it over and over. But then they try to get it to fly up and fall into the trash barrel. When they start to roll the barrel from the edge of the orchard over to the yard, I tell them to put it back. I tell them they are spilling ashes and partly burned trash *all over the backyard.* They look at me. They keep rolling. This is called *pushing it.* As in, *You boys are pushing it now.* They run back to the catapult and set it up and try again. The brick misses and lands with a *thunk* in the newly planted garden. They discuss distance verses height and set up again.

I wonder what the point of this is.

"You guys better stop. If you mess with Mom's garden, she'll be mad."

"But if it goes in the barrel, it won't be in the garden," Tom says, as if this answers everything.

They set up the barrel again, and this time, they decide to try two bricks. "Yeah, two bricks. More chance to get one in the barrel." Rick says. He's good with mathematics.

But when one jumps on the opposite end, the bricks don't fly as high. My brothers flush, embarrassed. My brothers stop, rub their chins and the backs of their necks, thinking this through. The next time, they both step on the end of the plank but not quite in unison. Mixed results. One brick flies up, and one shies off into the grass. This testing goes on. The bricks get changed; the plank gets differently balanced. The yard becomes scattered with bricks. I tell them to *pick them up and put them back.* More bricks. Once, in an attempt to get the bricks to fly higher, they both leap on the end together and then fall off.

I laugh at them; they throw me dirty looks.

I shut up for a while, feeling the tension run through me, wishing Mom would hurry up and finish with my little sisters. I stand under the crabapple tree, practicing the curtsy and talking to myself, building a story about my soul, which is something as beautiful and holy as the grown-up Shirley Temple who wears the gown with wings. My soul will fly, wispy and pure. Twirling maybe.

I watch my brothers only as much as I have to not because I am not interested in what happens—I actually wish I had thought of it—but because they won't let me in. They are beings unto themselves, contained in the physics of the fulcrum. An invisible sphere surrounds them like an oversized *Sputnik* satellite, the one the Russians sent into space with no living being inside, before they sent up the one with the dog. Now I imagine my brothers riding inside a capsule of their own making. They are circling the Earth, throwing bricks.

What happens next is inevitable.

The catapult process improves with each foot smacking the plank, sending a brick into orbit—until one brick flies up so high that it thuds onto the roof of the porch, then tumbles off into Mom's rosebush. The next one stays on the roof. I stop prancing, look at the brick, and figure it's up there for as long as the house is standing, which, given the wear and tear from my brothers, might not be as long as we'd hope. I figure that a brick on the roof is close enough to *breaking a window*, so it's my turn for my big girl voice, something I have recently perfected though its effectiveness has yet to be proven.

"Okay, you boys, stop that right now."

Again with the look, again the shrug. They shift the plank on the cinder block, deciding they will try to increase the force of liftoff by both stepping onto the plank hard at the same time. They'll keep their balance this time by holding onto one another across the plank.

I have spoken to air.

Whap. Their feet slam the plank.

The results are spectacular: the bricks fly high dark spirals against the Saturday sky, coming down with satisfying thuds. My brothers are thrilled; they jump up and down, yelling in a language that I know comes from outer space. What is it about making things fly through the air? But isn't this what I have wanted for my soul? I am deranged with jealousy.

I yell over to them, "You stop or I will tell Mom!" I sound almost fierce, even to me. But they are riding on success. The bricks scatter farther, fall harder.

I kick the tree trunk in an unprincessy manner. I'm not mad at them as much as I am aware that I can't do what I am supposed to be doing. I'm starting to feel that awful feeling of being trapped, unable to move. All I want to do is play soul in a twirling skirt. Still, I have to be able to tell my mother that I tried to stop them. While they set up the next round of flying bricks, I think.

I cross the lawn and kneel down at the end of the plank, which is already set with a single brick that will fly, they announce to each other, as *high as a spaceship*. I lean over it.

What possessed me to do this?

Impersonating the calm voice my father uses when he is disciplining them, I say, "Stop. Now."

Did I expect that, in the face of their big sister's poor impersonation of an authority figure, they would put the physics lesson away and slink into some still poorer version of ground-bound play? They are making bricks fly, for heaven's sake; they are sending up spaceships.

But I don't believe they will hurt me.

I bend over the brown brick set on the end of the plank and think this will put a stop to it. But they will defend their right to fly bricks no matter what is in the way, even their sister's head. Is it one or both of them—probably both—who raises a sneakered foot and brings it down hard, no holding back on this because maybe, just maybe my head will fly off? And won't that be cool? It happened once to the goblin on *The Shirley Temple Fairy Tale Hour*.

But then I am inside another twirling, inside the spinning, a wild turning, blind and dizzy and lost, a stunned silvery skirt inside my head. Is that also when my soul starts to spin away, become something less simple, something turning wildly with betrayal? Then there's heat and a tearing in my face and pain so sharp and clear that I can't breathe, and when I do breathe some wet and salty thing fills my mouth, streaming over my face.

Blurry, it's all blurry. I sit back in the grass and scream.

At some point, my brothers concede that I won't stop, and this will interfere with future experiments, so they might as well call Mom. My mother comes running, and there is a small look of shock when she takes in the scene. But she is calm; she is efficient. She uses the dish towel, ever present in her hands, to mop my face. I see the blood soaking the towel and scream harder.

Slowly my soul returns. When I'm down to gasps, Mom looks over the yard scattered with bricks and absorbs the rudiments of the process. "You let them do this?" She leads me unceremoniously into the house where she packs my nose with ice. I lie on the couch, my head pounding, holding cold rags to my face, trying not to cry because it makes the bleeding start again. Through the afternoon, we watch as the dark bruises appear under both eyes and slip like melting warrior paint down my face.

There is a place in the middle of my nose, just below the bridge, where all the skin is gone.

How much later does the calendar come into play? At some point I realize that I am supposed to model at the 4-H Achievement Day in a week. Something in me rises, and the tears slip down my face despite the ache. My mother walks into the room and asks, "What now?"

"I was going to model my new skirt."

"Why wouldn't you?"

"Not like this." How can she be so stupid?

But my mother is not letting me get away with anything. She knows too much about hardship, not to mention my vanity.

"We'll put makeup on to cover it." This she says with a smile.

Makeup. And that's that.

I never get to tell her what I felt when the brick hit me, that strange loss of something precious that for a moment I thought was a soul but was merely my brothers exposing me to an object not from outer space, not from heaven, but from the hard dismantled walls of old foundations, the way of the world.

I will be hurt.

Later, I do model the twirling skirt for the first time. But it does not twirl. The polished cotton is too heavy for twirling. The makeup does not quite cover the yellowing bruise, and I am confused by the lights, clumsy on the stage. And every time I look in the mirror, even after the scab falls off my face, I see the small distortion—me but marred. It surprises me, the face in the mirror. Even at that young age, I know I will be forever distracted by a bump on the nose.

JACKIE, FEBRUARY 1962

We don't like the president of the United States, but we like his wife. She likes antiques and old things. My mother gives over her political grudges, the hard-nosed conservatism that runs through farm families in old bloodlines, to take notes on old dishware and lamps. She gathers magazines and newspaper articles about historical furniture.

But tonight is special: the first lady will be on TV.

My mother and I sit side by side at the dining room table. She is cutting out a pattern for my sister Marijo, laying it out like a map of the world. I am cutting valentines but only when she's pinning the pattern because we have only one pair of scissors. My brothers have lost the other. We trade off using the scissors. I cut out the cheap valentines—why couldn't she get the shiny, pre-cut ones?—and worry about Valentine's Day. She cuts the pattern for Marijo's new spring dress for church. While she pins the next piece, I cut and write notes on the valentines. We trade. Outside, winter light fades over the barns. My siblings play in the snow. Dad has taken them sledding so she can make this dress.

Be my valentine.
Your friend,
Anne

I add notes to these disappointing valentines so that my favorite friends will know I really like them, and the kids I don't like will still have a valentine even though I am not sure I want them to talk to me. Then there is the other side of the coin: will anyone give me a valentine? What if there are none in the envelope with my name on it that hangs on the bulletin board at school? Or what if they are homemade? I hate the homemade ones even though my mother says they are more meaningful because someone took the time to make them.

This kind of remark, I have learned recently, will make me feel guilty. I am supposed to be a better person. But valentines are a terrible worry: who to give to and who not to give to? Who cares for me and who doesn't? It is a battle of who and who not to love, who to be loved by. It's not really love, even I know that, but it feels as important as love. It gets all screechy inside of me, and I hate it, and then on top of that, I feel guilty for not loving everyone, even some of the girls in the 4-H club.

I would like to talk about the valentines, but my mother is busy with the pattern, which is a complicated one. Maybe it will be an Easter dress. I can see that this will take her attention, and she will be impatient if I ask now. I wait for the scissors and for the special TV show about the White House, which has been put together by the first lady. The TV has recently been put on a cart so that it can be rolled from the living room to the dining room, where it is tonight.

At last, my mother glances at the TV and the clock, then turns the knob on the old Zenith. There is the static moment. I put down the scissors, pick up the pencil. She returns to the table, studies the pattern, picks up the scissors. The screen clears. From the TV, a black-and-white picture appears showing the White House when it was first built. We look up, look down, waiting for the beginning as music plays. I wonder if this will be boring.

Then the voice. We both turn our heads, pulled to the screen. Still the picture of the White House, but the voice rises behind or over the picture. It is something soft and beautiful, and it feels unreal. My mother puts down her scissors. I drop the valentine to Lydia. We listen. Here is a saint's voice plainly explaining the history of the White House but, just like a saint, saying something without words.

Even my die-hard Republican mother, who believes in never wearing anything too showy, in choosing colors that don't show dirt, in saving every penny and reusing every piece of clothing, likes that Jackie dresses beautifully and walks gracefully. I do, too. We like to see her slim frame in pictures, so unlike our stocky bodies, and we always notice her "wardrobe," a new word for me. We pay attention to her pillbox hats with little veils, her Chanel suits. My mother shakes her head at how much money those cost. We study her beauty, not quite sure what to do with it because there is so much of it. My mother is quick to judge uppityness, but other than asking if Jackie's wardrobe is paid for with tax dollars, my mother does not judge her. Instead, she watches. And so do I.

 But now her voice. Jackie has a voice like . . . it takes me a while to decide . . . like dark chiffon. She speaks carefully; words become flowers, delicate and slow to bloom. This is how the first lady becomes Jackie, a whole friendlier thing, but at the same time, her voice adds mystery to that friendliness. It fills the dining room, soft and glowing.

The next thing I notice: my mother stands still, listening. As much as I want to listen to Jackie, I want to watch my mother, scissors poised in her hand. This voice has stilled my mother, stopped her ever-swift movement toward the next pot of soup, the next broken bone, broken machine, broken heart. Something has quieted her nerves, something from the TV, from the outside world.

I stack my paper hearts, listen to the voice, and watch my mother listen to Jackie talk about American *antiques and collectibles*, how she will gather them for the White House, how she thinks the White House should have *the best things*.

Then she appears on the screen. I try to do two things at once: watch my mother study the face, the dark hair, the heavy brows, her classic dress—lean lines on her slim body—and at the same time watch the screen. Here is something I have never seen before. She is like a model but not a model. She is beautiful but she isn't quite certain. She, the first lady, is nervous and a little scared.

In that crowded dining room, my mother and I stop trading scissors. We do nothing for the rest of the hour. We learn all about the White House. What I finally decide is that the voice is really smart, and I like that, and I think my mother likes that, too. At the same time, her voice makes her seem like she could be hurt. She seems like someone who is . . . I search for the word . . . shy but doing something brave. Oh. Is that what my mother hears, shyness in this bold thing that Jackie is doing? I want to have what she has, the way of making people—no, of making my mother—listen, even though she is not strong.

Is this how valentines are sent to an entire country?

Has she sent us a valentine? *Be mine?*

And we will. Oh how we will.

When the show is over, I stare at my valentines in their cockeyed stack. I wish I could make one for her. I wish I could send one to her. The first lady has shown me my mother listening. Because she is graceful and brave in a quiet way. Because she cares about how she looks and about her house, the White House, the house of the country. She wants it to be the best so she is doing things to make it the best. She is showing the country, even my mother and me, how she will do that. I think about this. She is showing my mother how it is to be done, and my mother wants . . . not the White House but something like it, here in our dirty, dust-driven farm.

Jackie is like my mother's 4-H leader, but it's not 4-H.

It's about how to be. And this is what my mother wants me to be.

I am not any of those things.

But I vow to try to be quieter, to be better.

Mom hands me the scissors. I am to take them and be quick and sure and give her back the scissors when I'm done.

ACHIEVEMENT DAY, 1962

So I blame it all on Jackie Kennedy.

My sailor outfit is a two-piece of navy blue linen: a sporty top and a slightly flared skirt that makes me look older than my twelve years. Smart. Perky. At Gambles my mother finds white anchor appliqués that I hand-stitch to the squared corners of the collar using a thimble for the first time. I wear a bright red bow in my hair and a matching red tie under the collar. This nautical theme was something my mother cooked up when she saw the pictures in *Look* magazine of John and Jackie Kennedy sailing at Hyannis Port. My mother is no fan of Democrats, but like most everyone in the country, she is paying attention to this first lady, and if the first lady is wearing sailor outfits, we here in the Midwest might as well try it. And uncannily, it works.

At that year's 4-H Achievement Day, I win a blue ribbon for my workmanship, my third in the four years I have been sewing. I win because of my mother's inordinately careful, though rarely patient, teaching. Despite my success with workmanship, I fail to gain any recognition for modeling, but this, the modeling, is what my mother wants for me. She wants me to be poised and confident in front of people—though not loud, a behavior she fears in girls. She sees both my thick gawkiness in front of people and a longing for attention that makes me, yes, sometimes, loud. But she takes the project on. She, who has never liked the spotlight, who has never been on the stage, who fears too much attention on herself or any of her children, trains me as a 4-H model because she believes it will at least teach me to walk gracefully, one of many things I seem unable to do with any finesse. "You'll learn to walk more elegantly," she says by way of explanation, straightening her shoulders, which signals me to do the same. But the entire endeavor is a challenge the size of our new barnyard not simply because of her reticence and fear of embarrassment but because of me. I am awkward with plumpness and dreaming. I have the grace of a half-grown heifer; no one would compare me to a filly. She sighs, broods into her coffee, and reads aloud from the 4-H bulletin: "Participants will be judged on outside construction, fit, and modeling ability with the main emphasis being the selection, modeling, and choices made by the 4-H member to enhance their color, silhouette, and activities." She puts the bulletin down and looks at me hopelessly.

The outfit is well constructed, the dark color complements my hair, and the details enhance the illusion of being somewhat put together, but not in a million years would a body actually sail in the outfit—as if any of us knew anything about sailing in the first place. So much for enhancing activities. Despite all that, the sailor suit is . . . what's the word of the day? *Adorable.*

My mother, against all odds, is counting on adorable.

Achievement Day dawns. A Saturday. She rolls my unruly hair so we can pull it back and tuck it into the red bow. After breakfast dishes, after the little sisters are set to play in the dirty yard, we practice again. She reads the narration. This is what the mistress of ceremonies will read as I model the sailor suit on the stage. She reads it, and I walk around the dining room in the same pattern I will walk on the stage. I remember the steps in one of a half dozen attempts as I wander in circles. The problem is that I have never been on this stage, the one at the old gym in Hart. I've seen it, and it seems bigger than the barnyard. She tells me to imagine the stage, and when this fails, she figures out the dimensions and maps a smaller version of the pattern on the checkerboard linoleum of the dining room floor.

She is right: this is about walking. Not running or skipping or scrambling, which are easy. Me, walking. First, I start at the table and walk to the center, pivot to the audience (the front window), walk halfway toward the front, stop, half pivot and walk a diagonal to the left (door to living room), turn my back to the audience to show them the back of the outfit where the little anchors smile in white, pivot, walk back to the middle, stop and turn again, touch the red bow with my fingertips, walk right across the stage (kitchen door), pivot the other way and gesture to the collar, walk back to the original place (table), turn again slowly all the way around, then off the stage. If you are really good, as one last step, you stop again just before you disappear behind the curtain and stand still to show the outfit one more time. I always forget that, and after any number of reminders, my mother decides not to worry about the last step.

She's right about another thing: I can't seem to walk, period. It's not simply clumsiness but a self-consciousness about where I am putting my feet. I forget how balance works. And pivoting in the slippery new patent leather shoes throws me; I actually fall over during one practice session. When I look up from the floor, blushing hard, untangling my too-big feet, she is not laughing. She takes a sip of cold coffee and puts it on the table with a sharp clink.

I rehearse again and again, and, slowly, I learn the sequence. I learn to walk the slow and careful walk that leads with the hips and not the head. I learn to pivot. I learn to hold my hands in a pretty way, thumb touching the middle finger. I am just starting to feel comfortable when she tells me I have to smile. Smile when I can barely place one foot in front of the other without stumbling? I can't smile. She's crazy to ask. When I try, I feel like something awful has happened to my face. I can barely keep the sequence of moves in my head, and she wants me to smile?

I can already tell this modeling will not make her love me in the way I want her to, will not make her so proud that she will put her arms around me, something I still crave. I have no hope. I lower the bar and tell myself that I need to do this just well enough so that she won't be embarrassed, so the shadow will not enter the room.

Here I am walking across the dining room floor, trying not to look down at my feet, trying not to let the checkerboard make me dizzy. I walk, turn, pivot, walk, but I can't do the walk-turn-walk-pivot-walk and add the smile. Here is the great tension of her coffee cup. She stares into it, chewing her lip. I wait, expecting her vinegar voice.

Instead she gives up. She looks up, says to me, "Anne, just be yourself."

I stare at her. How can I be anyone else? How is that possible? When I practice with those words in my head—*be yourself*—it feels like more pretending. How do I pretend to be myself? And if I have to pretend to be me, who was I in the first place? Even I know there is something about that idea that doesn't work. I'd rather she lost her patience than tell me this so kindly.

Late in the afternoon, we drive to the old gym in Hart. With dozens of other mothers and girls, and even whole families, we enter the crowded, high-ceilinged gym with the worn hardwood floors and the stage built along one side so that the building, which always smells like a basketball game, can also be an auditorium. Today the room is lined with exhibition racks. We pull my sailor suit from the display rack where it has hung with its blue satin ribbon for two days. We carry it down to the dingy locker room under the bleachers where I change with some forty other girls from all over the county. Chatter and fear runs through us all like heat lightning. I dress, so embarrassed about changing in front of people that I am almost late to the lineup. I carry the hair bow back up into the air and light. My mother meets me, looks at the outfit, and sighs, saying, "We should have brought an iron." Then she fixes the bow, finds my place in the line along the wall, hands me the narration card, and without a smile says, "Don't forget to smile."

She disappears into the crowd. The lights go down. People seat themselves. The mistress of ceremonies takes the stage.

I am standing in a line that moves slowly into the stairwell leading to the backstage area. Many girls are ahead of me and then not so many. I stand in the dark of backstage for the first time, waiting so nervously that I want to suck my thumb, though I haven't sucked it in a year. I watch the younger girls go ahead of me. They are cute in little skirts or aprons, and I know the *adorable* score must be pretty high. I am wondering if winning anything, even a prize for modeling, is worth this feeling of being alone in the middle of a crowd of so many girls. How will I walk in front of everyone? How will I not shame my mother? And smile? And be myself? I want to throw up.

One of the volunteers calls me toward the edge of the stage. I hand her the card that she will give to the MC. I stand behind the curtain and stare out into the light, trying to imagine the pattern of steps. With no checkerboard to guide me, how will I know where to turn? The little girl in front of me walks out and promptly forgets to listen to the narration. She doesn't remember to point to her apron when directed. She doesn't turn to show the bow in the back. She messes up. But as she leaves, the audience bursts into applause. She is adorable. I feel like I might faint. I can't seem to breathe. My rough, unmanicured hands tremble a little.

My name is called: "Anne Oomen."

I need to walk now.

I step into the light.

I walk a few steps onto the stage.

I can't see anyone. The lights are so bright, I can't make out faces. I know people, my mother and others, are out there sitting in folding chairs. But I am in a bubble of light that blocks them all. I can hear the moderator begin the description of my sailor outfit, the Jackie Kennedy outfit, so I walk to the center. The light stays on me. I turn to the audience, but really, I am turning to the light. I feel its heat on my face, and it is not unlike the summer sun. I lift my face to it. My spine straightens. Is that when playing dress-up in the yard connects to 4-H modeling? A story happens inside of me. This is like dress-up. I do *not* have to be myself. I am not me—or not the me I know. I am someone who remembers the pattern. I walk, listen, pivot, point to my collar, point to my bow, turn to show the little anchors, and keep my face to the light. It is blinding and at the same time safe. I feel free to be the model who is walking in the light where I can't see anyone but where everyone can see someone who is not me but someone better than me, someone dressed like the first lady on holiday.

I come to the last step on that stage, and the me who is not me remembers to turn and look out toward the darkness. For just a moment, I want to stay on that rough stage where I am the center of attention, not my mother's attention but the attention of an audience beyond the light. The moment doesn't last—it can't—but it is like nothing I have felt before, that first time when 4-H, in this strictly monitored ritual, lets you feel a little power.

It is almost like being loved.

Later they call my name, and I return to the stage to accept the certificate as winner of the junior level review.

Later I dream I am Jackie Kennedy in a sailor suit.

Later my mother will inform me, worry slackening her entire face at what she has seen, "You smiled the whole time. You looked like you liked it."

THE HEM, 1962

My father doesn't want John F. Kennedy as president, even though he is Catholic and so are we. Even after he is elected, Dad worries about the communists, who are mostly Russians but also Chinese, who are a different kind of communist. He thinks Kennedy is soft on communism. The other guy, Richard Nixon, may have lost the election, but he was not soft on communism—so Dad says. My dad was a sergeant in World War II, so he knows about communism. He says we need someone who will fight communism and not let it spread. He says it is a secret menace in the country. I know enough not to ask what a secret menace means, but I think about it because it seems to frighten him. When he talks about it, his calm voice gets stern. His sternness says, "This has got to be stopped."

At school we get a comic book called *Treasure Chest* with a special comic series called "This Godless Communism." The comic tells about how communism starts and how it grows. Communists can't go to church. One night Dad looks over my shoulder as I read. When I turn the page, he puts his fingers on the panel that shows a man beating another man, a man who was in the *fight for freedom*.

"It comes to that," he says and walks away.

Sewing comes faster now. I can sit at the sewing machine, hold the fabric tight, and sew a seam straight. I can gather a waist and French seam a seam. I am still learning to fit a bodice, but that will come. My mother still rescues my mistakes, catching the wrong cut, untangling the tangled bobbin, sighing at the sleeve that must be reset one more

time. But slowly I learn how to do the hard things. Except for hand-
work, except for hemming.

There is an autumn evening after supper when I am sitting at the sewing
machine while my mother and father watch *The Huntley-Brinkley Report*.
It is that time of year when they come inside and sit together, when my
father is not going to the fields every day, when my mother is not split
between house and harvest. They listen to the news together.

I'm not listening. I am trying to hem a dress that she has made for
me. On *principle* my mother doesn't like just giving us anything. We have
to help; we have to do something to get what we want. We have to participate. So I have to hem it. To complicate principle, this dress is made
of special fabric so the hem has to be a hidden stitch, not just a regular
stitch. She will teach me if I put those darned comics away and just concentrate. So I am concentrating.

Hemming is a folding up of edges, a tidying, a catch and pull, catch
and pull. It is done with the silver wand, the needle, thin and hard, sharp
and cold. My fingers slip. The thread knots. Hemming is a dark line running crookedly along the outside of the skirt. "A blind man could see that,"
she says. She pulls it out and I try again.

She takes the skirt of the dress and turns it over to reveal the underside with a part folded over. She says, "I've stitched the raw edge and
pinned it. Hold it just so." But it slips. I can't hold it straight and manage
the needle at the same time. She stares at me. She sighs and takes the
fabric to the ironing board, steams it into place. The color comes high in
her face, and as she looks down she is so pretty with her auburn-and-gray
hair thick in its roll, but her eyes are determined.

She puts the skirt back in my lap. She shows me how to hide the
knot at the seam by tucking it in. I like the knot hidden, the tiny secret,
a roughness tucked inside. She shows me how to catch the smallest bit
of the skirt front, a needle's tiny bite, then another bite of the folded
edge, then pull the thread but not too tight. "Go back and forth from
the layer that will be the outside to the layer that's inside. Catch just
a little fabric each time. Keep the stitch on the inside." Then she sits
beside me, and I catch the skirt side and catch the hem side and watch

for the pins. She turns the fabric over: too much of the "catch" shows on the outside of the fabric. She tears it out. She says, "It's got to be invisible. No one can see the stitches."

I hold the thread and needle and concentrate while the news blares in the background. During the Texaco commercial, they get coffee and she finishes washing dishes. She calls my brothers in from raking leaves. She feeds the little girls a snack. Then *Huntley-Brinkley* again. They are only half listening, moving through little chores.

Change, when it comes, is first about a stillness. The clink of the dishes stops. The voices from the TV shift in tone. Now just the TV, just Huntley and Brinkley filling the air. A special report. My ever-moving mother and father stare at the TV, alert but without moving. Brinkley is talking about missiles, about the Soviet Union, a place called Cuba. A dictator named Castro.

My father gets up and paces. My mother rubs her forehead, says, "Oh my God." She never swears.

"This is what happens," he says.

And I look at his face. I feel a strange buzz running through me.

The next day at school we all hear about the missiles that are aimed at our country from the island called Cuba, which is a communist country. Cuba is not on our side; it is on Russia's side. Or Russia is on its side. Cuba is very close to our country, right by Florida. In current events class, we learn that Kennedy wants Khrushchev, the leader of Russia, who is a communist, to take the missiles away from Cuba. Khrushchev says no. Khrushchev and Castro are friends.

Every night my parents watch the news. Every night I sit with the dress and try the secret hem with stitches so small they will be invisible. I sit there so it looks like I am trying to do something useful, but my body buzzes, and the stitches show. My father talks to his friends from the war. I overhear him say, "We could have a third." And to my mother, "We have to be ready." He touches her shoulder. She nods.

When I get home from school the next day, my mother is in the basement. I walk down the rickety steps all the way to the musty back room with the stone walls. My mother is stacking gallon water jugs on the shelves. She has rolled the winter blankets up, and they are resting on the old bed Dad uses when he can't sleep in the summer heat. She is moving quickly.

"Is this a bomb shelter?" I ask.

"Help me stack these." She hands me canned beans to shelve.

"Is there going to be a war?" I place the cans on the shelf in a crooked line.

"Of course not." She picks up the broom to sweep the cracked cement floor.

I feel the buzz turn into a racket in my ears. She sees my face. "They are going to take care of this." She throws sacks of hard peas on the shelves with a loud thud.

The next day, after current events class, we practice a thing called "duck and cover," which is about the bomb. We cover our heads and hide under the desks. We have done this before, but it was just to be safe, just in case. Now it is not just in case. The missiles have bombs, are bombs. We know this because all the newscasters, even Walter Cronkite—whom my dad doesn't like—say so. The newspapers, stacked on the counter, say so. But I don't understand. It's still far away, isn't it? Is it because they have seen something that I haven't?

One night, I am working on the hem. One in three stitches is really invisible, but the rest show. I have to tear it out again; I know this before I show her. Dad is glued to the TV. More than once he has said, "Never on our land . . ."

Does he mean the farm? Our land? I work up my nerve. "Are they coming here?" I ask. His answer is hidden somewhere on the floor, which he stares at.

Another night I ask him, "Dad, what did you do in the war?"

He shakes his head, says, "Not much."

My mother says proudly, "He was in communications."

My father brushes her off. "Radios. Most of the time I was in charge of the radio."

I try to figure this out. I ask the next question. "Were you in battles?"

He was. He tells me that while staring at Chet Huntley, who is announcing that Russia considers the U.S. naval blockade "a step toward nuclear war."

Buzzing in my fingertips. In my head.

"Where?" I want to know where his battles took place.

"Africa. And Italy." Places across the ocean. Not like Cuba. Cuba's close. He stares hard at the TV.

My brother Tom is eating popcorn. His mouth is full, but his words are clear enough: "Did you kill anyone?"

My father, my calm and clear father, turns to him, his jaw hanging open. He doesn't say anything. My mother gasps, then says briskly, "Time for bed." It's not even seven o'clock.

Did he? Did my dad kill someone in the war? The movies always show soldiers getting shot or blown up. Under the sound of my brother chewing popcorn, there is silence. I look down at an invisible answer. Or is it? Am I seeing something in a line of unseen things?

After that, my brothers ask and ask about the war, and each time my father changes the subject or my mother distracts them. As I stitch, another question occurs to me: would he do it again? If they, *the Reds*, came here? Who are they anyway, these communists? What is this war?

One day, over dishes, I ask her, "Why won't he tell us?"

She breathes slowly. "He doesn't like to remember."

"Because bad things happened."

"Bad things happened."

"Even with the radio?"

"The radio got blown up."

It takes me a minute to see where this might go. "So he couldn't call for help?"

"That's enough now. I need you to set the table."

When you get the hem just right, you can see, only if you look really close, the tiniest catch on the outside of the dress. From a distance my mother says, "It's there but the eye barely notices." But the wonder is on the underside. When you flip the hem over to look at the inside, all you see is the seam at the top of the hem. All the stitches are hidden under the fold. It looks like that hem shouldn't work, like there is nothing there to hold up the hem, like it is being held by something magic.

That's the secret; that's the invisible part of the hem. Only if you fold back the edge can you see the stitches, tucked in, safe.

The days pass. Halloween is coming, but no one talks about costumes. Everyone is talking about the Reds. My brother finally announces that he wants to be the devil. No one laughs when I say, "You already are." My mother scolds him. *Be something good.* This is hard for Tom to think of.

There are now sacks of potatoes in the basement, white eyes staring up from the basket. Also lanterns and oil, soap and tubs. One night my father cleans his hunting rifles and carries them down there, too, with boxes of bullets. My brothers are excited because there might be a war. My mother shushes them, but they just go out and play the war games where she can't hear them. They shoot each other. The buzz in my body seems like it's there all the time now.

How many days does this go on? Is it five or seven or ten days later?

One afternoon, my father comes into the kitchen with a quick step and a small smile. He slaps down a newspaper on the counter by the percolator. My mother looks at him and, standing next to him, unfolds it. A headline shouts in black type, "Reds Back Down." My mother puts her arms around him and kisses him so hard, he has to pull away. Then he puts his head on her shoulder, just resting it there. They hold each other tight, standing there, leaning on the kitchen counter.

Mom stops gathering bedsheets. All the food gets put back into our regular kitchen cupboards. The guns go back to their locked case. Dad stops pacing. He returns to the fields, hat tipped back.

On the news, Huntley and Brinkley seem to say that we have *won the crisis*, but at the same time, it was *a close call*. They talk about it for a long time. Things will have to change: a *hotline* will be established so the leaders can speak to each other. There is so much talk that the hem becomes a quiet center.

I pull the thread, and at last it eases cleanly through the fabric, then tucks itself under the lip of the fold. I stitch all the way around, casting this stich in quiet time after so much buzzing. When I flip the hem, I see it: all the stitches are hidden. All those tiny places where one thing is hooked to another are covered by the fold, straight as a ruler. But they can't be seen—as though they weren't there at all. My mother comes by, touches the line, smiles quietly. My father leans back from his chair, touches her hand, asks for a coffee. I understand at last: the stitches are so invisible that they become not real. Except when I touch the fabric, I feel it, the tiny knot, the strand of thread running under, and the faint buzzing that remains.

RESUSCI ANNIE

"And if you do a demonstration, you might win an award. You may be able to attend the State Achievement Day in Lansing." *Demonstrations?* At the monthly meeting, the county extension agent, Andrea, tells us the new thing in 4-H is demonstrations. She stands at the front of the church hall where all the local 4-H'ers are gathered, cranky and sweaty at the end of the school day, and all the group leaders have come despite the encroaching holidays. We sit on the folding chairs among sprays of battered pinecones, only half paying attention. Andrea gets all the news from Michigan State University, which sets up all the 4-H activities throughout the state. This makes her important. My mother talks to her often.

Andrea announces, "Demonstrations are a way to showcase your confidence in a skill and teach someone else that skill." And then she says, "The best demonstrators will go to Michigan State University to compete."

That does it for Mom.

I will become a 4-H demonstrator.

But on what will I do the demonstration? On the way home, my mother and I are trying to figure this out. After we eliminate all the easy things, such as dish towels, aprons, and place mats as childish, we come to a silence. I can tell she is thinking. I like this and it scares me. What is she going to come up with?

I think of something to head her off. "I could do the invisible hem." I know all the steps to keep that little secret.

She ponders the road. "The pictures would have to be pretty intricate," she muses.

"There have to be pictures?" This is sounding hard.

"Weren't you listening? Posters for the steps of whatever you are demonstrating." She's dodging ice, and the car swerves for a second. But then she says, "Nope, that won't work."

"Why not?"

"It's invisible."

"But that's the point?"

She looks sideways at me like I've sassed her.

Oh, does that mean it would be hard to show something where the point was that you can't see it? I think it would be magical to demonstrate something invisible, though it does cross my mind that the judges might not appreciate magical things, even so practical a magic as the invisible hem. And, besides, it's not really magical, just invisible. This has been a problem for me—that I think about invisible things. My mother doesn't know this, or if she does, she doesn't let on.

By supper, she has thought of something else. She has remembered right there in the dead of winter that I, her moody child, am happiest when I am swimming. She has remembered that when I am taking swimming lessons, I stay focused and don't think about the invisible things. I have learned to do the sidestroke, the breaststroke, an awkward crawl, and, finally, the thing called the survival float, which is about as interesting as mud, but it's important if your boat sinks and you get caught for hours in the ocean.

Like that's going to happen in the Midwest. Lakes freeze here.

But she dives right in. She loves the survival float.

"If you demonstrate the survival float, you can make posters of each of the four positions. You can set up real-life situations and show how important this is. Even nonswimmers can do the survival float. You can show with your own body how your hands hang down."

"I will look exactly like a monkey."

She throws me the look again.

My mother has no greater fear than big water. Her version of a good swim is to walk in the shallows barely up to her thighs, squat to her shoulders, stand up gasping, splash her face, and walk out. Perhaps because she is so afraid, she has insisted on all five of her children learning to swim at the swimming hole, a dirty pond in Hart where we come home grimier than if we'd spent a day in the fields. She has watched every lesson with her hand over her mouth to keep from screaming that we are drowning. But she has made sure we learned, and in the process, she has learned the names of all the strokes and knows which ones we should use and when. The survival float is a version of the dead man's float but one step further. It saves you before you're dead.

"This is practical," she says. "This is life and death. And in the demonstration, this will show that you care about people." Meaning that I don't? But it's true: I don't really know what I care about. I'm just not quite of the same world as she is.

So the survival float is my first demonstration. I painstakingly make the posters, four large-sized placards with each of the four body positions.

The first is the float. Facedown in the water, you let your body hang down and hold your breath. This is the dead man part of survival, because you stay still and don't struggle. Your body is *naturally buoyant* and will float if you let it. Like the drowned, I guess—though I've only seen pictures. I often wonder how you float for hours, but my mother assures me that she has talked to the swim instructors. It has been done. In the next step, you slowly raise your arms but not your face, then bring your arms down hard through the water, which forces your head up and out of the water. You take a big breath, tread water, then let yourself sink back into the dead man position. You don't lose energy, you won't sink, and you won't become exhausted. Each step is broken down into smaller steps that I talk about. You can do this for hours in almost any kind of sea. After all the demonstrating, I must allow time for questions.

When I complete all the posters and all the notecards for my points, I have to practice. I set up on the ironing board, posters leaning on the laundry baskets, and *present* for my brothers. To their credit they listen, maybe because my father is also watching from the table. They laugh only when I slump my shoulders and show how the first position, the dead man, looks.

"She looks like a monkey," Tom says loudly.

When I ask for questions, Rick wants to know, "What if there are sharks in the water?"

Tom chimes in. "Yeah, sharks would eat your feet, and then what do you do?"

My mother says I have to be ready for all kinds of questions.

Sharks?

At the next big 4-H meeting we all practice with an audience. Everyone who wanted to be a demonstrator gets to show how far they've gotten. We carry the posters to the front of the meeting hall and set them up on card tables. There are demonstrations on how to groom animals, butcher chickens, and knit a scarf. The butchering chickens one gets lots of questions from the boys, who especially want to know what to do if the chicken doesn't know it's dead and takes off running in circles.

When it's my turn, I talk through the steps. When I get to the dead man's float, the kids laugh because I look like a monkey, but the adults like it. Afterward, Andrea says, "It's okay if they think you look like a monkey. It means they will remember the position, and that means they might save themselves."

I think I love her.

But someone says, *It's too short*, and suggests I extend it with a life-saving technique like *mouth-to-mouth resuscitation*.

Everyone laughs. My mother flushes.

Andrea says that it's a really good idea.

The club pipes down.

Mouth-to-mouth what?

My mother *thunks* a huge suitcase on the dining room floor.

She says, "She's in parts."

She says, "Go ahead."

I kneel, unsnap the snaps, and lift the lid and the foam that protects her. There she is—the head and neck of a woman. The body is snugged into various compartments with tubes, balloons, and a kind of blue jump-suit—all divided up in the suitcase. But it is the face, the head, that stops me cold. The head is like a doll's but more real than a doll's, life-size, lips slightly parted to reveal the opening of the mouth, her eyes closed, every-thing still. But her face looks . . . mysterious. Beautiful.

My mother looks over. A small gasp, then she says, "Well . . ." A long silence.

Then my father walks in and takes us in. He has been drafted to help put her together. He kneels on the linoleum beside me. He looks at us both and says, "Now, now. Let's just see what we have here." He lifts the head out of the suitcase and holds her up, turning her this way and that, and almost tenderly begins to put her together. The spell is broken.

You thread the tubes and connect them under the chest cavity. You inflate the body and attach her torso. You put the cavities in the right place and connect them to the tubes. You pull the blue coveralls over it all. You dress her to look like someone just pulled from the water, someone for whom the survival float did not work, someone who only knew the dead man's float.

My father is careful. She is not ours; she is borrowed from another county. She is expensive. There are only a few Annies in the whole state, and we are responsible. If anything happens to her, we have to pay hundreds of dollars. We get to borrow her for practice, and that's it.

All through putting her together, I think the magic will happen and she will rise and walk, but when she is assembled, she is a dummy in blue coveralls. Perhaps because I have seen how all the parts go together, she looks less real.

I think it will be easier now.

Until we practice. My mother looks at the directions, nodding. Perhaps because she was a nurse, this all makes sense to her. She shows me how to tip the head, open the jaw, place my mouth over Annie's, and blow so that the chest inflates. Then she demonstrates how to exhale, watch the chest deflate, and blow in again. If you don't get it right, the airway clogs. I watch the chest inflate and deflate, inhale and exhale. It's my turn. I practice the tipping. Annie's face is always cool, and she smells like plastic. I lift her neck so the airway opens. I bend down and blow into the opening. Her chest does not rise. I try again. It does not work. Have I broken her? Why won't she breathe for me? My mother says, "The air is leaking out. You have to make a seal with your own mouth. Take a big breath and blow in, harder than you think, and blow in slowly."

I breathe air deep into my chest, so far down that it hurts. I place my mouth over Annie's. Her mouth is now sealed, so I blow in slowly and steadily. The chest must rise. The chest must fall. Keep it steady. Try again.

For the three days that we have her, I practice.

After the first day, I ask the thing on my mind: "Why is she a girl?"

And my mother tells me, "Because men who have to learn to give mouth-to-mouth, like lifeguards, don't like to practice on a male dummy."

I don't know why I understand this, but I do. Still I say, "But it's not like kissing."

"No, it's not, but that's men for you."

On the second day I ask why Annie's face looks the way it does. Mom hesitates and then says she heard that the face was molded from the face of an actual drowned woman. "The doctor who invented her said that Annie was inspired by someone who drowned."

I look at her, lying now in the corner of the dining room.

Later I ask, "What was her whole name?"

"I don't think they know."

"Why not? Who was she?'

"I don't think they know."

"But they call her Annie."

"It's just a name they gave her."

"It's not her real name?"

Mom is impatient with this line of questioning. "I guess. I don't know. We just have to use her. Keep practicing." My mother wants the real Annie to remain invisible.

I stare at Annie. Someone didn't know her name and so gave her this one? A name something like mine, a version of mine.

I keep practicing, but I can't get enough air in her to make her chest rise. It leaks, becomes ragged.

Is it Andrea who gives me another detail of Annie's history? Some-one says, *she may have taken her own life.* Annie drowned herself? I have never known anyone who did that. Never known it could be done. I think about breathing water, and if I think too hard, my own breath becomes ragged. I wonder if I could die from not breathing right.

As the days pass, I still get her to breathe correctly only about half the time.

The last night before the demonstrations for real judges, I practice alone while everyone else watches TV. I go through the survival float and then onto Part II, the demonstration of mouth-to-mouth. She is on the rug of the dining room floor. I kneel by her and place my mouth over hers and try again. It doesn't work.

I sit back, trying to figure out how to do this thing.

What is it that possesses me to move her? I slide my arms under her and slowly struggle with her weight, which, though not like a real person, is heavy for me. She is clumsy, and I am afraid I will dislodge one of the tubes. I lift slowly. I carry her to the dining room table and shove her onto it. Next to the table, I can lean over, take the big breath I need to take, and breathe into her. I want her to not hiss. I breathe into her, thinking of her standing at the edge of the swirling water, sad as nighttime. Slowly her chest rises. I lift my head. Her chest falls. She is hot with fever. I lower my head. I breathe into her again. Here she is, looking at the river rushing quickly, deep and hard. I breathe in, deep and steady. Her chest rises. I lift my head. Her body exhales. She wants the cool of the river; there in the cool of the river, her fever will leave her. I lower my head again and breathe into her. She has been hurt and she knows he will never return. Everything is like broken glass for her. The water is smooth against her feet. I release the breath. She exhales. She walks into the river; it is cool. The current catches her. I begin to feel the rhythm: inhale, exhale, inhale, exhale. There it is: she is breathing. She walks to the river because her sorrow is hot, and she must stop it. She is not afraid, just taking care of the fever. The water cools her. She relaxes. She exhales. She is in the current, and it is very fast, but she is not afraid because the heat is leaving her. She is cooling now, carried along on the current, faster and faster. I inhale, and she lets her face fall into the water. I exhale, and I know she is going to drown, not on purpose like they thought, but because . . . inhale, exhale, inhale, exhale. I keep it up until I know I can do it again and again. I don't want to stop, because as long as I am breathing into her, she is breathing in that long and deep river. She is still a little warm. But I am hot. I am full of her story. I can't stop.

Is that when my mother arrives? Is that when she comes in from the living room where *Gunsmoke* is keeping everyone in place? She watches and nods but then watches some more, and at last she says, "That's a good angle. That's what was wrong." And I keep going. Soon she says, "That's enough, Anne. You don't want to hyperventilate." I keep breathing into Annie, seeing the end of the story now, the end I don't want to see. And my mother touches my shoulder and says, "Stop, Anne. You know how to do it. You can stop."

And when I do, I watch her exhale for the last time. Her chest does not rise unless I breathe. I want to cry for her loss; I want to sob that I cannot make her breathe again. And I am so relieved that my mother is there, pulling me back, that I could cry about that, too. I look up at her and say, "I wish she could have learned the survival float."

"Well, that would make a good closing line," my mother says.

And using that line, I win a county award for my demonstration.

That summer, I will go to Lansing, to Michigan State University, for the first time. I will see the state capitol for the first time, and I will win an honorable mention for the demonstration. The criticism of the judges? That I needed too much equipment to make this work. Still they liked the premise, the idea of teaching lifesaving. I think it odd that no one can see the story I am telling each time I breathe into her. And each time I try to teach her to survive the fever and the river, my mother's voice calls me back.

Why is it that when I get the certificate with its fancy gold edges, I feel so sad? I feel like I should have saved her, should have taught her the survival float before she drifted into the other float that no one returns from.

JAMS, 1963

Strawberries

What, for heaven's sake, will impress the jam judges? What will make my plain pint jars with their scarlet, cherry, and blue-black berries stand out from dozens of other jars of jams and jellies from all over Oceana County? What will earn a blue ribbon at the county fair? Not only does 4-H train us to dress ourselves in decent clothes but also to feed a family. And in our world, jam is a food group. And here, just as with the clothes, workmanship and appearance count. This is summer 4-H, not winter, not sewing. This is not about making clothes look good; this is about making mashed fruit look good.

While my brothers raise cows or pigs and my sisters show horses, I am stuck with jams. While they train animals to leads and anticipate selling them for money, I do what we do almost every day on a farm: pick something ripe. Not that I want to raise animals. What I want is to read *Nancy Drew* mysteries and watch Westerns on TV: *The Roy Rogers Show*, *The Lone Ranger*, all the heroes. Or daydream. I could drift for hours on the couch. My mother says, with real nervousness, that I am *so lazy, it's sinful*. We have discussed this sin in catechism class at St. Joseph's. *Sloth, sloth, sloth*—one of the seven deadly sins. Of the seven deadlies, this is the one I am most likely to go to hell for. But my mother has ideas: she has 4-H, and she will fight this. She will lead me back to whatever it is I am supposed to be. She has decided this summer project will be good for me. She will have me make not just one but an array of jams, a rainbow of jams, made the *old-fashioned way*, everything by hand from start to finish.

Why?

This project will take all summer, will reward me for steady work, will make me proud (pride, another of the seven deadlies, but I don't bring this up), and then we will taste the rewards of my work and earn praise for cooking something sweet. My father and brothers will love the sweetness (gluttony, yet another of the seven deadlies, is the word that comes to mind).

But why?

Because it's exacting work. You have *to be precise*. There is little *experimentation* in jam making. I know the source of this. The last two sewing projects have earned only red ribbons, mostly because I hurried, took shortcuts. I was experimenting, so in each of the projects, I had tried something different that did not follow the pattern. She had warned me, and I did not heed her (pride of a different sort), and so it went badly. She did not like that I did this, that I had altered directions, broke the pattern. She said I was being too big for my britches (pride again).

But jam? Why?

She is tired of red ribbons. She wants me to have the experience of a blue, maybe even the purple champion.

For a long time she didn't know what to do, but then she figured it out.

"The old-fashioned way?" I am skeptical.

"Your report will explain it all: every step of the way, the right way, the precise way to handle fruit. Process is as important as the finished product. The judges will love it."

Where does she get this stuff?

"Just shy of soft," she instructs as if I didn't know as we straddle the rows and bend over the strawberry plants, picking from the viney strands that rise almost to our knees, lifting the runners, rolling the leaves over to see the plump dollops of red fruit glistening with dew, shiny with tiny stars.

The field is a neighbor's you-pick operation. My sisters are in another part of the field, picking with more concentration than me. The field is laden with fruit just shy of ripe or past it. Still, this is the time we have, a Saturday morning in June to make the first of a half dozen jams. I bend to pick heart-shaped globes, and for every one I drop into the stained boxes, I eat one. The sweetness is a magnificence my body has craved, succulent in the mouth. I am eating and picking and eating. I am always hungry these days. The sweet, the sweet. Gluttony?

I look up and across the fields running with the wide lushness of early summer, away from the rules of school, away from the catechism that haunts me, away from the news where it seems like everything is changing but us. We are safe. Except . . . I don't always feel safe. Sometimes I look at the news, and it all feels far away, but then some little thing will catch my eye, like the faces in the pictures from *LIFE* magazine that show people marching and a dog biting a man who is marching.

I tell myself that today I am picking strawberries. But this is how fruit picking is done, with half a mind on what I am doing and half on memory; half on worry, half on sweetness. My mind is wandering in slow circles, first on one thing, then on another.

The soft strawberries smudge my fingertips like thin blood. I study them. Like my first blood just last month, this strawberry smear across the fingers—long after every other girl in the class got her period. I had worried my period would never come, this thing that was supposed to come and change my life. *Please, Blessed Mary, mother of God, give me my period.* Once I wondered aloud at lunch when the Blessed Mary got her period, and my girlfriends looked at me and burst into uncontrollable giggles. Charlene had said, "She never had one—that's why she's immaculate."

All winter in that second floor classroom of the Catholic school, learning about the seven deadlies, it had not come. When I would throw my books on the table and tick off another girl's name—*she got hers*—my mother had little patience with my worry. "It'll come soon enough, and then you'll be stuck," she said without any sympathy at all.

Dawn edged its way slowly into the bathroom of our old farmhouse from the high window overlooking the stained tub. Tom and Rick yelled for me to *finish in there* because the *bus is coming.* (It was not.) I sat at the edge of the tub, looked, and looked again. The feeling of being rewarded for waiting, for my prayers and patience, was so immense that I teared up. I was older than other girls, but that morning, when I shoved the door open a crack, yelled at my brothers to get *out of the way,* and asked mom to come, I felt as shy as a little girl. Despite all the education she had offered about what would happen, I had no idea what to do.

Her face fell when I told her, and for a minute I didn't understand. Hadn't she wanted this? She had told me over and over that she wanted me to *grow up.* And I wanted that, too. But her expression reflected a more practical concern: just the week before she had taken the box of sanitary napkins—given to me as a gesture of reassurance that it would come—and she had used them all for her own period. There were no sanitary napkins in the house. We stood in the bathroom, me wondering if she had ever really believed it would come for me so she felt free to use them, her wondering how to solve this problem. She hollered at the boys to *shut up a minute,* then with quiet practicality showed me how to construct a makeshift sanitary pad with layered toilet paper. It was a lumpy thing, and despite a safety pin, it didn't stay in place. It shifted like something alive. Still, I felt her concern and was grateful.

I left for school with mincing steps.

I had forgotten the girls' baseball game that afternoon, a game played on an open field to the east of St. Joseph's School, a field on that day permeated by cool wind and sharp spring sun. I couldn't play my usual position of catcher. I couldn't squat, suddenly overcome with a need to protect myself from something I could not name. With the team huddled in the chilly breeze, I asked if I could play outfield. No one minded since Mary Ellen was actually a better catcher (not that I was any good at outfield, either), and that would help us win, which happened so rarely that it was nice to think we might have a chance. But I figured with everyone focused on home plate and the pitcher's mound, maybe I wouldn't look like I was shoving the makeshift pad into place.

I had forgotten about the boys. The boys had finished their game first, and so they came and loafed behind the foul line to watch us play, their eyes strangely attentive, mocking, their stance disinterested. In contrast, we didn't look at them, but our bodies stood straighter. Carly, the pitcher who had real and shapely breasts, threw back her shoulders so far that she could barely pitch. I stood as still as I could, hunched. Would the boys know I had my period? We aren't supposed to ever tell them, because our periods are private, but how could I ever keep mine private when the pad was sliding all over the place and my face was sweating with worry?

With the innings slipping by as slowly as the decades of a full rosary spoken by an old priest, I found that when I did have to move across the field, I couldn't move fast enough. I missed every ball that came my way in that far right position. The balls would drop out of the sky, and I would be unable to guess where they were falling and would run the wrong way, turn the wrong way, glove outstretched as though catching rain. Or the balls skittered across the grass and I would bend to scoop them up, but they would skip just beyond the cup of leather. Here I was, shuffling across right field, *a woman now,* chasing a ball that would simply slide past my glove. I felt so tired that I wanted to fall down, curl up on the grass, and sleep.

Something else was rising in my body. In the book my mother had given me, *Growing Up and Liking It,* from the Modess company, it stated: "Almost every girl feels some sort of discomfort in her lower abdomen. The feeling ranges from almost undetectable twinges to cramps (which are muscle contractions). Don't be alarmed." I had never had a cramp in my life. I had lived the simple bloods of scrapes and cuts, the unwelcome but harmless badges of bruising. The broken nose had healed without a scar. I didn't expect to cramp, even though my mother had said she had cramps until she gave birth to me. In all the pictures and the booklets, no one told me about the fierce red chain pulling down through the lower back, tying itself with fire under the abdomen. I was thoroughly alarmed.

We were back in the classroom at the end of the day, into current events where we were learning about a civil rights bill, which some people wanted and some people said no, that it was not the right time. I couldn't raise my hand to ask the one question I had, which was, "How do I make this stop hurting?" I didn't care about civil rights or any other rights because this was so wrong. Once home, I doubled over on the blue couch, tearing up as I told Mom about losing the game because I'd missed all three fly balls. And because—this was closer to the truth—I was so disappointed not in the game but in this first period. I had waited for this with all my heart. I hadn't known what cramps meant. I hadn't understood.

My mother gave me an aspirin. I could lie down, though not for long, because you know I tended to take advantage. "This is how it goes," she said. She did touch my forehead, but then she was gone to the kitchen, to the little girls, to the garden. I lay there and turned on the TV. There was something happening in the South, all kinds of trouble with negroes. I watched the trouble vaguely. People were talking about this man Martin Luther King, Jr. They were marching again, men and even some women. Did those women have periods? Did they have cramps? How did they, out there on the streets, keep it a secret? But in the end, the TV could not distract me, no matter how strange the images. And ten minutes later, my mother was looking down at me, saying, "Get up and try to get some work done. It will get your mind off it." But it didn't. When the chain pulled and burned, I had no words—me, the one with words. And even when I walked tentatively to the kitchen and tried again to explain how it hurt, she told me, "Offer it up to God for your sins." Offer it up? I couldn't even think of my next step, let alone of God; the cramps made me vomit.

In that strawberry field, my skin heats not from the sun but from this dream gone wrong. I'm tasting strawberries but dreading this other thing. About once a month, they had said. But nothing of what they had said about this *becoming a woman* had been as predicted. As I eat another strawberry, I'm thinking that the game was just before the end of school. It's been a while. Maybe it won't come back. They said it might be irregular. And because everything about becoming a woman has not been like they said it would be, I want them to be right about this, because I don't want it to come back. I had not felt proud, had not felt like a woman. I felt pain and a tiredness that made my bones ache. It had all been lies.

I stare at my fingers smeared with sweet fruit that reminds me of blood, one thing connected to another. Down the row, my mother lifts her head, shades her eyes, and scolds. "Can't you move any faster?" But she doesn't mean it. She loves being here, too, with my sisters and me in this no-clock time, away from the house and its noisy demands. She's finished her own row and is returning to mine to meet me, the sun touching her hair, her hands, and the fruit as she shoves each basket forward. I fill my quarts, but I keep tasting, wondering now if those boys ever have interesting things to say, thinking about their stares, how one boy at school dropped his pencil, and when we both bent to pick it up, our hands touched and he smiled at me.

Then Mom is so close that her head nearly brushes against mine, her half gray, half auburn hair escaping from under its faded scarf and almost tangling with my brown flyaway curls as we reach for the same berry. She looks at my basket and rolls her eyes. I have picked only three quarts to her six. But on the side of her mouth is a red mark, a flicker of berry.

I ask, "Did you eat a strawberry?"

"No, of course not." She says sharply, but I see that she does not mean to be sharp. She shakes her head, as though annoyed, but she doesn't take it back. It is a small lie, only of the venial sort. She looks pointedly at my small haul. I sit back on my heels; I wonder if my mother is even capable of one of the seven deadlies. As I watch her swift-moving hands, I know she is not capable of sloth. And it comes to me, squatting in the sunshine, that her deadly sin is wrath. But even that is not quite right because her wrath is not random. It is wielded, like in a holy war. She is determined that I, all of us, must be good, and she must set the example. She must show me how to live. She cannot admit to eating the sweet berries. She can't let me see that she loves this pleasure as much as I do. Only when the work is done, only when we rise from our knees and gather my sisters and carry the baskets down the sunny road and pay for the quarts at the stand does she show me. Her hand lifts a ripe berry to her mouth with a quick smile. She takes it with a small pucker of her lips, almost a kiss. I want to laugh; I want it to last forever.

The worn kitchen with its east window pours midmorning light onto the sink, onto the linoleum's green and gray squares. We have washed and hulled the berries in cold water, dried them on frayed dish towels, crushed them with the old potato masher, and added white sugar. We have poured the raw jam into the old stainless steel pot, which is almost black on the outside but inside is as shiny as a moonlit night. We have not added the special ingredient called pectin, which assures us that the jam will thicken. That is *too easy*, because my mother determines that if we do it the old-fashioned way, we will impress the judges. We want to do it *the hard way, no shortcuts,* so when I write the report, the judges will know that I understand some of the chemistry of the jam-making, and this will add points to my score for the blue ribbon.

The old way fails.

Is that when I go to the bathroom and realize the fear of the morning was based in some inkling I didn't know I knew? Or had my thinking made it come again? Was I being punished for being lazy or for . . . oh, all the sins, large and small?

The hot kitchen steams with the scent of cooking strawberries. Now I am stirring the pot at the stove. I have to stir down the boil because the mash looks *a little thin.* I stir slowly, reducing the mash. After awhile, a stirring inside me wants to be free of this. I feel trapped, and my arms burn. My mind drifts again. What is happening here, me caught in this stirring while my brothers raise a steer that will earn them a hundred dollars at the fair? How much does the champion jam maker win?

She interrupts to check on the stirring, studies the mash in the kettle. "Keep it up. Sometimes it thickens as the moisture reduces." This setback fills the kitchen. She leaves to hang a load of wet laundry.

The metal spoon spirals and bangs the long moments in the kettle. I turn on the radio: more trouble in the South, wherever that is, something about freedom fighters.

Do they make jam there?

The next time she checks, she sighs and wipes her hands. "Let's take a look." She ladles the mash into a glass pint jar. She lifts the hot jar to the light. At the bottom, it's a clear bright red. I can see through it, like Jell-O. The upper half is dense with the fruit that should fill the entire jar.

The jam is floating. The condition of floating, I learn quickly, is the cardinal sin of jam makers. I see in her mind the blue ribbon turn into the red that matches the fruit. In short order, my mother leaves the kettle and makes a half dozen phone calls. She even speaks to the county extension agent. When she returns from the phone, shaking her head, she says, "It won't be easy." She comes back to the stirring, stares into the pot, "Sometimes it doesn't work, but there's no choice now."

I don't tell her that my body is starting to ache.

"Like this." She shows me how to ladle the hot mash into a scalded jar. She pours to within a quarter inch of the top, twists tight the caps with their inserted lids, and without setting them to cool, she slowly turns the jar upside down. The mash rolls in the glass. She places it upside down on the counter. It looks wrong. But this is how to do it.

Every ten minutes according to the kitchen clock, I turn every jar upside down. Ten minutes later, I turn every jar right-side up. As the jam cools, it thickens a little each time, and if you keep the fruit moving through that cooling jam, it suspends as it thickens. With each turn, I watch the fruit move more slowly to whatever the top is—which may be the bottom or back where it started.

If it works, the mash eventually suspends evenly.

The radio has a voice that turns with worry. I turn it off. I want to turn everything off. I turn the jars. Each time, the crushed berries float to the top.

I stand in that kitchen heat, staring at the dozen jars, counting minutes, turning jars. Each time she checks, my mother's disappointment hovers until at last she abandons the operation. I stand before rows of floating fruit. What happened to the morning with its sweet mouth? Is this failure a punishment for sloth or one of the other deadlies sneaking into our kitchen?

No, this is about my body.

The slow burn settles in my abdomen. The first period was not a fluke. My period has come again and will come with obscene regularity just as predicted until I am old. And these cramps will keep to the same schedule. No one lied about this part. And no amount of sloth, wrath, stirring, or being good will make a difference. The months will turn right-side up, then upside down, forever and ever amen.

Cherries

A month later it is cherries. We pick the tart cherries in high summer, in July, the month of heat. Even in Michigan, we have heat waves, and the orchard is big enough to stop the breeze. The trees are hot in the orchard, and shade is small. The straps that hold the full cherry buckets pull against my shoulders and back. I hate the unwieldy buckets and the even more unwieldy structure of the ladders. My body feels unwieldy, too: heavy, clumsy, and slow in the heat. I think I am the only one who cannot stand up to this work, and I feel ashamed, but shame doesn't spur me to pick any faster.

I can hide for short periods of time in the branches of a cherry tree; life is simple there. Trees and heat, reach and drop. Hide. But there is no hiding really. Someone will call, will ask, *Where is Anne*? Someone will answer, *Third row back, fourth tree, topping*. I top trees because it is slow work, and I am slow, and so the two seem compatible. Is that what she sees, why she comes? Because come she does, striding swiftly down the broad rows of trees in headscarf and jeans, her stained blouse, the one with cut-off sleeves, pulled taut across her back. She arrives at my tree, stops, hands on hips, staring up with a frown. I know she will ask if I can't *move a little faster*.

She says, "Pick out a few good quarts from the lugs on the truck."

She says, "Bring them to the house."

She says with a small smile, "We'll mix them with some sweets."

She says without any wrath, "We've only got one day."

I scramble down before she changes her mind. I wonder where she got the sweet cherries so early in the year, but I also know this will be special. This will impress the judges, a jam with both sweets and tarts. Then she's off again, and I am left to find the truck where I sort out three quarts of ripe tarts. When I get to the house, she has three quarts of sweets sitting on the counter, and I realize she must have traded at the processing plant when she delivered the last load of full lugs. Despite her pleasure, I am afraid to ask. She is impatient because she is torn: drawn to the heavy harvest out in the orchard but knowing we must do this today while the fruit is fresh.

After lunch, after dishes, after she has checked on my sisters and sent everyone back to the orchard and my father has nodded to her before he leaves, she brings the cherries to the back porch where she can still see the orchard, where she can hear the distant voices and the truck when it moves. She brings two old-style bobby pins, like the ones my great-aunt Mary uses in her braid, but these are used for canning. I know what's coming.

She has tried to teach me before, but I have been too clumsy and have torn up the skin of the berries. She doesn't like *beat-up cherries* for her canning. This time, she shows me again how to poke the curved end of the hairpin into the tiny belly button of each cherry, slip it around the pit, and bring the pit out like the small rough seed it is. But she doesn't scold when I tear the skin. She says, "It's okay for jam. Jam doesn't need to be perfect, not like canning."

She stays with me until the rhythm sets in my fingers, and then she leaves me on the porch in the sun, pushing the hairpin into the tiny crevasses of the cherry and bringing out the hard pit. The cherry deflates softly each time.

The pulp cries with juice.

In the lazy sun, my fingers feel how to work the pin, easing into the flesh around the tiny pit. My hands fall into a rhythm, this pushing in and bringing out. My hands turn sticky. The sun heats my thighs and hips. Everything feels too bright. My whole body hums with summer light.

I stop. I feel like I should move, not just my hands but my body. My thighs are too warm in my cut-off jeans and in that place where the blood comes. What is happening? My hands drop into my lap, and there is a brief upside down spinning. I am suspended, floating for a second or two in the heat and light.

This can't be right.

And all the way from the kitchen, my mother has sensed my not rightness. She has sensed sin, because she bursts onto the porch and stands in front of me. "You get busy, Anne. If you want this blue ribbon, you get busy." And I blush hard, because she has confirmed sin with her voice.

But which one is it?

She gives me no time to think about it. "Right now," she says, her arms crossed in front of her. I become nimble and pit all six quarts in record time.

The day powers ahead according to my mother's plan. In that hot kitchen, we crush the cherries, tart and sweet, and pour them into that fine old pot that has seen a thousand jams. We pour in all those broken orbs of sweetness and sourness, and this time she says, *not so much sugar*, because you know we are already adding *these sweets*.

Is it because she is low on sugar?

Then the stirring. When at last she pours the test ladle, red-shredded stars, bright scarlet and dark maroon, suspend perfectly. The dense fruit hangs balanced, the color so beautiful that we both sigh. I pour it all into jars. Sealed with wax, we admire the look of mottled reds in a tidy row.

That night, at supper with a loaf of plain bread, we open a test jar and taste the cooled jam. We learn the truth—sour is greater than sweet. The tart cherry flavor dominates the sweet with a determination that makes even my father pucker and gasp. My mother shoots daggers at him and says, "Well, at least this one didn't float."

He nods deliberately, silently slathers more on his bread, and looks at her steadily as he takes a bite but does not smile. She turns to me and says, "A discerning judge will recognize the old-fashioned taste." She carries on, ignoring even my little brothers who are pretend gagging. "The flavor is complex."

My father chokes.

So this is complexity. What was supposed to be sweet has turned so sour that you can't take it in? Is this how it works? Sweet is what we expect, but sour is what we get? When one thing tastes a way it wasn't supposed to, we find the words to cover it up, to make it something else.

We call it complex.

Wild Currants

The quest escalates, rising from the never-to-be-exhibited floating strawberries of June and the *complex* cherries of July to late August, when the Oceana County Fair happens and all this work *pays off*.

This time it's wild currants.

They are hard to see, like the beginnings of a change, hidden in tangles.

They ripen in August like tiny grapes in the old fence lines, at the edges of woods, and in secret places in the pasture.

"We don't really have time for this," she says, hurrying to gather baskets, but we have to find them when they are ripe, then pick enough, which is a problem because they are *not plentiful*. Once picked, I will carry out the too-familiar ritual of stirring, cooking down, pouring, and then assembling the whole display with neatly labeled titles. Finally I will write the 4-H report on these *unique* jams.

All through that long jam summer, we have thought of the fair. From the news of freedom fighters to the fruit picking in heat, from the marches and trouble in the South to the not-to-be-mentioned, so-thick-it-couldn't-be-spread apricot, the fair has loomed in the future, lumbering with judgment, ever nearer. She is worried because we have decided not to show the strawberry. She thinks we can get away with the plum jam, which looks like crumbled oak leaves in the jar but has a strong and pure flavor. "At least it's not pucker jam," she says, admitting at last how sour the cherry is. She says we will create a *texture of flavors*.

This jam, this wild currant, is, my mother says, *the crowning glory*. "Because no one uses them anymore," she says. They will be the contrast that makes all the other jam flavors stand out. And the currant is more purply so will add another color to the display. When I ask what they taste like, she says, *sour grapes*, and part of me sighs—just what we need. She has refused to use one ounce more sugar on any of these jams than is absolutely necessary and insists on no pectin, because she is always trying to get the jams to thicken in the natural way.

The problem is that no one grows currants any more; thus they are only found wild, as in *gone wild*. "Just like everything else around here," she says as she climbs into the car and we embark on yet another search for the mysterious fruit.

We look first at the abandoned homesteads. The grapes may have once been domestic. A hundred years or so ago, they may have been planted and pruned to mix with apples in the making of hard cider. She remembers some of this from her childhood. We climb into the rusty station wagon and drive around the dusty old two-track roads. We park in weedy easements and stroll oh-so-casually into the backyards of gray farmhouses with no glass in the windows. We explore the edges of ancient apple orchards. My mother knows these places: *failed farms* where people have not lived since the *Depression*. I think about these old farms, these haunted places with the wind rushing through them. The dried-blood red of empty barns, if they haven't fallen in, seems like old sorrow. Even the birds, flickering dark and feathery shadows in the trees, seem distant and lonely.

We are on one of the north roads driving to a place she has just remembered, listening to the ten o'clock morning news radio when we first hear it. Jackie Kennedy has given birth to a little boy. We smile at each other. Her pregnancy has been on the news for months, though she has not been. My mother likes that she keeps these things private. She thinks that's a good way for her to behave. We have been excited by this prospect of a baby in the White House, especially a baby to this mother, the Jackie we like.

Then the newscaster says the baby was born premature.

"What's that mean?" I ask.

"Too early." She says, her mouth tightening. She pulls over then, staring at the black-eyed house set back in overgrown trees, leaning in the heat. She shakes her head, sighs. Like always, she says, "Say a prayer."

Hail Mary, hail Mary in my head.

She climbs out; I scramble after, thinking we will head behind the ramshackle barn in the far back. But she is scanning the old farmhouse; she is not looking at the fence lines or the old garden sites. She looks for a long time, a small battle happening on her face.

"Shall we look inside?"

For the currants?

I want to ask her more about babies born too early, but my mother is on a personal crusade. She crosses the yard, marches right up to the back door, pulls aside some old vines, and walks into the old kitchen. After a moment, I follow her in, my heart beating hard. Here are buckling floorboards, drooping ceilings, pigeon and sparrow droppings, and everywhere the sense of something lost. She tells me to watch out for rotten spots in the floor, but she moves briskly as she opens grimy cupboards one after another. Most shelves are scattered with debris—an old baking powder tin, a rusted spoon—but here and there, she finds a bottle or a tiny glass jar. She looks at these closely for bubbles. If they have bubbles, it means *they're old*. She fingers these but leaves them. She's after something, but what?

She heads for a door, peeling and warped, and pulls it open to reveal steps. *Is she going to the basement*? What is she going to find there? She steps down into the darkness. I hear the steps creak, and she calls back, "Don't come down here." But after she disappears, I follow her halfway. I'm scared for my mom. What is driving her down there into that cold hell? What will I do if the floor falls in on her? When I hear her rattling among the decayed beams and abandoned tackle, I just know there are rats, bats, spiders, and who knows what else. I'm trying to be brave, but it's not in my nature. The sound of glass clinking carries up, along with mustiness and mold, dust and rot. How is she able to rummage in the dark? Metal bangs and cans fall over. I hear her favorite expression, *oh shit*, and just as I am about to call out, she appears, floating in gray at the bottom of the steps, looking up, cradling canning jars covered in thick layers of dirt, the contents still sealed.

She calls up, "Come take these." She puts them on the steps and goes back into the darkness.

I step down a few more steps to lift the gray things in my arms. Through holes in the foundation—this is how she must see her way—I stare at my mother's moving shadow silhouetted in a dark haze. What is she doing? Why? At home we have 227 jars with everything from green beans to red beets. We don't need this old food. And this food is so old that it might be antique. And that's it. She is looking for jars to be used for canning. No, not just canning. For the jam. She is taking these jars to make the jam look even more old-fashioned. This will impress the judges. Old-fashioned—the right way to do things. But as I stand with old fruit in my hands, I wonder . . . is it possible that my mother . . . is stealing? And I'm . . . helping. I know this is supposed to be wrong, but it's a wild feeling. It swirls around in me, a small thrill and fear and . . . ? Is she so worried about money that she'd save a penny by taking the jars? Or is this something about claiming the charm of old things? Is this her version of what Jackie did in the White House?

I turn the jars in my hands. The remains inside are black and lumpy.

Is this really stealing if no one wants them?

I trudge the jars up and out to the car, into the sun. I spit on the small ones to clean them off. The raised letters spell "Atlas" on the front. From one of my mythology books, I remember that Atlas held up the world.

So, this is how it's done: we will take the fruit to the fair in stolen jars. Will they hold up the world?

Out of that haul, we gather a few quarts, several pints, and three precious half pints—the ones that are perfect for jam. As she starts the car, she is so happy that she hums, something she does when she rocks my littlest sister.

"Mom, what did we just do?" I gesture at the jars. I stare at her.

She stares back, baleful. "This is gathering." She turns back to the road. "A kind of antiquing."

This new word entered our vocabulary after Jackie Kennedy explored the basement of the White House and found all those antiques. So now everyone is *antiquing*. My mother is just doing what Jackie did, right? Not exactly.

This makes no sense, but it doesn't seem to matter.

She turns on the radio. The news is full of the Kennedy baby, Patrick Bouvier.

The baby is not doing well. The baby has been taken to another hospital. Not the hospital where Jackie is.

"What's wrong with it?"

She sighs, her humming gone. "It's a blue baby."

I know what this means.

"Will it die?" I am remembering my aunt Barbara's baby.

She doesn't answer.

I stare at the small jars, the contents wrinkled and strange with age.

We don't talk about it anymore, but we listen to the news all the way home. The only other thing we learn is that Jackie got to hold the baby before they took him away to the other hospital. I think about this, how it might hurt to have a baby and have people take it away from you.

When we get home, the washer has backed up. I wonder if this is a punishment. Because sometimes Mom overloads the wringer washer, and because the washer backs up every few weeks, my father has to walk through the orchard down to a spot a couple hundred yards south of our farmhouse, the place called the drain field, a sunken area that is always mushy and full of stink. We all avoid the drain field, because even we who are in daily contact with dirt hold some instinct about it being unclean. Even as children, even with my brothers' fascination with all things scatological, we know the waste of the washing and poohing and flushing ends up there. Since the farm began, which is since time began, this place has existed, and even when my father put the new tub and toilet in the bathroom, he ran the drain pipes down to this sinking place.

For whatever reason, it is not a desert but an ill-scented oasis. A dense thicket of wild shrubs circles it. On the edge of this green stink, my dad wades through the brambles with the long snakes to clean out the pipes. He, the person who must always be aware of the weather both in his fields and in his house, notices the dark grapelike bunches, draped and ripening, tumbling over an abandoned bedstead dumped there in a previous age. My dad carries them up into the kitchen and waits patiently until the scolding about his stinky boots is over. Then he pulls them out of his pockets and slyly asks, "These what you looking for?"

And she says, "Oh, John," with that disgusted grin and gathers them into her hands like gold.

That's how I end up mincing into that fly-riddled thicket with a scarf over my mouth, standing in slime, picking a bucket of wild currants. The clusters of tiny purply orbs seem to have thrived on the household runoff. The bushes are dense with clusters. I try not to wonder how this place, this sinkhole of waste, might taint the flavor. Still, these tiny purple-to-black pearls, set in tight clusters the size of a baby's fist, are stunning and perfect.

I bring the wild currants to the house, dump them in the sink.

My mother says, "Be sure to rinse those a couple of extra times."

I rinse until my hands are raw, then mash and dump the currants into the pot. I know the process by heart now: turn up the heat in a hot kitchen; wash and scald the old jars, the contents which have been tossed and buried; then stir.

Always with the stirring.

They will tell us later that the baby was perfectly formed. They will tell us later that he was put into a huge machine, some thirty-feet long, to help him breathe.

They will tell us later that when it became clear that nothing could be done, they placed him into his father's arms.

The radio plays softly in our August kitchen. We keep listening for the reports. The wild currants change their shape in the pot, becoming thick at last.

I stir, and the radio announcer's voice comes into the room. That voice. That tone again.

The newscaster announces that the Kennedy baby has died.

My mother stops wiping down the counter. I stop stirring. We look at each other.

Something has been stolen from us; something that was ripe with promise has been taken from us.

The dark mash rises in front of me, swirling with change, and as I have been taught, as I am coming to understand, I must stir it down. After a minute, we go on working. I realize the mash smells like communion wine.

Later, I add half the sugar called for because nothing can be really sweet in this jammy world. Later, I skim foam and pour jam into scalded "antique" jars lifted from the bowels of an old house. Only days before the fair, I will scribble my mother's optimistic adjectives in the report: *rich flavor, dark substance.*

By then, I know I will earn a red ribbon on this project. I know my mother and I will go to the 4-H building after the judging, stand before the long tables of showcased jams and jellies, and look quietly at the rows of jars, at the tacky red ribbon. I can almost see the way she will stand over the report on the winning jams, look up, and say, *Oh my gosh. She used honey!*

But in that kitchen moment, while stirring the wild currants, hearing the news about Jackie's baby, the very air, thick with the winey scent of grapes, seems to shift, announcing change. My mother and I have been thieves. The fruit is transformed. Kennedy, who saved us from the Cuban Crisis—even my dad thinks this is so—cannot save his family from a blue baby.

I lift the mash in the spoon so old that it may be antique and taste, searing my mouth with wild currents.

DECISION, 1963

I have never before made a decision like this—if I've ever really made one at all. The 4-H club has become a part of my life, my way of thinking, but the decisions associated with it are about appearance and the domestic arts. Despite all my mother's personal attentions, it hasn't quite worked as she dreamed. For six years, I've done every project, from the dish towel to the jams to demonstrating on Resusci Annie, a dummy, how to give mouth-to-mouth resuscitation. I've made skirts and dresses and tops. I've learned to put in zippers and buttonholes and pleats. Sometimes I win blue ribbons, sometimes red. I go to meetings and I've even gone to Lansing as a club representative, to Michigan State University, to the annual Exploration Days.

This time the 4-H project is home decorating. I will cut out pictures and draw table settings and put together the colors of place mats and napkins with scraps of bright green and red fabric that I think will make a nice summer table. To be honest, we've never set a table with place mats and napkins in our lives, and the likelihood of starting now is about the same as going to the moon. I am not having any fun with this project, not since Mom told me I can't put checks with polka dots, even though the colors look good together.

She shows me pictures of some of the winning projects in the same category. Nope, not anything like those. I am not like the other 4-H girls and not just in table settings. I like to sew but not to follow a pattern. I like to model but not to prepare the reports on the projects. I love to read but don't get good grades—though the sisters who teach me say I am smart enough. I have friends but feel lonely. My parents are trying to figure out what's up with me.

My mother shakes her head at my choice of colors.

"Looks like a poinsettia." She is standing by the table, which is covered in scraps and cutouts. "Maybe you'd like to try something more neutral?" She points to the soft beige plaid to go with a cream linen.

I look at her with that look; I can't help it. "I'm trying Christmas in July."

She looks at me, chewing her lip. The silence lengthens. My mother isn't silent unless she's thinking something through, something hard. Then she floors me. She looks down at her dish towel and says, "Maybe you'd like to try Marywood Academy?"

Light and shadow shift on the table.

"Marywood?"

"The Dominican mother house in Grand Rapids—where all the sisters live. There are aspirants there. Some girls there are interested in being nuns."

I am so shocked that I slice clean through the picture of the Golden Wheat platter I'm cutting out of a catalogue.

"A nun?"

While I tape the two pieces together, my mother says, "You don't have to. We just thought . . . You could talk to Sister; she'd tell you about it."

"Grand Rapids is way past Muskegon." I've got that much geography figured out. It's two or more hours south of Hart, somewhere in the middle of the state.

"Well, you'd live in a dorm, with other girls your age."

"I'd live there?" In Grand Rapids?

"Just for the school year. And you could come home once a month."

"What would I do there?"

She sighs, exasperated. "You'd go to school, Anne. And to mass most every day. You'd get a good education from the nuns." She pauses as she sorts through the pages I've cut out. She picks a black-and-white checkerboard that looks like a Purina sack to me.

"It would be for your freshman year in high school. If you didn't like it, you would come home. It's just something to think about." I know this isn't what she means. She looks up. "We wouldn't send you unless you wanted to go. It's expensive. And we have to prepare. There are entrance tests to take and . . ."

So she has thought about this. A lot. I know why.

Something has gone wrong in my world. Not just my dreamy side taking over when work is to be done. Not just my periods and sleeplessness. There has been an incident.

While I was babysitting in a new place, a farm in another township.

A hired hand, after chores were finished in the barn, had come to the house where I had put the little ones to bed. As was often done for hired hands in our house, I gave him some food, leftovers I found in the refrigerator, and talked with him. He stayed and stayed. Perhaps I talked a little too loudly, tried a little too hard to be grown-up. Then he asked for aspirin, and when I went to the bathroom to get it, he followed and touched me. And other things. These other things were not the new word I learned, *rape*, the word everyone says in hushed tones. But he had done some things that made my world full of the shadow. I was ashamed.

Amazingly, I had been able to tell my parents. I had walked back into our house and told them what had happened. I could do this because, even though I was an odd duck, as my aunts called me, I knew my parents would protect me. They listened, and my mother and father, in the ways of country people, took care of things. Once they knew, the right steps were taken quietly on their own. Now the hired hand was no longer in the region. And I was busy doing what they said to do. I was spending a lot of time trying to forget. I was succeeding. I was going about my days, and everything looked normal. After all, I had not been *robbed of innocence* as they described in *True Confessions*. But because he had touched me, because something serious had happened, I understood it like a pond. There was dark water running under it all, but instead of closing thought, it opened thought—to fear. To curiosity. I wondered what would have happened if he had kept going. I feared it, too. It had to do with the kiss, the way he had kissed me. I tried not to think about his mouth, but then I would. It was real; it was not real. And I was to distract myself from these thoughts, these bad thoughts. But of course they came anyway and made me more reclusive, more irritable at my daydreams being interrupted. And oddly, I became more religious, at least on the surface. The 4-H club had been no help with this. It had been the silence of church I wanted, not the club.

And so, my mother's suggestion is not unfounded.

"I don't know," I mutter, startled. I'm cutting again, trying to decide between green checks and a garish orange instead of red.

"You may find it's a . . ."—she takes a long time to say this—"a better place for you."

A better place? Is this about getting rid of me?

But no. They have thought of something that will help me feel safe and help me with the worrying. It occurs to me that maybe it is where I belong. I am interested not so much in the nun part but in the idea of someplace else. *Just an idea,* she repeats as the days pass. But once the idea is there, it floats around the rooms and wafts after me at school. I like the majesty, the dramatic rituals of church, and prayer means something to me, so maybe, maybe I would find something I am good at there, something more than reading and daydreaming.

But I look around at all the fields, at our beautiful old yard and worn barns. I elbow the oak dining room table, covered with projects. I think of my little sisters and even my brothers, and I know it is impossible. I can't leave. I am here, and I will always be here. This is us working, doing our projects, and even though the world gets in sometimes, we are safe. Aren't we? But my mother's idea stays, hanging on like a rainy fall, waiting to turn into something else.

We are sitting on the second floor of St. Joseph's Catholic School in science class in a room housing thirty farm kids, fifth through eighth grade, taught by one tough Dominican nun. Large double-hung windows to the north let in the chill, and the east windows scarcely let in any sunshine in November. The spacious room is crowded with the restlessness of kids in new winter. I sit toward the west, nearest the wall and bookshelves, though I long to sit near the windows. It's after lunch and we have watched Mr. Science on the education channel on TV. Now sister breaks up the history classes according to the grades.

The priest comes to the door and motions for Sister. We all watch as she crosses the front of the room, her heels hard on the linoleum, her beads murmuring bead words inside her flowing white habit. She steps out, and suddenly the door closes. We look at each other. The door is always open; Sister is always in view. A minute passes. The boys are already reaching for some small weaponry, some secret way to wound, when the door opens. The priest enters. He comes into our classroom for two reasons only: teaching the religion class or scolding. The boys still themselves, their faces edged with guilt. He doesn't even look at them; he takes us all in. He takes a breath. He pauses. Something in his face is about to break. I know these moments; I know something terrible is coming.

I don't remember the words. But I hear the tone of voice in that drafty room filled with Catholic farm kids. I could make the words up, say the likely thing, but it is the tone that sears, a voice holding alarm under a cloak of its opposite, calm. I had heard that tone, rhythm, pitch of voice placed just so every time I had been told of a death.

He tells us that President Kennedy has been shot.

I sit up at my desk.

We are not sure how to react. Many of our parents do not like this president because even though he was Catholic, farmers are not Democrats. But we know by the way Sister stands by the door, holding her beads at her side, her lips moving even as she listens, that here is seriousness, something far different from liking or not liking. We can almost smell it, sharp and acidic; there it is, the danger that enters through the ears and goes straight to the nerves—every one of us electric with alertness right there among the catechism books and saints' posters.

The priest leads us in the Lord's Prayer, *our father, our father*, and then he is reaching up to the TV stand in the corner, flipping on the TV, turning it up. That same voice is everywhere, every voice on every channel, as he turns from channel to channel, that voice, that rhythm, that quiet pretend—the mask danger wears until it wants to show itself.

Within ten minutes, word comes not that he has been shot but that he has been *assassinated*. A hissing word, those hard *S*'s. Assassinated means killed. He was killed in Texas, in a car, shot in the head. She was with him, wearing a pink Chanel suit, a pink hat. It was sunny there.

It is cloudy here, gray spotted with flashes of sky. We had Mr. Science that day. We had felt safe learning about—what was it?—the composition of water.

The busses take us home early.

Two days later.

At Sunday mass, we pray for the Kennedys, for Jackie and her children, for the new president, Johnson, who was sworn in on an airplane. And for the dead president. Out loud we pray, *Lord, have mercy on his soul.*

We pray for real for our country. It seems strange to me that the words in the 4-H pledge—*for our country*—are now everywhere in church. A crossing over. Leaving church, everyone is gentle with each other, and some women cry. I know the farmers will pray while they feed the animals and while they walk the fields. We have gone more quiet with this praying.

After church, while Mom irons a white tattered tablecloth for Sunday dinner, the table is bare, waiting to be set. Nothing is spread there: no sewing, no button basket, no mending or even fruit to be peeled. Not a 4-H project in sight. Our table, bare.

The TV is on. It has been on since he died, though the sound is turned down low. My dad is asleep, having worked a night shift to make extra money. He is worried that the assassination will give the communists a chance. My brothers have been sent to the barns where they may or may not do their chores. I don't know where my little sisters are.

My mother and I are alone in that dining room with a bare table.

The TV is on and on and on.

The man who killed Kennedy, Lee Harvey Oswald, is to be taken to a prison. We want to see him in person. I don't know why we do, but we do. It is about to happen on live television.

My hands are on the oak table, fingers reading scratches and nicks but feeling mostly the smooth surface. I am running my hands over it, palms flat, like I am smoothing fabric. Mom turns up the volume. A big Texan announces that Oswald is coming. I watch, my hands still moving slowly over the table. Mom is there, too, but she is ironing. Oswald comes through the doorway. Lee Harvey Oswald is being led through a corridor in a police station somewhere in Texas. With my hands on the oak, I watch this man who killed our president.

He is walking, two men at his side. He looks small. He looks ordinary in his sweater. How could such a small man kill the president?

It happens quickly. Another man steps forward, his back to the cameras. A popping sound, familiar and clear. Oswald's mouth twists open; his shoulders hunch. Then bodies block the picture. Hands, just hands and bodies and feet and shouting. And the announcer says over and over, *He has been shot.*

In the second just after, my mother looks up. She hasn't seen what I saw. "Someone shot him?"

I nod. I can't speak.

"Oh. Oh." She sits down.

My hands are on the bare table. I can't seem to take a breath. I have just seen a man killed on TV, and it feels like I have seen it for real but not for real. The two feelings are running side by side. This is real; this is not real.

This is real. A man was shot. This man was shot.

Finally, I inhale. I don't know what to do. I turn to ask my mother, "Should we pray? Should we say the rosary?" And my mother, my deeply religious mother, says, "Not now."

She doesn't want to pray. She just stares at the TV.

We sit in long silence, listening to wild voices. The words run through me, over and over: *He has been shot.*

"Are you okay?" she asks, suddenly looking over at me.

I feel so grateful to her that I want to cry, but I nod, then say, "I feel bad." Confused by my own words, I try to find the next ones, but she says, "Me, too."

She turns back. The look on her face is not calm, not angry. My mother is scared.

To keep my hands from shaking, I trace the grain on the table; it swirls and moves on, swirls and moves on. We are here, I tell myself, here in our plain dining room with our plain table with nothing to clutter or cover it: no project, no food or clothing, no buttons or scissors, no pledge to head or heart or hands or health hovering in the work. There are only these lines: narrow and wide, dark and light, some straight, some wandering, some lost.

I have seen a man shot.

My mother is afraid.

Nothing is safe: not the president, not even the president's assassin, not home.

I don't know what Marywood is or what it means, but it is not here. Is it then that I decide?

I trace a single line with my finger. The bare wood is full of motion; here and there a knot like an eye stares back.

PART II: SEX

... nothing will ever dazzle you like the dreams of your body ...

Mary Oliver

GOING PUBLIC, 1966

The yellow school bus, gears grinding and windows already slid to the grimy halfway point, roared down the hill from the west, stopped, ill-tempered and impatient, September dust roiling like a smoky cloud of dragon's breath at the sand-burred and burdocked corner, and loaded all five of us Oomens into its slammed-open vertical door, then roared off to the north to pick up Grays and Smiths, our Oomen cousins, and on to the Vandenheuvels' farm. It would carry on then, toward Crystal Valley or Elbridge or Twin Bridges, depending on what mileages had passed and what rerouting had been done, and it would pick up, along the way, thirty more desperate kids than even we were at the time.

The bus was the way to the world, to an education my father believed in desperately, which he had been forced to give up in his second year of high school. But his sense of dedication toward education was coupled with his deep Catholicism. That meant my father believed in a Catholic education, not a public education, for as long as he could afford. The quandary: there were five of us in school now. So he felt he'd given me what he could by sending me to that convent in Grand Rapids for my freshman year of high school. He hoped this Catholic education would take, but I had come home. He made clear that he loved me, was not disappointed—and turned the lens of Catholic education on the younger ones. He trusted me to keep the oaths. I should have tried harder.

On this day, this September, we all climbed onto that bus, and miles later, my siblings would climb off it and enter St. Joseph's Catholic School in Weare Township. But I would ride on and climb off in town. I would enter a public institution. The nuns and the church would protect my brothers and sisters, but I was about to go public.

Though 4-H would continue to be a part of my life, this was not 4-H. This would be learning to use what 4-H had given me—though not quite as they had planned. I was a sophomore. I was green, fresh out of that year in a convent, where I had lived and prayed and realized nun-ness was not meant for me. I had learned this much: since I wasn't cut out to be a nun, I wanted to know about love and sex. Not in a conscious way—though I had wildly romantic fantasies—but as love and sex sneak under all things young in the body.

I had prepared for this day. I had sewn several outfits—staying up late after the Oceana County Fair, 4-H meetings, daily chores, and the demands of late summer harvests. But one outfit, the one for the first day, made from a remnant, was a dress so short that my mother threatened not to let me out of the house.

"It looks cheap and it's immoral. How can you go out like that? " she asked, wiping her hands on a green dish towel, staring at my knees as though they were news.

How can I not? I might have said, but I wasn't that clever. Instead I told her that if I had been able to pay full price for a piece off the bolt, I wouldn't have had to scrimp on the yardage and guess. I said, "It wouldn't be so short, Mom, but I bought a two-yard remnant for a pattern that needed two and a half yards." That sentence, or a variation, would become a refrain.

And she said, "You don't expect me to believe that? You're just saying that so you could make it that short." But she knew I had saved her a little money in a house where we would be nickeled and dimed to distraction, saved more than a little by making my school clothes while she and Dad were still trying to pay tuition for my brothers and sisters at St. Joseph's. So when I slunk away to the sewing machine, she sighed and *tsked* and said it was a *good thing* my father was working midnights at a factory to keep us going and also keeping up the farm and all—to remind me how hard everyone was working and of my *eternal laziness*—so he wouldn't see me leave for school *in that getup*.

The getup, a dress of narrow bright orange and yellow stripes racked with red dots and made of cheap cotton, did not cover my knees, and my legs had grown long that year, so the dress had the effect of an orange Popsicle, and though, like all the Oomen females (and orange Popsicles as well), I would run toward a softness in the middle, the sleeveless shift slimmed my hips. The tossed-on sloppy sweater was just there to cover my shoulders until I entered the long hallway of Hart Public High School.

As ordinary as my parents were, the word *public* scared them, and I knew, too, that it was something of a cliff over which I was to fall. There, in public school, my parents could not siphon my activities toward a 4-H club, to their own kind. They could not as easily filter my friends, and these new friends would be of different congregations. They would be of different parishes where my parents might not know these children's parents. They might even be of different churches entirely, protestant churches. Then there was always the possibility, one supposed (though it was unlikely), that these kids might not attend a church at all. They were the most dangerous.

I was as naive and uncertain as a girl can be, but I had, under the guise of saving money on that remnant, made the dress as short as I could and still get out of the house. In 4-H (and Marywood), the hem of a dress was supposed to touch the floor when you were kneeling, as if praying had something to do with the length of your skirt. But at public school, the rule merely invited rebellion, and who in public school would stop a new girl, one it was rumored had been to a convent, and ask her to kneel to check the length of her skirt?

Other than climbing on the bus in the orange dress, I don't remember that first day clearly, except that after an hour on country roads, we approached Hart, a small Michigan town with maple-lined main streets and hometown shops and a tiny theater and a grand funeral home—the only structure of its kind. We tumbled off the bus into a young high school, a new one, built on a single floor with a single long gray hallway lined with lockers and a couple dozen shining gray classrooms. We stumbled with first-day madness, a hurried, barely contained hysteria, under the awning that was the yawning mouth of this thing called high school, carrying spiral-bound notebooks and pencil boxes with Beatles faces laughing bizarrely across the covers. We lined up for books, lined up for locker numbers, and lined the long hall to try, for the first time, the combination that would always make me nervous. I flicked the numbers in a combination: first left, then right, then left, and, with a *click,* the lock unlatched. If you were cool, you could unlatch and drop the lock against the metal door with a satisfying bang. It was a matter of honor to learn this as quickly as possible.

I don't remember the order of my classes, except there was biology and geometry in the morning. Somewhere throughout the day I took French and history, then English with Mrs. Fram, a tiny woman of mythical stature who was so fear-inducing that we did not want to cross her ever, and yet we would, everyone one of us. Later it was she who would report an even shorter skirt to my mother, saying I did not know how to sit properly, which said more about her prudery than my lack of grace. That said, it was she who would open the subtleties of language to me.

So how, on that first day and after all those years of projects, did I reconnect with the one friend who was not a 4-Her? And a protestant? I found Lydia, who had been my best friend in third grade, standing in the lunch line in the cafeteria, a line that ran past the seniors' lockers, which were the lockers closest to the cafeteria, another ranking I would not understand for a while. She was dark-haired and red-sweatered and already talking with a boy who stood nearby and waited for her, leaning against a locker, slit-eyed and cool. She was talking to him and then not talking to him, and when he came too close, she glanced around and saw me and pulled me in to stand next to her. She said to the girl behind her in line, "She's new. She's got cuts." And so I cut in and stood in that crowded line, filled with sudden gratitude and pride. But then Lydia went back to talking and not talking to the boy. As the line moved away from he-who-leaned-and-stared, she looked back, smiled, turned away, but then looked back again. She stared until he smiled in an embarrassed and awkward happiness, and the word came to me unbidden and fully understood: flirting. This was flirting, and I watched carefully to see how it was done. Watching in that long hall, I thought there were not a lot of important words in flirting. And the words that were said held other meanings under the tongue, melting like a hard candy or menthol lozenge. The word *innuendo* would be on my senior vocab tests, but I had it by the tail right there, watching the looking-not-looking between Lydia and the boy and hearing the short sentences full of something other.

This was Hart Public High School in 1966. Though Kennedy had died, there was a war going on, and Bob Dylan was singing about "the times, they are a-changing,'" the town itself was still caught in what was mostly 1956. A few shades of *Rebel Without a Cause* had drifted in, and there were always bad boys and wild girls, but even if that had not been the case, we believed, or our parents believed, that we were mostly good kids from mostly decent families—though one must be ever vigilant. Still, there had not been a murder, except among the migrants. (They were different, weren't they? So we assumed.) There had been few deaths by car accident, except among some youngsters who started drinking too young, but they were from the families out by Silver Lake, the ones who lived too near the nudist camp—as if that explained anything. There had never been a suicide in my memory. And with the exception of the high school band, there had never been a march against anything. As late as 1966 we were still blinkered, unaware of much that happened beyond the bus routes spidering through the townships, beyond the county lines. But in those three short years of my public high school experience, the danger felt in the secret hems of our short skirts would rise another inch each year until the secrets of women's legs were revealed, a bare inch below the crotch, and we would stand in the flood of knowledge of good and evil. Even if we had been delayed in our comprehension of that decade, it would always seem to me that in those three years before I graduated, the fashion, then the heart of the nation, rebelled against the times, the everything-that-was-long-before, including long skirts.

But right then, we were still narrow-minded, full of wonder that we could not define, did not even know was there. A president's assassination had been the beginning of a rite of passage, though few of us understood to what. There was a war, and people were dying. I suppose I knew that, but I was not sure what it should mean to me. I had gone to a convent school, aspiring to something noble and pure, and instead I had fallen in love with a character on TV, a spy from *The Man from U.N.C.L.E.* My first crush, combined with wild yearnings, battled the remnants of Holy Communion and the 4-H pledge. Though I would be appalled and ashamed of being a bad girl, I did not really want to be good anymore.

There was something else: the kiss. The kiss mattered. The kiss was the precursor and teaser for everything sexual. When I was fifteen, the kiss asked the unarticulated questions, the ones that woke me in the night in an undefined sweat. Not politics but the kiss—my first step toward the changing world. But because of what had happened to me, it was there but it was smoke. Or chasm. I had had a poor experience that I had carried to the convent and tried to forget. But the shadow was still there. I could only say, "The kiss." What I imagined was perfect but set against an imperfect experience. In-between the two was a tension like wires humming through my body.

Through 4-H, I had learned to make ever more bright dresses with simple lines that I could stitch up in just a few hours, so that I could answer the hunger rising in me. I had taken it with both hands. Look at me. Notice me. Love me. Standing against that were the oaths: *head and heart and health and hands.* I pledge. I pledge. *Our Father who art in heaven.* These were the promises I had made every year since I was seven or eight. Between 4-H and the church, I was, as my father had wished, committed to the good. But here in the long hallway was flirting. Here was a skirt so short that if I bent over to pick up my books and lifted them to the top shelf of my locker, the snaps of the garter belt that held up my stockings would gleam. This was the danger. This was going public.

THE CLICK

That first year, Lydia took in me and my striped dresses. At her cafeteria table, I found a place to sit. I practiced flirting with her brother, Ted, a junior almost ready to earn his driver's license. I went to my first party, a side-yard picnic at their house. I danced beside a fire pit and popped my first Tab, a soda so carbonated and artificially sweet that I choked. I looked at the boys.

I also looked at the girls, for I knew already that looking was important. I had learned that in 4-H through the annual Achievement Days in which I had modeled on all those public school stages. I knew you had to depict a look in order to be looked at. Even as the country prepared to leap off the deep end of fashion absurdity, the looking was *what it's all about*. If boys, girls, friends, and friends-to-be looked at you with admiration, surprise, and amazement, and if you carried yourself just so—like the model I had been taught to be—and added a bit of cool, then maybe they would all like you. If I dressed right, maybe they would love me.

Lydia and her Elbridge Township friends had welcomed me, but I thought that they were the fringe. It seemed evident from what I learned in the cafeteria. The cafeteria tables, folded-up, Formica-topped behemoths of structural amazement, dropped like wings at eleven o'clock each morning, then folded up and rolled away to the side in time for wrestling practice. Just before lunch, all down the hall, you could hear the janitors collapse them, tables clanging against the floor where some four hundred kids from the north end of the county would swarm to eat casseroles and hot dogs and canned vegetables.

Here, in this cafeteria of hard linoleum flooring and high fluorescent light, without apparent order, there existed an at-first-invisible hierarchy. Kids appeared to mingle with a factional craziness, except under the surface an order lived and breathed more strictly than if we had been assigned our places. Here I learned that if I tried to switch tables, I would be ignored.

It had to do with light.

I sat down with my sack lunch in Lydia's second row, third table from the wall. I saw other clusters of kids at other tables—poised and blonde, taller and more handsome, so *far-out* that they could not be touched. They sat at tables under the windows along the west wall. In that light, they flirted, lunch an afterthought. Although it was indirect at noon, light still poured in on them. Light formed a shield around them, or so it seemed.

The other thing I saw was that their clothes were different; their clothes were bought in a store.

Over time, I learned the rest.

There was the word *clique*, but I heard it as *click*, with a hard American pronunciation, not the French but something snapped shut and closed. Even then, I understood it as the quick sound of the imagination being cut off from friendship, even love. Its opposite should have been "public," inferring common identity, but in actuality public high school covered a schism so long-standing that it was a scabbed over and half-hidden scar of the local culture. Most cliques that evolved in public school evolved from place, from the knowledge that where you came from made you who you are. I was a country kid from good dirt farmers.

They were called townies. It appeared to me (true or not) that kids from town bought their lunches and carried their trays into the light. They got haircuts in beauty shops or at barbershops—not at the kitchen table. Some had cars as soon as they got their licenses. In my unsophisticated judgment, I thought that townies were all cheerleaders and football players, the kids of the proprietors of the stores lining Main Street, the kids of grocery store and gas station owners. I thought what made the townies a walled-in clique was that they lived near each other, only blocks apart. They knew each other. We country kids not only did not know them and did not have means to know them; we did not know each other. Thus, I mistakenly saw them as whole, complete, and impermeable. Still, I couldn't help but hope that perhaps the walls were not impossible to overcome.

In those first days of public school, sitting at the cafeteria table with Lydia and her brother, Ted, and kids who all hailed from various distant townships, sitting among those of us who were behind in everything because we were simply trying to learn each other's names, I felt the first thinning of that oath to be loyal to those who took me in. I saw, and those dear country kids saw, too, the way I looked with longing at the townies' tables.

After a few days, I tried hanging out near their lockers. I ignored the Elbridge Township boy who liked me because he was shorter than me and his boots smelled of a barn—I who had grown up in barns. Later, when I tried to make friends with cheerleaders, lingering near their desks, contributing odd remarks to random conversations, they were not rude but focused on their own interests. For a while, I stood alone in the lunch line, unwelcome in either group, my stripes vertical as bars of bright anxiety about what I had tried and failed.

Those country kids must have seen some small worthiness in me or else they simply knew from longer experience that this behavior had to be tolerated until I learned who I was. They took me back willingly enough, though I never went back to them as willingly as they took me in. It was still there in me, that utterly ambitious need to be seen by the others, to cross the lines, to sit at someone else's table.

I wanted to be one of the ones who would not let me in.

As far as I could see, waiting daily for the tables to open their hard wings, dressed in one handmade dress after another, there were two ways to break through. One was to be so cool that there was no question that you should be seen. This involved more money and cultivation of airs than I could muster—though a certain style could be mine if I was watchful. The other way was to have a townie boyfriend.

His name was Carl.

UNKISSED

Darkness rushed into the October evening as overhead lights flickered on their brilliant eggs of light, and there in a field of dark grass, boys dressed in new red-and-white uniforms lined up, clenched with an intensity we could feel all the way to the bleachers. Though I should have been glad to sit with my family at my first high school football game, I abandoned them. I wanted this new world spreading like a circus before me. I skipped down the bleacher steps for *a closer look at the game*, tossing back my words. It was a lie. Other than understanding the rudiments of a touchdown, I knew nothing about football. I was enticed by pom-poms and banners, thrilled to mingle with kids in varsity jackets chanting, "Red and white, fight! Fight!" In the cool autumn night, under the country sky that had always before been lit by our single yard light, this light of a high school football game widened to a lake. On a field marked with white stripes, boys hurtled themselves over the lines, bumping and thrusting in animal fierceness. Crowds swirled between the concession stand and the end zone. The Pep Club rose again for each down, waving pom-poms like loose-petaled mums: *hit 'em again, hit 'em again*. There was no weight to any of it, only light and lightness, hands clapping, cheers like wild prayers gone to unruly shouts. I floated in wonder among the bodies, sniffing frost, overcooked hot dogs, bitter coffee. The sweat of boys.

It was heady and strange, and I was in it.

When the band marched onto the field in formation, playing a rousing rendition of our school song, I was drawn, a child to glitter. The beat was as fierce and clear as the game itself. I followed the rotund *thud-brush, thud-brush, thud-brush* to him, high-stepping onto the field, drum slung around his shoulder in a red harness. The feather in the high hat shuddered each time he struck the membrane. He turned and saw me, looked straight at me. Eye contact. Warm. Like that, spark of brown eyes igniting every ounce of ignorance I held, flaring among the blaring. Without missing a beat, he turned back, marched into formation, straight-lined and sharp-cornered. He kept the beat all the way across the field, but I could no longer hear the music. It took me all of ten minutes to find out who he was.

School spirit—that was my excuse, much to my parents' alarm, for attending every home game after that. I flaunted a tattered red-and-white pom-pom, joined the Pep Club, gathered with other misfits on the gray bleachers. I sang the school song with high-pitched, off-key gusto. But it was all a warm-up for halftime, the real game. Then it was a dash down the wooden steps through the crowds to watch the band gather in formation. There—yes, he saw me!—an abundance of eye contact. He was good at making eye contact. I learned to make him the singular audience, make him look at you. Me. I did. He did. Oh, there under the world of light and incomplete passes, we looked at each other. That was all.

How to make it more?

Homecoming. That single word meant the world, meant an October game so important that each class built a float. A float. There was, as training for the world, a sophomore committee to build what was to be the finest float of all four classes, a red-and-white pirate ship of tissue flowers with cardboard cannons full of bright confetti that would plume out at the moment when a drum signal fired. These floats would be driven onto the field on homecoming night to receive the prizes. The class committee would construct this schooner-to-be on a hay wagon (who knew?) that would float like a boat (that's why they called them floats!) across the football field during halftime with everyone looking on. The class that won would be awarded a trophy for the year. He had signed up to work on the float committee. I insisted (after a heated argument about gas, miles, and my parents having to pick me up in Hart) that my parents let me sign up for the float committee to support school spirit. They were flummoxed and resistant; I wore them out.

A flatbed wagon in a barn at the edge of town, cast-off lumber and cardboard, fifty boxes of tissues and more coming. Paint, rusty tools, and staple guns. A box of mismatched nails. These were the materials of the project. Parents could watch from the dim light, distant and smoking but this was to be ours, the committee's float. Parents could supply burned popcorn and an occasional hammer, but they stayed to the side, talking about the new quarterback. I made tissue flowers with the girls—dozens of peony-sized red and white flowers—for all of half an hour before I figured it out. The real work was building the cabins and quarterdecks. He was there, his dark head bent over a two-by-four, muscling a rusty handsaw.

I was a country kid. I knew nothing about building—all of my manual labor having been about fields and harvests—but I trusted my body. I could manage physical work and use it to my advantage. I climbed up onto the flat, crawled in among the boys, and picked up a hammer. When they stared, startled at invasion, it was he of the dark eyes who said, "Yeah, hand me that board." With that, I was in. If the girls noted it, they did not feel threatened enough to say a word. One father asked if I knew how to run a skill saw, and I said, "No, but I can sling a bail of hay." He left us alone.

The pattern set, I would enter that dusty barn on the outskirts of town, not even stopping to speak to the girls. I went straight for the boys on the wagon who moved aside and made room for me, though I did little but hunt for the right sized nails and hold the boards in place as they tried to figure out the rudiments of carpentry. If once, during those long nights on the wagon, laughter slid across the rickety flatbed at some small joke I made or he made, then full-moon joy filled the bay of that barn on the edge of a Michigan town. And if one night some gawky sophomore who would not come into his own until basketball season of his senior year suggested that maybe the committee needed me on tissue duty, he spoke up and said, "She's not like that." I could have cried for the pleasure that raced through my body. I could have kissed him, wanted to kiss him, wanted to send him poems of longing and heartfelt gratitude. I had no idea what a real poem was, what it was supposed to do, but that's what they were about. Weren't they?

Through this poor apprenticeship I developed a different skill, a particular flirtation that subverted the look-don't-look mode of the lunch line. Instead, this was flirtation side by side, looking together at something to be accomplished, kneeling on a ramshackle wagon, shoulder to shoulder, staring at a two-by-four and a tape measure. It was how your arms might brush against each other, skin to skin, or your elbows bump, or how both of you together, holding the handle, might raise a hammer to bring the head down on a spike so oversized that it split the board.

It could not last. And, too, the float failed utterly, those boys having no more real knowledge of construction than I did, living as boys often do on brawn and sudden inspirations. As it evolved, the elegant pilothouse supporting the mast became a kind of squat box covered with cardboard from toilet paper cases. (Where did that come from?) The Charmin toilet paper baby glowed through the thin white paint because we didn't have enough primer to cover the cherub face, nor had we enough tissues from the fifty plus boxes to cover all parts of the bow. The mast, which was supposed to be poised gallantly upright, leaned backward at a precarious forty-five degree angle. We had forgotten the height restriction due to the power lines at the edge of the football field until some gentle father, realizing our ambitions and seeing the discrepancies between what we dreamed and what we were building, decided not to let us electrocute ourselves.

When homecoming night arrived wrapped in mysterious wind, mist, and fog, we took it as a sign of atmospheric cooperation. When the wagon paraded slowly onto that field, we were filled with all-out, unprecedented hope. But the white-and-red-tissued sides of the ship, seen from a distance, looked like bubbling froth or, as my mother would later announce, a pirate birthday cake. The pirate sail, a king-sized sheet, had been punctured with tiny cuts so the wind would pass through without tearing it away from the flimsy mast. But instead of the grand spinnaker we had envisioned, the sail snapped violently in the growing bluster of that night. The small cuts did not hold but tore open, then ripped full-out. The entire lower half of the sheet, on which were a cleverly drawn pirate mouth and jaw, sheered off in the wind. The pirate's face, the twisted *argh* of a mouth flapping wildly, mouthed windy inanities. The eyes looked oddly surprised at the absence of the rest of its visage.

About the cannons, the coup de grâce that would nail us the class prize, we were felled by the nature of confetti and drizzle. Our plan had been clear. Before the game, and after many tests, generous handfuls of bright confetti had been stuffed into each cannon tube so that when they were fired, they would explode with a flurry of fireworklike mystical fluttering. But because the tubes were tipped upward, the atmospheric spit betrayed us just before halftime, sluicing down the uptipped cannons and into the cannon bases. The confetti absorbed the rain as only snippets of cheap Christmas paper and torn-up tissue can. When the pirates onboard, shouting as triumphantly as ten-year-olds, shoved those carefully selected bathroom plungers through the cardboard cannon tubes to create the much anticipated explosion from the cannons—instilling awe and evoking applause—the cannons looked as though they were dropping raw sewage onto the field. Imagine the plunging apparatus becoming stuck inside the now swollen cardboard tube of the cannon, and the entire cannon, complete with plunger, coming unhinged from its stapled and duct-taped moorings, and plunger, tube, and sodden confetti dropping unceremoniously onto the field, trailing behind the cumbersome cake of a ship, whereupon a coach, who just wanted to *play the Goddamned game* described the situation in phrases to be repeated with relish for years. I imagine it was he who finally sent some second-string players out to pick up the messy stuff before the refs began the second half.

Stuck in the end zone, we, the committee, waited for our sinking ship to come in. We pushed back our moppy hair and watched with awe and despair as, for a finale, the flailing eyes of the sail tore free of the mast and flew, an object of mockery. We descended into a state of chaos and accusations. *Whoever thought that would work?*

We came in fourth, behind even the freshmen.

I was too young to read the signs.

The float had done its work. Carl and I had a bond—though its molecular structure was as weak as wet tissue. Our bond—the complete

embarrassment among those of us who had pounded nails on the float—
held for a while in shyly chagrinned but thrilling grins. We were com-
rades in failure. We'd fall in step in the long hallway and knock shoulders,
shaking our heads at each other, startled that the world had not seen the
vision we had seen for the tissue-flowered pirate ship.

I thought maybe we could be boyfriend and girlfriend.

I thought maybe we could kiss.

I was afraid to even think of the other thing, the thing called sex. I
knew little about sex except the technical rudiments. Though I was raised
on a farm, the ruttings of animals belonged to the animal world, not to
my dream-sodden one. For me, the kiss, the one true and real kiss, was
what mattered. From Walt Disney's *Sleeping Beauty* and *Snow White and
the Seven Dwarfs*, from romance novels and Westerns, from my own family, I had taken the kiss as a token and wonder, miracle and ordination.
And the thing in my past? It was gone, wasn't it? I could start over and
have a real first kiss. I could be awakened, couldn't I?

I learned about the last three rows of the bus from Lydia, who told me
during a rare sleepover after another side-yard party at which someone
had set off a cherry bomb to send up a tin can that rose high into the dusk
and then came down from such a height that it chipped a windshield. She
told me that the last three rows were where the kisses happened. Those
were the seats where kids made out in the back of the bus, and that new
term, *made out*, slipped out of her mouth and into my brain like a snake.
Yes, she said, one could make out on the bus. *You know, celebration kisses* at
having won a game or *consolation kisses* for a loss. Never mind that the guy
hadn't actually played the game, wasn't even on the team. You were part
of the clan who had won or lost, and you felt the win or loss as deeply as
the quarterback might, right? And even if, like me, you didn't much care
what happened in the game, you could pretend, and that would be reason
enough for the kiss. I was afraid of and adored the whole idea. Desire rose
like a flood. Danger sat like a living creature right there in the last three
rows of the away-game bus. Sweaty palms, blush, blush—the whole thing.
Oh please let it happen.

A bright Friday afternoon in the great hallway of Hart High. Because the
band didn't play for away games, he was riding the bus. He grinned and said,

"Wanna ride the bus?" Was the game against White Hall or Montague? Who cared? I begged my mother to let me ride the bus. Certainly, I assured her, I would be with a crowd of Hart kids. I would ride on the bus, not in some beater car. She gave permission, albeit grudgingly. She knew nothing about the last three rows.

It was as Lydia predicted. Almost. After a game I don't remember, after a game I may not have even seen except that I was physically present for it—*who did win*?—I climbed aboard a yellow bus on the edge of a dusty field and sat, third row from the back, and waited with my crush on my lips.

His form rose from the steps at the front of the bus, slim-hipped and long-legged. He strolled through the garish interior lights, easy and confident, between vinyl seats. Strolled like a summer's day. How did he do that? He nodded and smiled at other kids who waved and looked to where he was headed, and when he sat down next to me on the brown vinyl and slipped his arm around my shoulder, some girls turned to each other, hands to mouths.

We waited quietly until the interior lights dimmed and the last desultory cheers faded. The grimy windows, pushed up to ward off the night chill blowing from the lake, promptly steamed up from the crowd. Condensation blocked the view of the now empty field, and autumn dust rose around the bus. I made a fist and lay the heel of it on the window, my curved hand imprinting a child's foot, and with my fingertip, I marked five little toes above it, a perfect baby foot such as you would find on my hospital birth certificate. He smiled.

We were in a Disney movie.

The bus shifted, as though driverless, into gear. If there was a chaperoning adult, he was invisible to us. I rested my head on his shoulder. I waited for the bliss of the kiss.

Why did I do what I did?

It would be laughable—if it weren't my first version of tragedy.

In a shadowy dark punctuated only by headlights racing beyond the glass, he leaned down, and when his lips were a breath away from mine, I slapped his face so thoroughly that he touched his cheek, surprise in his eyes. Then a flicker, a tightening of jaw. He pulled away, slipped his arm off my shoulder. I felt it crumble, the entire ship that had set sail weeks before, made of tissue that could not hold. I grasped my own hand in my lap as if it would rise again and I would have to hold it down.

I didn't mean it. It was unnatural. It was a slap against my own body, against all the dazzling longing. I wanted to be wanted, wanted to be remembered in the hallway between classes, to be asked to dances, to be taken to games, to sit in the last three rows of the bus, over and over. I wanted to hold hands, be kissed, be taken in. To have played this role against him was to betray myself even more than him—and to lose him whom I never had.

How many years was it before I understood that he was a perverse stand-in for someone else? How long was it before I could see how I had projected the one emotion I had never acknowledged? But then, right then, I only knew this much, and this stopped time: I had lost him at my own hand.

That autumn, Huntley-Brinkley announced that President Johnson would send thousands more soldiers to Vietnam. My teacher in current events class explained the ramifications of the war with concerned tones. My father watched the news with a furrowed brow. In light of that world, what was a fifteen-year-old girl's first heartbreak?

Only the biggest thing in the world.

I moped on my mother's blue couch, replaying the bus scene over and over, blushing as though my own face has been slapped. I sprawled, wrapped in a Grandma afghan, running my fingers through the loops in the crocheted gold and brown, TV blaring news of marches and war. I dropped bad hit tunes like "Hold me, Thrill me, Kiss me" onto the hi-fi. I was stunned, *driven to bed with the vapors*. It's cliché until its real.

But it came to me finally that he didn't know that I didn't mean it. How could he? And if he didn't know that I didn't mean it, could I take it back?

On the Monday following the away game, I rode the bus to school, stepped out from the lockers, and faced him. There among throngs of kids, I reached out, touched his arm. I said the words: *I'm sorry, I'm sorry, I'm sorry. I didn't mean it, didn't mean it.* He looked at me briefly, nodded, then faded sideways, slid into the masses. He walked away. The warning bell rang, locker doors up and down the hallways banging with the kind of force that says, *No, no, nope.*

In the days following, how many times did I step out from those lockers to fall into step with him and try to apologize? How many times did he nod and walk on? I stopped him in the halls, in the cafeteria. I slid into seats near him. And though he was never rude, he also never gave me any more attention than necessary to politely leave my presence. He didn't sigh or push me away; he wasn't mean. When I spoke to him, he looked off down the hall at one of the display cases where dusty trophies were set behind the reflecting glass. I checked the reflections to see if I was there.

I thought obsessively about this turn of events. I took a new tack.

A demonstration of atonement.

I knew all about demonstrations from 4-H and atonement from the church.

Dress for penance.

Didn't the saints wear sackcloth, hair shirts, whatever they were? Weren't the habits of the nuns meant to demonstrate humility? And 4-H had given me the means to accomplish this bizarre endeavor. In 4-H, you learn to fix things. You can make what fits wrong, fit right. You can dress to express. You can change history.

One morning, I float solemnly down the stairs to the dining room, cowled in silence, refusing breakfast. I wear a baggy navy jumper, a gray amoeba-like sweater, and dark socks dragging down to the ankles. My siblings stare. The next morning I don the kind of plain skirt and mud-colored blouse that no one, not even the Mennonites from Shelby, would wear.

I am 4-H penitent.

My mother makes a careful observation: "Those colors are more subtle than what you've been wearing." I nod, full of perverse piety, and slip out the kitchen door dressed like a celibate pigeon. I find the blue-and-gray plaid uniform skirt from my year at Marywood—only a year ago? I don't roll the waistband over but let the wool pleats fall in meek submission below my knees and put on a sweater the color of a rejected hen. Too bad I don't have a veil. My mother, on the other hand, is thrilled about the skirt. After all, they had *paid nearly $25.00 for that skirt.* I should get *some* *good wear out of it*. But as I leave the house, she stops me, lifts my chin, and says, "You've got dark circles under your eyes. You're running around too much." If only that were the case.

The next outfit, a remade brown skirt that falls to the floor worn with an old maternity dress cut off to be a tent top, just plain embarrasses people. In first hour, Ted looks me over, says "Whatcha trying to do—be a nun?" Oh irony. Then he ignores me. Instead of communicating a message to the Lost One, I am becoming invisible even to those who have been loyal to me. If the dress is the message, what I probably communicated was an "oh that's who you really are" message.

Finally, after my teary-eyed confession into the black sleeve of what I think is a mourning blouse (my last effort at dressing for atonement), Lydia tells me, with the bluntness of a truth-teller, *Nope, he ain't coming back. He's got someone else. You better stop that stuff. You better get over it.* How much later is he seen walking the halls—oh this cut to the quick— with a beautiful junior from our own church, a country girl who had become a popular varsity cheerleader?

After Lydia's news, a public self slowly rises. I return to the old gang— yet again. They sigh. Ted shakes his head but says, "Hey, Dutch" (his nickname for me), and scoots over to make room at the table. Remorse lives on like a live worm in me, but one day, I traipse into Gambles. Without asking my mother, I buy enough bright red-and-white checkered fabric for a new miniskirt—though it looks like a tablecloth for an Italian restaurant. And when my mother frowns and says, "Valentine colors? In the fall?" I deny it.

"Nope. School colors. For spirit days." Not even a star 4-Her gets to do the past over, not for all the sewing and dressing down and atonement in the world. But if you can't change history, you can still dress to express. I live a common duality, a public self who laughs and claims school spirit and a private self who wants to be a valentine. At my own hand, I remain unkissed and undeserving of the kiss, but my longing for the kiss still twists into light and fabric and color.

A PRINCE

If I couldn't achieve belonging with a boy, could I break in with style? Create a look? Like in 4-H but not a 4-H look? If I couldn't have the kiss, could I have the look? Of course, I got the style thing mostly wrong. My tendency toward bright colors without a sense of what colors looked good on me led to combinations of such garish clashing that when my mother asked what I thought I was doing, I said, using a brand-new word as justification, *It's psychedelic,* and she, with uncharacteristic wit, said, *Or psycho.* My mother thought I should have paid attention to Jackie Kennedy, now out of mourning, sharp and classy. Instead of her aloof elegance, I was looking at bold and brassy—the mistake of overstatement. It would last a lifetime. One day I wore a vivid blue dress glaring with wild red and purple daisies, like dyed popcorn, overly enthused. I cinched it with a ratty patent leather green belt I had stolen from my mother's closet, and even if it wasn't quite hip-hugging, it passed muster as such. I was back, festive as the NBC peacock, but without a Carl, I had no place to focus. What I needed was not a kiss but a miracle.

It might have been Don—one of the boys in the cafeteria gang—who looked at my outfit with consternation and said, "You should join the drama club."

Drama Club was a club as 4-H was a club, but the word "club" is all it shared with 4-H. With little more in common than *Robert's Rules of Order,* Drama Club was a 4-H club turned on its head. At the first meeting, held in the cafeteria, I looked around the gray-toned room at the motley mix of kids who belonged to this thing. Members ranged from the truly odd to popular townies, from a smattering of awkward country kids to some I finally slotted into the really smart category—National Honor Society. Here was a democracy. At last, an equalizer, a leveler.

We were all here for one purpose. We wanted the light.

A burst of applause, a loud rapping on the tables. A teacher, the drama coach, stood before us with a sly smile.

"What's going on?" I leaned toward Don, watching this preamble unfold.

He bent, conspiracy in his voice, and said, "The show. The play. That's Mrs. B. She's about to announce." These words, *the show*, were a clear bell among buzzing fluorescents, a sweet and dangerous arrow in the cacophony of the cafeteria. I waited with all the others, holding my breath though I had no clue why. And when she named it, the title raced among us like lightning, heating the room.

The play was *The Miracle Worker*.

The cheering went on longer than for touchdowns. We clapped and banged the tables, suddenly better than we had been. This was a show about saving someone, bringing someone into belonging. We all felt it and we wanted to be the heroes. But really, there was only one role: Annie Sullivan, the miracle worker. Right then I knew that I would become another person, the one who saved the blind. I would become Annie.

Oh, to be Annie.

Annie. I would be Annie. I was Annie. I turned to Don and said, "Call me Annie." He looked at me like I was crazy, then said, "Sure, if that's what you want." And throughout the rest of high school, I gave up on plain Anne and assumed the charm (so I thought) of Annie.

B's classroom is packed. Twenty would-be Annie Sullivans crowd in with a dozen or so would-be Helens with such ferocious interest that, for the first time, I feel how competition could become a green dragon turning its scales to catch brutal lights. I had read the play and had acted in my bedroom every Annie scene including the physical fight to teach Helen to obey. I had scared my sisters and broke a chair. I am ready. When my name is called from the list I have signed, there is a titter. *Annie will read Annie.*

I walk to the front of an open space in a classroom in a small American town, lift a script from the pile on the desk, and begin reading against a senior girl, blonde and pretty, who is reading the role of Helen's mother. What comes to the surface is not shy, is not underplayed or awkward, but loud and brittle, with such terse anger that everyone in the room looks up from their scripts—which I interpret as a good sign. I have their attention. Instead of the complex determination of Annie Sullivan, a voice full of self-righteous conviction. I give it my all.

We trade parts, and I read the mother not with caution and concern but with the same how-dare-you attitude at the top of my lungs. When Mrs. B asks if I might try to modulate my tone, I read faster, with more energy, thinking it just the chance to reveal my range. I can only imagine what others saw, a brash sophomore shouting to the point of spit at powers that were not powers in the play because she couldn't shout at the powers that actually held her back. The few tentative claps should have told me differently. I thought they were all just stunned—which may have been the case.

I stay to the end, come back all three nights, but am never asked to read for the leads again, though I offer several times.

On Friday, the day of the cast posting, I race off the bus, down the hall, and run my finger down the list. *Annie* is not Annie. At last, toward the bottom, I see that I am assigned not the one who saved the blind girl but the role of a blind girl, one of the pupils in the school where Annie studied before going to Helen. I will appear in a single scene, one that Mrs. B may have written into the play so she could cast more kids, building the club. Four girls in plain brown uniforms will walk onstage, our hands held in front, fingering the light, staring directly off the stage. We are to have no focus whatsoever on Annie but will hold the pose of listening. Our hands may reach for her, touch her, but our eyes will never see her. I will put my heart into staring into space, pretending to be blind.

Again, irony, never my forte, is lost on me.

Through my entire high school career, I was never cast in a lead, playing only extras and bit parts, never able to overcome the overdone. But I loved the club because here were kids who were more like me than not, who felt a little too deeply, were a little too foolish or over-the-top or quiet, driven by the light of the stage or the power of the story. Some were townies, some country kids, and some were altogether different, like Don, who flirted like a pro but had the kindness of a true friend. I had no real talent, making acting an act instead of an art, but I had found my click.

So it began. During rehearsals, I stood on the dark side of dark curtains waiting for a cue to move into the light, where I would pretend not to see by staring, unfocused, at the light. I stood inside the folds of curtains and waited for a signal that I was not supposed to see. Others stood with me in that spill, playing out our small backstage dramas while we waited to play the onstage one. An older boy with a nice smile stood near. I pretended not to see him but then tipped my head, offered a sidelong glance, a barely practiced flirtation with this older boy who played Helen Keller's father, a boy of such good heart that he fell for me despite my shallow qualities.

His name was Earl.

"*Who* asked you?" My mother, incredulous, stood in the middle of the kitchen with nothing in her hands. The breakfast dishes were stacked and waiting.

"Earl Banic."

"To a dance?"

"The Christmas dance." This was important. "Mom, he's in the drama club, and he's captain of the football team." I knew if there was a chance in hell that I had to get this out of the way first, and I knew, too, what she would say.

"I don't care if he's captain of the angels of the Lord. You know the rules." It was a predictable response, but still she would have heard that he was a captain of something. That out of the way, I launched the next stage.

"Mom, you know his dad. He's Dr. Banic's son."

"Dr. Banic's son." Her response was not so much a question as a statement to be mulled. She moved to the kitchen counter and picked up a half cup of cold coffee in the spill of uncertain November light. She took a sip and stared at the barnyards.

My mother had worked as a nurse before marrying my father, so she knew every doctor in town. She respected doctors; in some ways, she adored them. Working for them had given her the first true respect and the first sense of a self beyond her farm roots. I could see that my being invited to a dance by a doctor's son had not been on her radar, had not even been a blip in her imagination. It meant something to her, this being invited by a doctor's son; it was something she would have to wrestle with. On some level I had known it would impress her, that under her righteous place as the wife of a successful farmer, her leadership role in a successful 4-H club, and an organizer in her church, she sometimes still felt like the embarrassed and ill-dressed daughter of a dirt farmer. But this invitation, she knew, was honor unexpected, and how it was handled said something about our position as a family. This boy from a very good family, a respected family in town, a doctor's son, had invited her daughter. I knew all this without a word being spoken.

On the surface, my only hope was to appeal to this side of her, the one who wanted affirmation for her family. I needed to get her on my side, which, after weeks of poor attitude on my part, would be a challenge akin to climbing Everest. But the image of the doctor's son was now standing in the air between us. Still, she knew she shouldn't be susceptible to such ploys. She had her place in the world, and the rules were the rules. This was a date.

"Please, Mom, can I go?" I held my breath.

"Your father says not until you're sixteen."

The mandate hung over my head, handed down from my beloved and gentle father who was as protective and strict and dear and utterly conservative as it is possible to be without joining the John Birch Society. He had forbidden me to date until I was sixteen. He had explained that with the oldest child it was important to set these things right, to make me follow the rules, first because it was the right thing but second to set an example for the four younger ones. He had said, "You don't need to go to those things." Meaning dates. He had said this with a quiet firmness. In other words, he forbid it.

Thus, the mandate. His first version? *Though shalt not date. At all. Not ever.* His protectiveness ran that deep. But finally he knew, as did my mother, though she was with him on everything, that not dating was as likely as not thinking or not longing or not farting. Sooner or later, it was going to happen. Version two: I was forbidden to attend school dances or date until I was *older*. Much older. Eighteen maybe. But as the first dance of the year, the homecoming dance, came and went and only deepened my dark mood, version three evolved: *when you're sixteen you can attend dances.* That was something tangible to look forward to. The addendum? Maybe *a year later* I could date. And all my dates had to be to public events. And chaperoned. And no wild parties. And no drinking. Ever. And no . . . I was barely fifteen. I would not turn sixteen until the autumn of my junior year, eleven months away—so much for tangible.

If there was a chance of going to this dance, it would be through my mother. I could tell she was leaning toward my father's point of view. I knew only one weakness.

"Mom, there's this dress I was thinking about from a new Butterick pattern."

"You don't need a new dress because you can't go." This bothered her. She pulled a bowl from the cupboard and was looking for the flour tin in front of her.

"The dress. It's kind of a hard pattern."

"You heard me."

"I might need some help. It calls for lace sleeves." She leaned against the counter, watching the cattle mill out the window. I had made a misstep by mentioning lace sleeves, sleeves of useless fabric, full of holes through which the light shines. She had led a life without lace.

"You don't have money for fancy fabric." A small crack? Not a complete refutation.

"I could babysit."

"You hate to babysit." True, I had not babysat since the incident, but by this offer, she knew how much I wanted it.

I rushed. "This dress is A-lined, with long bell sleeves. I wondered if you could help me with the zipper in back. I've never been good with those long zippers, and you always get them to lay down so they're invisible." The need to make the zipper invisible, so it wouldn't be noticed, wouldn't *suggest* anything, like the possibility of being unzipped. And the plea for her help? Ruthless.

"You just have to press and pin everything first. You always skip that; you're in such a hurry." A second crack. She was imagining how to do the zipper.

Barbaric manipulation was the final salvo.

"Mom, what will he think if I tell him no?" This was risky, because it implied lack of will, but she heard what I meant, which was, "What will his parents think if I refuse him?"

"I'll talk to your father."

Breakthrough. But she was also worried about me.

"How would you get there?"

"He has a car."

"A car." More contemplation of the flour tin. "How old is this boy?"

"I don't know. He's got his license." I was trying to avoid the real answer.

"What grade is he in?" My mother was no dummy.

I stood near the bread bin, opening and closing the tin lid. "Well, Mom, he's a senior."

"Oh shit." She abandoned the bread making and made a pot of coffee.

I made plans to buy my first dress-up fabric and that single yard of white lace.

But my father said no. My father said he didn't care if the Archangel Michael had asked me to the dance. (At least he hadn't said Gabriel.) My father said if I wanted, he would call Dr. Banic and explain that I very much wanted to go with his son but that he, my father, was sure that Earl's father and mother and Earl, certainly, since he was so mature, would understand that I was too young to go with a senior—too young to go with anyone, really, not yet being sixteen.

The look on my parents' faces was firm, tight-lipped, clear, and unwavering.

There were tears, scuffles of pouting, a skittish cat of anxiety running through our house, me mooning on the bed, shouting at my little sisters, and my brothers shaking their heads and asking to go fishing in November just to get out of the house.

The answer, like a compass point, remained steady. My parents joined as a couple, an American Gothic of will.

I prepared for the worst.

I spoke even less.

I slipped in and out of the Mood of Morose.

I skipped rehearsal because I didn't want to face Earl.

I felt so undone that I wore slacks to class. I, as someone who could make a straight skirt in three hours flat, never wore slacks.

Is that when she cracked?

A school morning in a tousled household scented with burned toast, cheap coffee, and milk verging on sour. The bustle and bicker of five kids readying for the bus in a November dawn. The bathroom door banging, breakfast dishes clanging, and lunches packed into Mickey Mouse pails. I avoid the oatmeal. Mom insists I eat. Tom, unwilling to get up until ten minutes before the bus, stumbles down with his pants unzipped. In a chorus, we all tell him. My mother in the kitchen, her unsympathetic, no-nonsense, get-over-it attitude reigning. During a gray interlude she announces that I *don't have to ride the bus*, that she will drive *me* to school. I stand still. No one gets special privileges. Or do they? I won't see how it works for years.

Just to test her, I ask, "You're taking me in?" She nods and keeps moving.

Tom never misses a beat. "Take me, too?"

Mom cuts him off. "I need to speak with your sister." Done.

Bundled, trundling into the frost-laden November morning, they leave.

I was alone with her then. Had my father relented? Had she found a way? Or was this the final and firm end of it and she was simply going to tell me to stop being a brat and grow up. She said nothing until we climbed into the cold station wagon. Whatever was to be said was important enough that she didn't want to look at me; she wanted her eyes on the road. During those crystalline miles along Jackson Road, she started by saying, "You're father has given permission for you to go to the dance." She sighed. "So you can go."

By the set of her jaw, I knew that wasn't the whole story, so I said, "But not with Earl. Is that what you're saying, because then . . ." It hit me, the pointlessness of arriving without a date to watch the boy who had asked me dance with someone else.

"Yes, I know." She was quiet, as if waiting for further irrational drama. I was good at irrational drama. The defroster roared, clearing the windows.

For once, I kept quiet. We passed the church, the cathedral of the county, its spire pointing high.

She took another breath. "But I was thinking. Since you have permission to go . . . I could take you in to your grandpa's. Maybe . . . Earl could pick you up there."

"At Grandpa Henry's?" Grandpa Henry, Dad's dad, lived in a little white house in Hart. He had retired from his farm when he turned seventy-five. His tiny two-bedroom with a screened-in front porch and foggy storm windows was next to the railroad tracks.

"And Earl could drop you off, and I could drive you home."

I was stupid. "But that would mean . . ."

"That he wouldn't have to spend so much in gas and drive all the way out to the farm. It's such a long way." What odd thinking.

"But Dad said . . ." And I stopped. I knew.

My father didn't know. He would never know. He would know only that I was going to the dance, as he had permitted, and perhaps he would know, because he was not stupid, that I would dance with Earl, but Earl would not be picking me up. So it wasn't a date.

But my mother's plan announced that I would have this date, that I could accept Earl's invitation. The plan unfolded like a scroll revealing a treasure. My mother would take me to Hart, to my grandfather's house, where we would meet Earl, who would pick me up in his car, drive the eight blocks to the high school, and we would enter the gym together.

I don't know what was greater, my astonishment at being able to go or my mother's audacity. Revelation cracked open in me. Even these rules of my father's, who one did not question because one knew they came from a magnificent love—these rules could be bent behind his back? There in that car, I saw how, if this could be done, so many other things could be done. I had arrived on the slippery slope of deception with surprise and a certain perverted joy, and I had absolutely no traction. I did not think about what this cost her.

She did the second astonishing thing of the day. She drove me to Gambles. We entered the fabric store together, before the lights were even on full. I showed her the Butterick pattern, and she sighed and said, *Complicated*. But she looked closely. Yes, it would be hard with those lace sleeves set on a velvet bodice, but at least *it has long sleeves*. And then, in the front window, among all the new Christmas fabrics, I saw a soft velveteen in a new color: maroon. She saw me looking and asked to see it. The fabric was the same color as the pattern cover and, yes, Christmassy. So I could wear it through the holidays. The clerk unrolled it on the counter, and together our hands reached out to brush the pile, a luxury foreign to us both. She winced at the price per yard, but she studied the pattern and estimated (luck and guess) that we could get away with a yard less. Then the lace, oh the lace. *You don't need a yard. Three-quarters will do, and in that new polyester; that's cheaper. Not the silk; that's for wedding dresses, for heaven's sake.*

Despite dithering about yardage and money, and despite the moral quandary, my mother knew the value of the maroon dress. The dress would be as stylish as anyone's; it didn't matter that we were dirt farmers and Catholics. Make them ask, *Who is that?* Make them raise their eyebrows and give a second thought on seeing the country girl with the doctor's son. She knew I was a reflection on her, and if she was going to go behind my father's back, she would do so with an ambition that would put the best to shame, she who had never had lace, not even on her own wedding dress.

She paid for that maroon velveteen without batting an eyelash, though she did say I should pay her back with babysitting money. I knew already that I never would. I was going to the dance. I, the girl who could not find a clique, was going to the castle with a prince of sorts. I understood she had waved a wand, and I think I smiled for the first time in days. I could tell Earl about the arrangement. I could explain to him so he would understand. It was a date, a sure thing, but at my grandfather's house, so it would be easy for him. And he would agree, and it would be *so cool*. I could tell my friends at last, and they would think it was *so cool*. I could stand in the hallway and sit in the cafeteria, and they would all know I had a date. And eventually Carl would know. And it would hurt, but it would be *so cool* that I was there with Earl and all, in a dress of maroon.

No one thought about the boy, this kind young man who played football, who was the doctor's son. No one thought about the color of his heart.

DANCE

In a small town, a high school dance had strict rituals developed over decades that still held well into the sixties. For boys, once the terror of asking a girl was over, their preparation was getting into pressed trousers, a decent shirt and tie, and sport coat. Their ceremony was of car, keys, gas, and the final obligation of flowers. Specifically, a corsage.

Weeks before, on the Monday following the homecoming dance, I sat at lunch with the gang, stung at not having attended the homecoming dance but managing to notice the girls from the court wearing corsages, flaunting carnations and roses like trophies. Then I noticed others, girls with shoulder ornaments of red and white flowers, fluffy tulle, and tiny plastic hearts spelling out *Hart* in fancy letters.

We were eating peanut butter and jelly, and when Lydia caught me staring for the third time, she informed me: "It's a corsage."

"Who got married?"

My ignorance was such a burden. "If you get invited to a dance, the boy is supposed to get you a corsage, and you wear it the following Monday so everyone knows."

"Knows what?"

She spoke as to a child: "That you had a date. So everyone who didn't go to the dance knows you had a date to the dance. And then they ask you who you went with. And then they look at the corsage and they're jealous."

Don reached across the cafeteria table to pick up one of her French fries. "It's a gift for going with a guy. Wish someone would get me one."

The table fell into an uproar, then awkward silence. What did he mean? I stared at the girls' blooming shoulders where red and white carnations clustered, caught with satin ribbons and sequins. Wearing that banner, a girl walked down the long gray hall, past the lockers, and everyone looked. Through the monotony of classes, kids *oohed* about the kind and color of flowers: pink carnations, puffy blue (blue?) mums. Even girls who wore their corsages with pride were jealous of each other.

For the boy, that corsage was the trick question. Yes, size was an issue—as it would be in so many ways—but also how many buds, how much ribbon, how sparkly, and of course the kind of bloom. Carnations, I learned, were traditional. A rose or two if your boy could afford it. But the critical point was the color match. The color could become a minor regional crisis, and all of it could be just too much for a red-blooded guy who'd rather play football. More than one mother took on the task to save her son from the carnage of a red carnation and orange mum clash.

Complicating this—there were only two florists in town. I learned that boys had to get orders in early to the florists, especially orders for roses, usually several days before the dance, and especially in preparation for the winter dances, because during winter in Michigan, roses, or any other special flowers, were trucked in from hothouses somewhere so far south that you needed a passport to go there. And the florist, Lydia further informed me, had to have time to do all the corsages. If the boy waited until the day before to order, the florist might have only those tiny unopened carnations or bedraggled mums and no special ribbon.

I realized the potential disaster was really about the color. What flower was maroon?

While my dad watched the first films of the moon coming back from a satellite, while my brothers and sisters were watching a new TV show, *Star Trek*, I worried about the corsage. I sat at the oak table and tried to do homework, waiting for the phone to ring, for him to ask, *What color is your dress?*

And what was the answer to that?

Earl took his time.

But then, after history class, where our paths actually crossed, and where our teacher, Mr. Cornig, had introduced a discussion about Miranda rights, which I had ignored because I didn't like a girl's name for a law, Earl fell into step with me in that long hallway. As was so often the case, his brown eyes were kind and warm, and he asked, "What color is your dress?"

"Maroon."

His eyes widened. There it was—*what the hell is maroon?* I could see that I would have to explain the color, but then, what was maroon? I felt like a moron.

He was a smart boy. "Like wine?" Smarter than I gave him credit for.

What was the answer to that? My mother made dandelion wine, which was yellow. Other than that, what did I know about wine? But then it washed over me. Perhaps it was inappropriate, but I had a point of reference: communion wine. Every Sunday—take this wine, the blood of Christ. Dark red. Close enough. I nodded. "Like wine."

The debate about Miranda raged in history class for the rest of the week. I didn't give a hoot.

Dances are carnival, festival, sacred ritual, and repressed sexual urges rolled into a three-hour span, narrated by a fledgling local band or a poor sound system attached to an RCA record player, held in a gymnasium decorated to within an inch of its life but that will never stop smelling of sweat and terror, no matter how many boughs of pine one sets into paint cans covered with red tinfoil.

Our job was to un-gym the gym. On Saturday morning, ladders, tables, chairs, lumber, and tools were hauled in along with scaffolding from the bus storage shed. Once the scaffolding was assembled, Don scrambled up the steel trusses with a roll of fine fishing line and strung it from on high to the tops of the folded-away bleachers. From that line, tinsel draped and glittery stars hung in long swaying loops to form a night canopy. Parents, drafted in panic, made unexpected trips to Muskegon where sparkly streamers and strings of lights could be bought with funds from some nearly empty class treasury. *Pay you back. Promise.* Katie, chair of our class committee, and Lydia arranged table favors of a single red carnation stuck in fake poinsettias, and the folding chairs each got a perky elf. The entryway popped with Christmas balls and tissue-paper bells. Lights borrowed from the old gym were hung with red and green gels. Some committee parent dragged in a misshapen tree—leaking pitch and needles—from a local farm on the edge of town. The tree was adorned with cutesy messages for the cutesy couples and topped with a candy angel. Our gym was taped, stapled, glued, and gummed into fantasy. Here was tacky tinsel and romantic illusion coupled with the loudest music they would let us play. We could enter the castle and come under its spell.

Was it while I blew up balloons—no helium in those days—that I asked Don, breathlessness covering another feeling, what band was playing?

"Oh," he said, knowing exactly what I wanted to know. "The one with that sophomore drummer." He flashed a wicked grin.

Could I make Carl jealous? The thought had never occurred to me, but once it did, it did. Could I dance close to Earl—the thought was scary—and regain Carl's attentions?

For girls, the ritual preparations are cosmetic. For each dance, the girls who could afford to made appointments at Wanda's Cuts or Cheryl's Salon. Though long, wild hair was beginning to mop its way into fashion, the sculptures of slicked-down bangs and upswept beehives still reigned, shellacked with enough hair spray to mummify a city. I knew, given what my mother had paid for fabric, that going to a beauty salon was about as likely as going to the moon. The girls who couldn't make appointments at the two beauty salons in town begged their moms for more Adorn or VO5 extra hold hair spray and clips and made themselves miserable with hand teasing fine hair into a shining foam of a home-done style. It usually didn't work.

But I had seen something of the future in *Look* magazine and rolled my medium-length hair onto orange juice cans to control its unpredictable waves, making it fall temporarily into a Breck-girl pageboy. And my mother, having learned that the new 4-H focus was on *accessories*, picked up the fabric scraps and pieced together a lace-and-velvet headband that matched the dress, a stroke of brilliance. My bangs covered my spotty forehead, my hair fell back from the headband, and my rough blonde hair glowed and curved under, perfectly framing my face.

That night, I stood in front of her dresser mirror and scrutinized this image. The maroon fabric was understated but also . . . what was the word?

Elegant? Was that possible? After all these years, had 4-H played a successful card? Beyond anything I had expected, the A-line slimmed in front and
back, the zipper lay flat as a good field, and the skirt length skimmed just a
quarter inch north of alarming. The lace caught the eye at each shoulder and
fell to the wrist. That night, in front of the mirror, I felt like the outside me
recognized some person on the inside who had stepped forward briefly into
my mother's chipped mirror, and that creature was pretty, and strangely
refined. I knew she would disappear.

Earl arrived at Grandpa's little white house in December darkness. My grandfather hobbled forward to the door, his huge mustache making his face more
ominous than anything my clean-shaven father could have mustered had we
given him the chance. Earl looked startled. Grandpa peered at Earl, put out
his hand, harrumphed, and said, "I know your father." My mother was warm
but clear about him getting me back to the house by eleven-thirty because
she wanted to get me home by midnight. The curfew was hers as much as
mine not just because midnight is always the magic hour when the ball must
end but also because my father, now working a swing shift, would be home
from second shift shortly after midnight. Both my mom and Grandpa made a
point of letting Earl know that his father was someone they respected. There
was a good deal of nodding and awkward smiling.

   All during the chitchat in that small living room wallpapered with
green fronds from some exotic island, Earl held a simple white box. With
the liturgy of introduction out of the way, he handed me that box. It was
bigger than I expected but light—well, of course, a first date. What did I
expect? It would be a lightweight corsage. I sat down to open it, but the
tape caught and I had to tug, and then a cluster of tissue I hadn't expected
popped up. I lifted it, and nestled in more tissue was a single white blos-
som, large and strange, a full moon of a flower with a dark throat that
could only be called maroon.

   Luck and beauty.

   My mother gasped. I could not speak. Earl looked away then, shrugged,
said he couldn't figure out pins, so my mother put her hands in, lifted it up,
and pinned it to the plush fabric at my shoulder, both of us shocked and
startled by a gesture of such extravagance set against our penny-pinching

ways. I looked at Earl with new eyes, full of wonder and curiosity. My mother's eyes—I knew this without looking—were calculating how much an orchid costs.

An orchid—I should have understood.

At the dance, we made the right kind of entrance, not too much flash, but then people turned and saw how the tinsel framed the couple in the doorway. And once in the ornamented gym, that castle of crepe and shine, I knew the orchid was a planet on my shoulder sending out a beam, turning heads.

Would it turn the head I wanted turned?

What neither Earl nor I had anticipated was that the corsage was so large, so stunning, that when we walked onto the dance floor in front of the band and stood face-to-face, it became a delicate creature between us. He could pull me close and crush the orchid (because God forbid I not wear it on Monday!), or we could dance at arm's length. There was really no choice.

The orchid shone off my shoulder, a beacon rising, some trick of the light, distancing us. If Earl was disappointed, he had too much class to show it. And when the band offered up "Everyone's Gone to the Moon," I felt like I had. I was on another planet, but it was not the planet of love. It was the planet of confusion. Because who was keeping the beat to all of this?

In the end, I was saved by the music—as so many of my generation would be. When the band offered up a poor but energetic rendition of "These Boots Are Made for Walkin'" I stamped my patent leather flats, which had been slicked with Vaseline for the event. We gave over to songs clumsily played but with a beat, for heaven's sake, and in the end, that's all that mattered. And we all raised our arms to the rising hit "I'm a Believer" by the Monkees. Who cared what we believed in? And if, sometimes, during those glowing slow dances, any of us in that rising generation thought of the satellite that had just orbited the moon, it was a small coordinate circling high above the crepe castle of our hometown gym. We danced until our satin was sweaty, our lace limp, our corduroys clinging. For the moment, I forgot about Carl. And the moon, at the end, was still untouched on my shoulder.

When finally we pulled ourselves away from the rushing craziness of the dance and drove back to the house of my grandfather, I was tired but pleased. We climbed the steps to the porch, Earl opened the old screen door to the winter porch, and we stepped into the silver light from the streetlamp falling on the dying geraniums. He pulled my hand away from the front door and turned me toward him. I never expected the swift and odd kiss, standing on my grandfather's cold porch while my mother waited inside. Here, the hands on my shoulder as he bent down. There, the warm-lipped peck. I was stopped in my tracks.

What flooded over me was not appreciation, not the princess at last seeing the prince, but its opposite. I felt only perverse betrayal. Again. It was all totally wrong. For this kiss, so unexpected that my slap reaction never even had time to kick in—thank God—was a further lie, something I had saved for someone else. And it was a poor kiss to boot, nothing compared to the kisses I had imagined. This kiss was not my kiss; rather, it was simple, unadorned, and he needed it. In the currency of favor for favor that still reigned, he deserved a kiss. I understood that much but did not want to make this exchange. I never felt his tender caution, only betrayal to him who kept the beat.

I wanted to go to the moon. I wanted to be someone else. I wanted to be me, whoever she was, without guilt for every move I made with a boy. But I was the girl who slapped faces, kissed the wrong boy, and thought Miranda rights was a movie star.

I felt so stupid.

YELLOW, 1967

Earl asked me to every dance that year, ignorant of my messed-up spirit. I accepted; what could I say? I could manage my own feelings about as well as a two-year-old. I wasn't unaware of his parallel to the prince in *Cinderella* or *Sleeping Beauty* or *Snow White and the Seven Dwarfs,* but I felt about as kin to those female archetypes as their cartoon counterparts colored into a coloring book with all the skill of a two-year-old. He was the prince who picked the girl of the fields instead of the girl of the cinders. I was the princess of duplicity. I went to Sweetheart's Ball with Earl, where he was not prince but king of the ball (as usual, the football captain). And my father, who would have been a stand-in for the powerful king, had been played again. But those fairy tales end with the kiss that awakens, the kiss that brings one to womanhood, full sexual awareness, etcetera, and so on. In about ten years, with a proper English degree, not to mention experience, I would finally understand that the kiss was proxy for sex, but at that time, gosh, it was sex.

After every dance, looming as that first orchid, was the kiss on my grandpa's porch, and I was the girl dating this lovely boy who was indeed a friend but did not hold my heart. I kissed him good-night but didn't like it, not because of who he was but because of who I was. Think of first kisses in the ideal. They are pink. This kiss was an old bruise, a kiss recovering from assault.

Then there was prom. Thank goodness for 4-H; I could make my first prom dress—though my mother did no small amount of work on it. That gown was yellow brushed satin, my first floor-length dress, with capped sleeves and a little poised bow topping an empire pleat that fell straight to the floor in the style that Jackie Kennedy had made popular. Geometric and clean, with a chain of white daisies, it was lovely, though my mother cautioned me about yellow, saying, "It makes your skin look sallow."

What was sallow?

For prom my father finally relented on his mandate. It had become obvious that some kind of dating was going on, and he wasn't fool enough to deny the obvious. He didn't know what to do with this thing that had slipped by him, defied his authority. I never learned if he knew about the Grandpa plan, but I wore him out with my own continued barrage, the need to go. I didn't think about his feelings. Grudgingly, with many man sighs, he gave his permission. For prom I was finally allowed a date.

That night, a new crunching on the gravel of the drive.

That night, a tall boy, dressed in a rented tuxedo, stepping into the mudroom where the hound sniffed his ankles.

That night, my sisters giggling in awe and my mother sighing with relief.

Then the exchange of flowers, for by now I understood I was to give him a boutonniere, which I hadn't known at first. Something yellow.

At last, the greeting of the boy by my father on our own land.

He gave Earl a steady look, and there was a brief discussion of sports, which was awkward because my father was a fan of baseball, not football, so he had to pull up some distant knowledge, which he did.

Photographs of us. The yellow dress. My expression, pink against yellow, serious as hell. Sallow.

Finally, into the car and the ride to the castle. We would be not townies and country kids but promgoers. Promenade. Earl and I would parade through that spring dusk into the gym and join a gang of kids caught in ties and tight shoes. It was a rough unity. We would drink sweet punch and marvel at the un-gyming of the gym to this year's theme, Brigadoon. And we would dance, shaking our bodies to sweat and breathlessness.

The band would turn up the volume and loosen the very air.

We felt wild; we were tame.

If we had listened, we would have heard not the dirty vibrations of oversized speakers but the underpinnings of that culture shaking lose. Outside of that gym, beyond the town and the lakes, civil rights workers demonstrated, a war escalated, and protesters marched against that war on both east and west coasts. But we were of the Midwest, or rather, not quite the Midwest but the Great Lakes, and not even the great cities of those Great Lakes but a small town set inland of those inland seas.

In that moment, what we heard was not the march of change but the beat of Aretha Franklin and Jimi Hendrix blaring out the open doors and over those newly plowed fields. We would be blind for a long time, but music was the first way we blew our minds. If someone could sing it, then eventually someone would latch onto the lyrics, and someone brighter than me would spread the word about every state of being from heartbreak to revolution. But not at prom. At prom we leaped and let that beat pierce our small souls. Blessed were we who did not know much, held in the castle, surrounded by our own narrow corn fields.

When we had danced so long that the invisible hem of my dress was dusty and my new black platforms scuffed, I was brought home in the dark spring night. We made our way into the farmhouse kitchen, stood in the light that splayed over the sink, and leaned against the kitchen counter. We kissed in the new green air.

Over that year, dance after dance, Earl was teaching me to kiss. Kissing was something we were figuring out. I was learning quickly. If there had been an Achievement Day for kissing, I would have won the award.

After prom, after school was out, after the rush of graduation, I found myself, as I had every summer since I was seven, in the fields. June meant picking asparagus, riding the picker, filling dirty bushels, sweating, and complaining. I looked up at the sun, wiped my eyes, and realized I was a junior. I was taller, more heart-confused, and a better sewer than I had ever been. I had learned to kiss but did not yet understand the kiss. Or myself. Or even where I was in the ranks of Hart Public Schools. My prince was going to college. I understood that he cared for me, and I cared for him but not enough, and the attentions I could offer, despite his good faith, were for all the wrong reasons.

Through the sweltering dust, my father yelled at me to pick the asparagus stalks *closer to the ground*. His words cut through me as I leaned toward the dirt, my hands breaking the stalks. As one act may subtly bring clarity to another, I picked closer and knew, having been hurt so deeply by the loss of one boy that it was psychologically impossible for me to be the one who would hurt him. I would need a reason to end this.

I turned to my father.

We had just learned that the U.S. was bombing a city called Hanoi in that country called Vietnam. The pictures on TV showed soldiers running through clouds of dust and smoke, and the sound of gunshots ricocheted around the room. My father left the living room and walked out the screen door to the front porch where the silver maple chattered in a warm June wind.

Yellow afternoon light. Dappled shadows.

My dad sat on the stone steps with his single beer of the day, staring out at the yard, the fields. I was still in my work clothes, and I sat down next to him. We could smell the work and fields rising from our bodies.

After a long moment, he came back, the way he did.

"What's on your mind?" For someone who didn't know me at all anymore, he knew me well.

"Dad, I need to break up with Earl."

A long moment passed while he adjusted his thinking.

"I like that idea."

"But I'm afraid to hurt his feelings."

"He's going to college, isn't he?"

"Yeah."

"Seems like he'd want that, too." This had never occurred to me. I looked at the light flickering on the stone porch. How would I feel if he broke up with me? I would be . . . well, relieved, I realized. But my pride would be hurt. Would Earl do that? No, no, he had just given me a charm bracelet. He wanted things to go on.

"Dad, I feel really bad about hurting his feelings."

"So he doesn't want to break up?"

"I think he'd like to be . . ." I took a breath. ". . . more serious." This word made my dad nod, sit up a little straighter, set down his beer. To my parents, serious meant not just that you were going steady but that you weren't touching anybody else, which means you were touching each other, that your touch and the boy's touch were exclusive and that meant

you were getting close to . . . *sex*. Past the kissing, Earl and I weren't anywhere near sex, at least not in my mind, but my dad had as good an imagination as anyone. And if his own lacked any specifics, Elvis and Priscilla
pictures plastered all over the news filled in the gaps.

"You don't want to go out with him anymore?" He raised his eyebrows.

"I think maybe he's too serious."

"Way too serious." He nodded toward his fields.

"So I was wondering . . ."

He took a long swig of beer, looked at me sideways.

"I wondered if you could say that you thought we had got too serious,
and that since he's going to college, you want us to break up."

He choked on the beer. After having set down irrevocable rules at the
beginning of the year, and having had to tolerate them being bent and
worn-out and finally broken until he wondered what authority he had in
his own house, for me to ask for his authority set him back.

"Dad, I can't tell him that I don't want to see him anymore. I just
can't." And the truth of what I was saying hung in the evening shadows.
Here was my immense appreciation of this boy and also the need to be
free. But there was also my own weakness and my wound. That was it. I
had been well treated, but I wanted out and couldn't do it without being
the one to cause the hurt. I needed to blame it on someone else, someone
who had higher authority. I needed my father to take back his power.

My father looked at me. "Why can't you tell him that you don't want
to date him anymore?"

"I think he thinks I like him more than I do. A lot more."

My father took this in. He liked Earl and had come to enjoy the
bustle in the house before the dates. He also wanted his daughter out
of the hands of a boy who was "serious." But he was also absorbing that
his daughter might have misled this boy and didn't have the strength to
be straight about it. He was seeing his daughter afraid to say what she
wanted (or no longer wanted) to the person who most needed to hear
it. He knew that was no good either. He stared at his fields, weighing the
matter.

It became clear. He wanted me out of range of "serious." He would
have liked me to be stronger, but he wanted me free of the boy who

liked me more than I liked him and out of a situation I was not mature enough to figure out. Perhaps he knew it was only the beginning of a series of mistakes for both of us, but because he had no idea of the true source of the trouble, he couldn't put the pieces together. He sighed, nodded to his fields. "I think that's a good idea. You tell him that I said now that he was off to college, it's as good a time as any to break this off. You've got two more years of high school, and you're too young, and it's too serious. He'll have other opportunities. And you're too young. Did I say that?"

He looked at me, and I realized that if seriousness is intent to accomplish something, he was as serious as one could be. And relieved. This he could do. In the helplessness he felt about watching me move too fast, too furiously, I had asked him to do something he could do. I had reestablished his authority when I most needed it—even if, again, I wasn't exercising my own will. He finished his beer, rose, and stopped. He let out another man sigh and said, "Tell him I said." Then he stepped through the screen door, walked through the kitchen, and out the back door where his tractor waited for him.

The trees rustled, and the fields looked long and wide.

Sometime that June, on some sandy shore, I gave Earl a memento ID bracelet in exchange for the charm bracelet he had given me. I told him what my dad had said. I led him to believe it was not what I wanted but that my father was firm. No matter whose authority I had used, it could not stop the hurt for him. But I felt a relief almost as deep as my father's.

SOMEONE HAS A CAR, 1967

I was cranky, moody, smart-mouthed, reclusive. Cranky. My body itched, and I was so resistant to farmwork that my mother, justifiably fed up, did the sensible thing: she gave up. She said, "Go apply at the Drift Inn." Work, yes, always work, but somewhere else. Maybe that would make me appreciate my blessings.

The Greens were good people from our church who owned a restaurant in that coastal town of Pentwater, twenty miles away. Pentwater was not Hart, not the county seat, but a *hot town*, a *groovy town*, a tourist town with that summer combination of wealth and wildness driving down its sunny streets to a wide beach and long pier. The Drift Inn was smack in the middle of the main strip. I bought the simple white uniform, better tennis shoes, and hairnets. Alice, the owner's daughter, trained me for two days. Suddenly I was off the farm and working in a restaurant.

On the street outside the bright-belled screen door of the Drift Inn kitchen, big cars fresh from Detroit thrummed over the hot pavement. Here were vividly painted automobiles tooling through town, slamming on their brakes, tooting horns, and everyone, inside and out, was looking. Unlike my parents' practical secondhand station wagons, these were what the sweet dishwasher boy called *pony cars*: white Dodge Charger, gold Chevy Camaro, red Ford Mustang. Finally we saw it, a cherry of a car, a blue-as-a-lake Thunderbird convertible. They pulled up, pulled in. They emerged like aristocracy. From the creamy white chiffon scarf protecting her blonde Marilyn Monroe hair to her strappy platforms, from his dark curls combed with a double wave to his slick loafers, this couple was far-out. They laughed the entire time that Alice waited on them. I eavesdropped, marveling at the confident way they ordered their food: burgers rare, fries crispy, Coke with extra ice. Alice bantered, asking how long they would be in town, how far they would be going, where were they from. Maybe from Chicago: they left a full 10 percent tip, returned to the car, and drove through the town, turning heads. But here's the thing: they kissed each other all through the meal, right out in public.

I was waiting on another kind of table. They'd come in from a green Volkswagen van with country handkerchiefs worn as sweatbands and torn jeans embroidered with peace signs. Here were boys with long hair arguing about *the system, the war.* They wore bell-bottoms with frayed cuffs and patches. Here were girls with feathers in their straight-to-butt hair who carried macramé purses woven with beads. The girls wore long skirts, bells tinkling on their ankles, and halter tops sporting mushroom appliqués. These flower children moved freely, loping and sloppy. They strolled in a slow way, leading with the hips, easy and mellow. They smelled of something Alice called patchouli, but when I asked to smell it in a store, it wasn't that smell at all.

Hippies. The word hung in the greasy air, and Alice whispered that they would stiff me because "hippies" never have any money because they didn't really work. Let them stiff me. I loved watching them, loved the way everything was *oh man, oh baby, wild, peace, peace, peace.* The rhythm, the inflection in those words gave them surprising new meanings. Again, unbelievably, this group kissed and not always with the same person, right in front of everyone. This was not something they were practicing. This was something they wanted so much that they didn't care what anyone thought.

Kissing. Cars backfiring with power. Tooling the streets. Too much.

I was tied to work, to the rhythm of the restaurant instead of the farm. To *better living.* But between shifts, I wandered down to the beach, stood in my mustard-spotted uniform and watched while, wearing bikinis and cut-offs in the sun and scented with Coppertone, lolling on the hoods of their cars or on the hot sand, every girl and boy was being thoroughly kissed.

I was not being kissed.

Practicality played an unexpected card. My dad needed our family car. He was working a midnight shift on top of farming, and if Mom had to pick me up every night at closing, what would he drive? And gas was a problem, and who was looking out for my sisters when Mom was picking me up because sometimes it was late? By mid-July she asked the Greens to put me up sometimes when she couldn't make the trip, and they said if I would work double shifts, they would gladly give me a room in their house. I could stay with them until things slowed down in August. It was an arrangement of astonishing trust, and I would betray it almost immediately.

Imagine night coming on in that town of lights and laughter and summer. The scent of menthol cigs, burgers, beer, and something that might have been marijuana. Streets full of people. Drift in, drift out. The *open* sign flipped to *closed*. Rush quieting. Cook bumming a smoke, kicking back on the back steps. Imagine yourself, back in the smoking alcove, counting your tips. Someone comes by, asks. Is it the dishwasher, this sweet guy whose older brother has a souped-up car? Yes, someone is asking if you want to go with them. They are taking a car, going to cruise around two-track roads for a while, and you are flattered and scared, and the dishwasher sees your face, knows you can't get into trouble, and says, *Naw, I don't drink, either*. They are just *tooling around*. Maybe they'll make a bonfire somewhere. Maybe they'll drink some Cokes at the place in the woods.

You feel like popcorn, expanding with sudden force. You don't think you can go with them, but then the scent of going is opening you, and you have to go. You wonder if there will be kissing. Could you let a stranger kiss you? You don't think so, but there are those cars, the engines throbbing—that's enough, that's fun. You tell yourself not to go ape, to be cool.

You change, pulling on cut-off jeans and a blouse you tore the sleeves from. You trade out the sneakers with laces for cheap flip-flops, let your hair out of its net, and say, *Yeah, I'll go*. It feels so good to say that, all on your own, without asking anyone, and when you come out of the restaurant onto the street, two or three other kids from the restaurant are waiting, too, all kids like you who smell of French fries and onions. You sit next to the dishwasher boy at the side door, in the shadow of the catalpa tree, and wait for his brother who has the car. Your small gang listens to the music rising, to people and cars, your bodies poised, waiting.

Up and down the street, doors and windows swing open, people talk and stroll and settle, and everyone knows each other even though practically no one does. But it feels that way. Everyone, all up and down the street, in their cars or sitting on benches, is listening to the radio at this time of night. *Music music music* from Frank Sinatra to the Beatles. Top ten. Top one hundred. This is *far-out*.

While you wait, the change begins like fog, rolling in so slowly that you don't notice change at first. Because of the radios—not all at once but in that brief time from dusk until full dark while you wait. The sounds shift. People in their cars turn the dials of their radios. Cook's back inside the restaurant, and you hear him turn up the volume as he does sometimes when he's cleaning the grill, so that he can sing along with some crooner.

This time it is not some crooner who wafts out the window.

You hear fragments, half sentences with an edge to them. Something about the city, that city, Detroit, the car capital of the world, where all the hot cars come from. Some tension is happening there, something with the people who live in Detroit, in those places—what's the word? —in the ghetto. Is this why people are sitting in their cars here, hours north, turning knobs, flipping now between the Monkees' new song and the news?

You sense a shift in attention as you sit there waiting for someone who has a car. But whatever it is doesn't matter enough. You are going with a bunch of kids, with someone who has a car, and you are looking at each other sideways and thinking, Isn't this cool? Yes, we are boss. We will have a gas. It will be such a gas. And you push it out of your mind, this dissonance that has coalesced into a radio warning. When the brother with the car pulls up, you rise as one from the stoop. Sweet dishwasher boy says, *Let's bug out*. The car doors open and you go. Never mind about Detroit.

Now, you hit the gravel back roads of Oceana County, dark and washboarded. Dust clouds follow your speed, and the car windows smear with the heat of bodies and laughter. Then two cars—one has joined you—following in your crop dusting. Here's a sweet cherry car, summer kids in that car, kids you don't know, and, yes, you really are booking down those old roads, screaming until someone slows at a dark place, woods on both sides of the road. Both cars stop, and you think there will be a Chinese fire drill, and you prepare to move fast. But no, the brother stops you with his hand, gets out, and opens the trunk. It bangs up like a door blocking the light behind you, but for just a slice of time, silhouetted in the headlights, you see their hands, an exchange, and you hear the clink of glass. Then the older brother gets in, turns, and says with a smirk, *You guys can't have any.* Then he tries to lay a patch, even though it's a gravel road, and your car pulls out, peeling too fast down the country roads just outside of this coastal town, the country of Pentwater.

You are scared but not too scared, though you think about the Greens' house, the small bedroom where you stay and wonder how you will get back there. But you are here now, on the road, with air whooshing through a side window, going faster. The radio is blaring *hot town, summer in the city*, and the other car is falling behind. Why is that? But the kids from the Drift Inn laugh, and you are all thinking, We are doing it, riding around the roads, tooling around outside of Pentwater! You look at the dishwasher boy, younger than you, and think how sweet he is and wonder if he is too young to kiss. You can't help it, but you don't kiss him because you are startled by this thought that you could try to kiss someone, someone you don't even know very well. You could do the kissing. What a badass idea. But it fits. Out there on the roads, it comes into your head, and you start to think about it. Could a girl really kiss a boy?

You tell yourself: don't be a ditz.

Brother twists the radio knob up again for the good music, but the news interrupts with more about the trouble in Detroit. *Yeah, it's a riot. What's a riot? Aren't we having a riot? Oh that's a riot. Isn't that funny—we are having a riot, and they are having a riot. Oh isn't that funny?* Then big brother dials in the music, and the dishwasher boy teaches you to car dance in the backseat, your arms banging against each other, and you laugh so hard that you just about have a cow. That hip joy goes on until the dust roiling in the open windows settles on your skin. Maybe you will kiss him.

Red light. Night punctuated by a flickering red, the flashing and the soar of the siren behind you. The gumball of light flashes in the same hard beat as your own heart. But your car is first, and the cop stops the car behind you, not yours. The sweet dishwasher's brother, who is driving the car, swears and says, *The pigs*. You wonder what pigs are doing on these roads at night. Did they break out of some farmer's pen? And then you realize this is a word you've heard the hippies use. The cops are pigs. The dishwasher boy says, *We gotta run*. And the big brother nods, says, *Yeah, get outta here*. So the big brother pulls over just far enough ahead and says, *Quick, hit the woods. Later. Dig?* Three people climb out so fast that the doors are not even shut when he pulls away. It's dark, no light in the woods, but thank God there's a moon. Crashing into the woods, scattering, breathing hard, breathing danger. You lose your flip-flops immediately, and think, *I will cut my feet running in the woods in the dark*. But simultaneously, being hurt would be better than being caught. *Caught? What have I done?* You are not drinking, not disobeying a law, just *tooling around*. Ah. You are with them, the people who made some trade. The clinking glass. Is that it?

What happens when you've gone with someone who has a car?

You run, body banging through the undergrowth. Stones cut into your feet. Tree limbs slap your face. Branches meet your body, bend open, slam back against your behind. You smell moss, wintergreen, and wild leeks. Far in, you sink into the sharp thicket, the detritus of deep woods. You lean against trees on the far side of the moon. In the dark. Breathing, breathing. Then not breathing so hard. You are not people but shapes, barely seeing each other, listening into the night, the dark. Mosquitos raise their piney whine. In the far distance, you hear the voices, but you cannot understand. The distant flicker of the police car makes trees look like they are slashed with blood.

Thoughts of kissing? Erased.

The air is humid, but you feel cold and are all shook up. You crouch in the swamp with all of your breath coming and going. After a while the faraway voices stop and the flickering red light moves off into the dark and down the road. You hear the sound of cars starting up and leaving. Have they left you? Have they taken the others away? What happened? Now no one has a car. No car, no way home. Where are you, how many miles from town? Far enough. You're not sure where. The dark is darker. You wait, looking at the small moon, at each other's eyes. Is this how people hide?

At last a tap, the sound of a horn. Short. Then longer. The sound puts the map back in your heads. The sweet dishwasher boy and others rise from the scrub and brush themselves off. You steady yourself against a sapling, touch the bottoms of your feet; your hand comes away wet. You are still scared, but the horn is the sign. Someone has a car, and it is calling you. You take a step and gasp, grit your teeth, then limp back through the trees. It takes a while, and you are shaking. When your feet finally touch the soft gravel road, the dust cakes on your soles.

On the side of the road, big brother leans against the hood of his car. He snickers and shakes his head as you tumble out of the woods. *Lose your shoes?* You don't speak but simply climb in. Big brother says, mocking them, *Cops just checked licenses, said get on home and don't be hanging out back here, up to no good.* Big brother chuckles, says, *He didn't even search the trunk.* And you think, No, he can't, because of Miranda rights.

The big brother looks in the rearview mirror, sees you are all still scared. He sighs, turns on the radio again. At first the top ten soothes through the speakers, but then the broadcaster's voice slips right into the middle of Frankie Valli's "Can't Take My Eyes off You," and the song fades. Yes, in Detroit, trouble rises, a dark moon. Right here in Michigan. You sit still, riveted as the newscaster describes people running. People run in the dark. You were running in the dark, but it was not the same. The riot is exploding.

You do not car dance. You are bummed out. Big brother gives up on all of you, drives you back into town, drops you off just down the block from the Greens' house so no one will hear the car door slam. You are back under the still pools of streetlights. You are back in Pentwater, a tourist town, streets gone quiet on a summer night.

You limp to the silent house. You close the back door gently, savoring slowness after all the speed, and slip into the bathroom, walking gingerly, hoping you are not bleeding on the rugs. You lock the door, step into the tub, sit on the rim, and turn the water on—not full blast but just a little—and let it run over your feet for a long time. You slowly turn your feet over and wince. You pull off the torn skin as you have seen your mother do, and you try not to cry as you see how hurt you are. Both feet, heels and insteps, and one cut between the toes. Nothing deep, but, yes, broken skin all over the place. You rinse and rinse and then raid the medicine cabinet and find what you need. You pour hydrogen peroxide, let it bubble over the still oozing cuts. You rinse again and then apply some iodine, gritting your teeth through the sting. You remove Band-Aids from their small box and use them all. As you do these simple things, your heart steadies, your eyes dry, and you think you will get through this. You vow you will never do it again, but you know this is only the beginning; you will do it over and over in many variations.

You will do it again because here is an action of your own. For the first time, you got into a little trouble—not big trouble like the trouble that is hurting people in Detroit, but your own kind of trouble. You were lucky and got out of it, though you had to run and hurt yourself to do it. Even though you didn't kiss anyone, you for once did something outside of the club, the clique, the farm. You were—this idea shocks and delights you—a little dangerous. This idea, more than all the rest, scares you.

The next morning I walk to work in tired silence, but I am where I should be, in uniform, on time, in my work shoes with an extra pair of socks. I refuse to limp or even to stop on my break, and I work with an efficiency I didn't know I had. In midmorning, sweet dishwasher boy slams through the screen door and winks, but neither of us speaks. I keep expecting some punishment, some scolding. By noon rush, I know that no one knows. More importantly, if they did, they wouldn't care, because they are glued to radios. The top ten is gone; they are listening to riots, to news that becomes worse as the days wear on and the heat rises. I rinse the shrimp, set up the silverware. I realize my small fear is just that—small.

Before the end of the week, Cook will bring a portable TV into the kitchen, purchased special, with rabbit ear antennas that he wraps in tinfoil and points out the window, and we will all watch the TV on breaks, bewildered by militia and murder here in Michigan. This is not like that war on the other side of the world. This is Michigan, not Vietnam. We see it again and again: people running, running in fear for their lives. We see that a riot becomes its own being, running in the dark. We see police shooting. We hear that people are killed, more than twenty, then more than forty. More. We see bricks shatter windows. Tear gas smears the air, and the flames, finally the flames, the flames roar through Detroit, burning the town where all the hot cars are born.

The riots push through Detroit and later through Milwaukee and much later through Washington, D.C.—the capitol of the country. They break out in other cities as well. Through that summer, when I go with anyone who has a car, the music I think I am listening to will periodically fade, and I will tense up, and the voices will give way to gunshots, sirens, tense reporters. Walter Cronkite discusses for the first time this idea of race relations, not just civil rights, and I watch as people, white and black, run in the night. While I slide my tongue across pistachio ice cream and drink iced Cokes, while I serve coleslaw and Campbell's soup, this becomes the other bitter constant of the summer. At night I go with anyone who has a car, and I ride around the empty moonlit back roads while the cities of my country riot. *I am just beginning to think.* I tool around, knowing how, like the ones rioting in the night, I can run if I have to. Even with all the small wounds, I will run. And why do I run? Because someone is after me. I am scared; I am drawn. All that summer I think about it—how we run, how I run—and I never try to kiss anyone, but I hold the idea of kissing like heat rising, like an explosive in my brain. Because if I can run, I can kiss.

EXPLORATION DAYS, 1967

After the summer rush, I came home to the farm as tense and alert as a strange new species. My running all those country roads had not quelled but fed the itch in my body, which now ran so deep that it was impossible unless I was moving, heading out, away from or toward the next thing. Where was I going? Anywhere. What was there? I didn't know, but I would go. Vague. Insistent.

That season our nation called the Summer of Love, with its frenzy of wildly free and broken ideals, became the Long, Hot Summer. I knew it only by the heat and dust of back roads and rumors. I never could have said, *I caught the spirit of the times*, because who really knew what that was in Oceana County? But still, that spirit, contradictory as it was, must have wafted through me, infusing the air I breathed with a strong enough whiff for a contact high. It did not make me mellow; it made me crazy.

My mother, through the rush of making coffee, fixing dinners, and doing laundry—not to mention farmwork, including looking after the chickens—took one look at my on-the-verge-of-wildness and shuddered. While she took care of her other daughters and tried to keep her boys from new bouts of trouble, she urged me to look to the future, get ready for school, earn money, take on ambitious projects. I could have spit. When it became obvious that there was no hope, she did what any self-respecting parent does: she turned subversive. She herded me back where I belonged.

To the good club, to 4-H.

"I think I'm going to die," I said as I flopped on the blue couch in the August heat.

She was at the ironing board, now set up in the slightly cooler living room, her hair plastered, face sweating. My impending death may have inspired her next move.

"Then go. Please go, for goodness' sake." *Going* meant to Michigan State University in Lansing to participate in the State Exploration Days to model the yellow prom gown at the 4-H modeling competition.

"But you're not going?"

"Not this time."

"But I can go?" I raised my head enough to look for confirmation.

She nodded into Dad's Sunday shirt, crisping the collar.

That meant what?

Exploration Days were 4-H's equivalent of Ed Sullivan's *really big shooo*, a competition where only a few of many were picked for statewide recognition. But go without her? Alone?

"You kid me not?"

"I kid you not."

I had been to State a bunch of times, but she had always been the chaperone. She had attended every meeting, every event, which was one reason I no longer looked forward to those events. But if I could go by myself to that college campus, stay in dorms on my own, hang my home-made clothes in strange closets, and leave the door open to admire them, I would be independent. I would prove that I could get myself where I needed to be and do what I was supposed to do. There would be chaperones, of course, and they would be as watchful as eagles. But they wouldn't be her.

You want to go. So go.

She was betting on some motherload of intuition and straight calculation about her girl and the big school while simultaneously believing that the club had enough built-in boundaries that I would be safe.

She had seen the cars.

No one had a car. I rode a rented bus down with a couple dozen other 4-H'ers from the county, all of us scrubbed clean but never quite shedding the scent of dirt. I carried a suitcase packed with homemade clothes and, in a plastic dry-cleaning bag, the yellow prom gown. I had been modeling since I was ten, and I had been to MSU for other 4-H projects, but this time I would model on a *runway*, with girls from all over the state. This was a step up, a step away, a golden moment to showcase my skills. I was going to a big university campus to model, and that was sooo cool, wasn't it? And of course, I'd take them by storm. It would be easy. And she wasn't coming.

What did my mother know that I didn't?

Not realizing there would be changing rooms in the building, I had dressed at the dorm and walked across that august campus in my gown, gathering blades of fresh-cut grass on the hem. I wore sneakers and carried my shoes. I can only imagine the vision I made, yellow pleat trailing limply in the heat. I reported to the registration table in a high sweat, wiping what little makeup I wore with a farm handkerchief pulled from a handmade macramé purse that my little sister Marijo had made and I had "borrowed." If I noticed the volunteers looking alarmed, or even amused, I took it for admiration. I pinned my number to my waist and made my way into one of Michigan State's cavernous lecture halls turned fashion arena. The stage area was wide but not deep, so the runway had been extended, an enormous canvas-covered tongue perpendicular to the stage in replication of Paris couture. It was bigger than I had expected. And so were the girls—not in size but presence. Polished, lovely. Some were dazzling. For the first time, I paused.

This was no county Achievement Day. Here a hundred or so representative models lined up along the side of the room in gowns, suits, and outfits so sixties' amazing that we personified a gaggle of rare birds, the ones paraded at the fair, tutti-fruttied, geometried and plumed, clucking for blue ribbons. We lined up and waited for our turn on that garlanded plywood ramp, surreptitiously checking our new panty hose and bouffants. Here girls from farms all over the state readied for the biggest thing Michigan State, famous for cattle if not always culture, had to offer. From the audience, mothers and leaders alike coached key girls, sometimes with contradictory information, hand gesturing to straighten sloppy bangs or to push up (or push down) the strapless bodice—that was a clear gesture—or, more commonly, to simply shush with fingers to mouth because we were all becoming, in plain sight of each other, so nervous that we couldn't shut up.

I found my place behind two "young women" (that's what 4-H encouraged us to call ourselves) who seemed older than me and sported a confidence I associated with experience. They were put together in a way I couldn't put my finger on—like maybe they hadn't walked over campus greens in sneakers and a floor-length formal. "Yeah," said the girl dressed in layers of chiffon the color of blue sky, "this will be so *challenging*." This was a new 4-H term. We were supposed to accept challenges, even embrace them, but she was being . . . what? Sarcastic?

"How come?" I braved the conversation, fingering my yellow bow, wondering why it would not lay straight.

"Lotta competition." This was spoken flatly by the girl dressed in a green polyester jumpsuit. We moved along the wall leading to the portal of the stage. I looked. *Competition?*

How do I compare? was not a question I had thought to ask.

Is that when they talked about the bears?

This was to be my first introduction and final understanding of the *runway*—two high-fashion 4-H girls talking about two other girls being mauled by grizzlies in "some park out west." The attacks had headlined the news, and everyone had heard about the fatalities. The news had frightened my little sister Patti into not going outside for days, but who in that line brought it up? It wasn't planned, was it?

"Yeah," said the girl in blue chiffon, "eaten alive."

"They were eaten?" I had not heard this part.

"Well, parts were missing." Deadpanned by the girl in the green jumpsuit, as though she was saying, *Have some gum.*

The line moved forward. It hit me for the first time that besides the entire audience watching as we prepared to take the stage, the judges were seated near the runway but with a full view of the lineup, like in some bad cop show. My mother would have pointed this out first thing. But we young women didn't seem to know that or were pretending not to. Having perceived the lineup as part of the backstage, not onstage, preparation, we acted accordingly—like girls.

"One had a boyfriend, but he didn't save her," said Princess Blue.

Considering what little I knew about grizzlies, I was not surprised. "He had to save himself," I whispered.

"Tell that to the girls," said Miss Green.

"Bears don't attack unless they're provoked." I was pretty sure about that. Why wouldn't my bow stay straight?

"So you're saying that bear was provoked?" Princess Blue asked. They looked at each other, bug-eyed and—did I read that right?—almost laughing.

We were hushed for the second time.

Princess knew all about it. "The girls were in different campsites. How did two bears get provoked at the same time?" She hoisted up her bodice, glancing down appreciatively at breasts so generous I had to look away.

"You might not know you'd provoked a bear in the dark." I was taking this far more seriously than I needed to.

"So the dark provoked the bears?" Again with the sarcasm.

"There were others kids, but they got away. Maybe they provoked the bears?" This from Miss Green, fingering her cuffs. I nodded.

"But they could hear the girl screaming." Princess Blue.

"Wouldn't that just kill you?" Miss Green looked sideways without expression.

Green and Blue looked at each other and started to giggle so extravagantly at the pun that they were shushed immediately, this time by a man in an MSU Extension Service badge.

In 4-H, when you were taught to model, you were supposed to concentrate, focus, stand straight, center your balance, review the choreography, and keep your chin parallel to the floor. Keep your cool, keep your nerves under control, and think about what the body had to do—the steps, the hands, your carriage—what my mother called spine poise. And while you showcased the dress, you wanted to show a kind of personality as well. My mother's definition of personality consisted of a never-let-up-for-a-minute smile and being clean and tidy. Anything more would be "putting on airs." All this had worked pretty well in Oceana County. I had dry-cleaned, then hand-pressed the yellow prom dress. But was I clean and tidy? The walk across campus in urban heat had wilted the crispness in my golden pleat, and though I had shaken out the grass, I had forgotten deodorant. As to the smile, I tried it out a couple of times with the girls. I tried to hold it in place, but it was like holding an ice cube. I was aware that I had been sent from Oceana County as a representative of the clean and tidy, but the only clear thing in my head were those bears. Miss Green brought them up again.

"One girl was caught in her sleeping bag." She said this while watching a tiny girl in a too-cute dirndl skirt and short jacket turn this way and that, prim as a teacup.

"Oh, I heard that." This from Princess Blue. "She couldn't get away, and then the bear dragged her into the woods."

I studied the runway, but I could only see the image of the girl trapped in the sleeping bag, struggling with the layers. I told myself that the runway was no different from the extensions for the Drama Club productions or some platform we made to un-gym the gym for a dance. *One girl was rescued, and a doctor helped her, but she died before morning.* The ramp was covered with white canvas that must have been last used by a lawn mower exhibit because that kind of wheel print crisscrossed some of the panels. White draperies clipped to the rims made the contraption look more "professional," a word we had heard a lot that day, but in a few places the clips had slipped off. The drapes drooped and revealed the hidden scaffolding.

We had been told, with no small amount of pride, that this was how pros did it.

The other girl had a terrible death.

I chewed my nails, watching girls disappear backstage, then reappear from behind the curtains and walk first all the way right, then left all the way, then to the center for a focal point. That would be where I would have to show my bow. If I stepped onto that runway that ran three-quarters of the way into the audience, I would have to walk to the end, look at my audience, smile and turn, then showcase the back of the dress as I walk back slowly so everyone can see the flow of fabric and absorb my poise. I could see the turn at the end was tricky. Many girls wobbled or stumbled on the pivot, swayed in the turning. All that space just hung there, like the end of a diving board, like walking a plank. The end of a night.

Is that when I finally realized that the lemony yellow of the gown did not fit my pink-toned complexion, even with the tan I had garnered walking on the Pentwater pier between shifts? My black shoes were too garish; white would have been better. I had donned a black headband and stuck fabric daisies into it. They weren't real, but they looked wilted. My hair was down when a gown like mine called for an upswept do, like a chignon. Along with the deodorant issue, what little makeup had survived the earlier walk smeared or dripped with sweat.

"Do you have any lipstick?" I asked the girls, not really expecting a response, but, lo, Miss Blue produced a bright red from her cleavage. It was so warm that I thought it would melt, but I smeared it on in front of everyone. When I caught myself in a reflection, it looked like a wound. *How would it feel to scream and have no one come?* I moved ahead. I watched the line of girls before me modeling everything from Russian-style coats to the new tent dresses. Still, most of the dresses modeled that day were gowns, and they were lovelier, more adventurous, brighter, and sexier— unheard of in 4-H—than anything I had ever seen. I fingered the bow.

Then it happened. One young woman took the stage in a curvy black-and-white striped midi coat. When she stepped out in the coat with her red platform go-go boots and a tiny red beret, I heard the gasp from the crowd. Her large eyes were accented with so much dark eyeliner that she looked like Cher of the singing duo Sonny and Cher. Her dark hair was cut short in a pixie style that the model Twiggy had made famous. But the way she moved made the difference. She was an exquisite, agile creature walking as though walking was a dance in tandem with narration. Her head was raised and level, and she led with her hips, her shoulders shifting, rolling forward with an even grace. She stopped at the end of the runway, held, *did not smile*, turned away, and walked halfway up the ramp. I thought she'd made a mistake, but no. In one swift but deliberate move, with her back to us, she unbuttoned the coat, pivoted back toward her audience, flipped open the front, and held it wide to reveal not just the matching striped miniskirt and tight black turtleneck but—another gasp—the red satin lining of the coat. She stood in her own scarlet silhouette, shimmering with a violence that became beauty, that invited you toward it, that you wanted to watch.

I knew she had thought about this effect: the stripes, the red, the association with the African zebra. Then that red—why did it take our breath?—not vulnerability but fierceness. Her look seared the crowd with—the word came slowly to me—the thing my mother would have disapproved of, *defiance*. And then she stepped forward, again the slow walk, again the stop and, stilled in her final pose at the end of the runway, she closed the coat. Only then did she smile, wide, warm, the kind of smile that says *I am who I am*. No apologies. She was a *young woman*, full-fledged and complete. Bears would bow to her.

I had never seen anything like it.

How had she done this?

Then she left the stage, and we saw the judges bend to their notes as one.

Quietly now, we went back to being *in line*.

I watched as Princess Blue and Miss Green each in turn slipped behind the curtain and in minutes emerged on the stage with huge smiles, stepping forward into the light, turning right and left. Princess Blue let her fingertips linger on the skin between her throat and the low satin trim that pressed the top of those breasts, and she smiled. I remembered that in 4-H modeling, your hands tell an audience what to look at, suggest a focal point. I couldn't for the life of me figure out what she was noting on the dress.

Oh, it wasn't the dress she was noting at all.

Miss Green assumed the literal in *jumpsuit* and walked out with such a spring that I wondered if she was skipping. She made a great show of the zipper jacket. Up and down, up and down. Was there a ripple of laughter, and did she join in? When Miss Green turned to walk back up the runway, she looked over her shoulder and winked.

You could flirt onstage?

I saw how the judges looked at her and noticed, for the first time, the men among them. They weren't all looking at the complex pattern, the beautiful fabric, or even her smile, but rather—and it came to me with sudden clarity—at how much *personality* she was showing them.

Then I was onstage. My black shoes scraped. All the stages I had walked previously had been solid, but this was hollow. How had I missed this? Most of the other girls had realized and adjusted. I hit the runway with those black heels, my heavy farmer step hard as a drum on the boards. My arms swung too widely, and my long legs took strides like a clumsy colt ready to head into a full gallop but not sure how. I could feel it, and I could not stop it. The yellow hem rustled but did not swirl. The judges watched me from hem level, necks craned back so I could see their mouths open a little. The runway was a path of tracked-up canvas. *Step lightly. Don't run*. But I had been running all summer. My footsteps were loud with that running. Even when I tried not to hit my heels, I could feel the stones of the swamp, the sharp twigs. When I came to the end, I *constructed*—the only word for it—a wide, hard-plastic smile that I hoped would fill the room. I thought my face would break into pieces. It was impossible, so I hurried, no longer listening to the narration for my cues. Nothing could save me. As I turned away and walked quickly off the stage, Blue and Green were already at the other side, whispering too loudly, guessing that the model in the striped coat, Zebra Queen, would take the state prize.

When it was over, I walked the quiet paths back across campus. I meandered through rare gardens still dressed in the yellow gown. I stared down at the metal labels for the exotic plants, reading the foreign words of genus and species, and not caring that I looked like a bedraggled, out-of-season tulip. I felt shadowy, suddenly ashamed. I had not done well. There would be no recognition; I was not to be one of the few selected to receive an award. And I had been unprepared to face the bears.

Where was my mother? I longed for her swift efficiency.

There in the garden of exotics, I also thought about the Zebra Queen. She had not succumbed to the ploys of the others. She had been unique in her utter confidence, her ability to say who she was. In her sexuality. How did she learn that? How did she know those things? I was confused by this new species. Of greater impact than failing was this idea: in her, I had seen something of what it would take to succeed at this thing called modeling, which was not just a beautiful dress or a ploy for the judges. She knew herself. She had showcased her individuality, her personal style, to her advantage. I longed to open the coat of a self like that, but it also scared me, and I knew I was not ready for anything like that self knowledge, that revelation. I wanted, suddenly, to sleep in my own room, with the closet door closed on all the 4-H clothes I had made over the years. I knew my mother would not have liked how the day had played out, but her basic plan had worked: I wanted to go home and stay there.

JUNIOR, 1967

My ninth year in 4-H.

My second year in public high school—after the convent, that is.

My first year driving.

The riots in Detroit and Milwaukee had left a residue of uncertainty that even Walter Cronkite, that intrepid newscaster whose TV voice now haunted every evening, could not allay. I could not have said the words, but the country was in a state of growing disillusionment. Images of marches and protests poured off the screen every night. We felt sorrow about the war, which was not our family's sorrow but which came to us in small insidious pangs—the son of someone in the next parish, an athlete from Montague, people we did not know well but knew well enough to say their names and tack them to our regional maps. We were losing them and the war. My father grew quieter in this less confident country. These changes coupled with what I had learned: that running in the dark, failing at the state competition. Those forces launched my junior year. I felt contradictions on the edge of my vision, but when I turned, I could never catch them.

What was rising in me was entirely different.

I knew it when I gathered the money from the tips and hours at the Drift Inn and went straight to Gambles and bought fabric for an entirely new wardrobe inspired to a great degree by the 4-H trip to Lansing. Mini-skirts. Jumpsuits. Bell-bottoms. I knew it by the time I dressed in the green-and-lavender plaid miniskirt and vest, fresh off the sewing machine table. I knew it as I climbed onto and off the bus and walked back into the long high school corridor with my short-short skirt and long hair now straightened in juice cans every other night, parted straight down the middle, pulled behind my ears, and swinging down my back. I knew it when I started classes and schemed all the way down the long hall.

There was one thing I wanted.

Yes, a boy. Not Carl—though that wound remained raw and real. Not Earl—the weight of that thought was a quiet guilt. I wanted a new boy, a specific boy.

His name was Nels.

Junior year begins with Nels, boy number three.

I don't know of anything in the unruly ambitions of the country that could match the unruly ambition, not to mention downright ruthlessness, of my almost sixteen-year-old self. I had been burned in the big world, and now I wanted something in this smaller one. He had to be special; he had to be good. It had to be.

Again I would first be attracted to high school titles, the only version of aristocracy I could know. He was a senior, president of his class. He had been an exchange student to Germany, been inducted into National Honor Society, and was the set builder for Drama Club. He was a townie but not like a townie, having lived much of his life in the country. He had all the respect and position to which I was susceptible. But mostly, and this was something I was just beginning to understand, he was someone I chose. I did not fall for him by naive accident as I had Carl. He did not find me, as Earl had found me. I chose him.

He couldn't have been a more impossible pick.

What had I wanted? The most common of things. Despite a summer of riots licking out of our radios and rifling our ears, despite my scrapes and unarticulated longings, despite Exploration Day and Zebra Queen, I had not matured. I wanted to go to dances. I wanted to be seen, to be the center of some small attention—that vestige remained—but not 4-H seen. Boy seen, as in boy scenes. I wanted a boy I truly liked, who I could rely on, who was popular and fun, who I wanted to kiss, who would take me to dances. And kiss. Did I say that?

Nels was to be that.

That simple.

It's never that simple.

That fall, Mrs B. rented a bus and took forty Drama Club kids to Grand Rapids to see the award-winning film *Doctor Zhivago*. I sat in the plush theater seats and watched a story altogether shocking. It was not just love but two kinds of love, real and simultaneous: Zhivago's love for the ever-patient Tonya, played delicately and darkly by Geraldine Chaplin; and his love for the robust blonde, Lara, played steamily by Julie Christie. Stunned and confused, I couldn't take my eyes off the screen. I was haunted by the way Russian history had played against these lovers. War and more war. Could that happen in our country? There was no revolution here. Or was there? People were marching. And soldiers had come to Michigan that summer, the National Guard, and now the war seemed closer because we knew families with sons who had gone to Vietnam. Still, none of that was near our farm. It was in Detroit, Milwaukee, Washington, D.C., over there, beyond the boundary of my county. Wasn't it? Here was Zhivago. Zhivago.

Oh God, the Russians.

And here I was, a 4-Her. Head, heart, hands, health. I was bound by the pledges—if not in behavior, then in spirit. I thought I had been following the Tonya narrative, patient and ever-bearing as a strawberry plant. But now a question overrode the pledges: was there love like Lara's in Oceana County? Was there love that big, that sweeping? What was passion, really? I looked around. Was love varied, as textured as fine fabrics? Could love change over time? What was the common ground between my parents kissing (which still happened, but now it bugged me) on the other side of the closet, and Lara and the doctor on the floor before the fireplace in the ice castle? Was it possible for a failed 4-Her to find a different love beyond the dresses and dances? The questions kept coming—wiggly things, random ideas ricocheting through me when I looked at myself in the mirror, which I did obsessively as I painted my eyelids with blue iridescent shadow.

I was on a cusp, staring at change, but had not crossed over.

I was a junior.

I needed a catalyst.

After a summer away from the farm, after the failure of Lansing, I knew what the catalyst should be. I zeroed in on one thing, a coalescing so simple and pure that it defied the times. I wanted to go to the homecoming dance with the boy named Nels.

Ridiculous.

Now imagine the long hall of September, the bustle of a school day, paisley miniskirts, patent platforms, hair straight to your butt, and eyeliner that made girls look like they had eye-whiskers. Before backpacks, book bags were the thing, embroidered or appliquéd with flowers and peace signs or the occasional marijuana leaf—though few knew what it meant. Here was the annual sorting out, lining up, realigning of lockers and locks—now old hat—slammed against the green metal doors. The ritual of return was laced with new cool. I had a plan, a plan to put myself in his way, to create moments for him to find me. I was sorting out Nels's schedule when a different and unexpected obstacle separated himself from the bell-bottomed throngs.

Here another boy approached, catching me off guard, a nice boy but not Nels, and he asked me to homecoming, and here I was, accepting him, hiding my disappointment. Why did I accept? I was afraid of not going at all. I was on the runway again, not having anticipated the unexpected. Since the world was apparently as tenuous as Zhivago's Russian history, he would be my backup.

And this is the worst of it: with one boy's invitation in my pocket, I continued to scheme. I had to move quickly. Many girls liked Nels, and a slew of senior girls were eligible for his attentions. Still, I had learned some things from Earl, Drama Club, flirting, Lydia, the girls at Exploration Day, and my own heartaches. I wanted Nels enough to use what I had learned. In this I would fulfill my mother's wish: I would show some gumption.

The kiss. From Earl I had learned its variety and nuance. And from Lydia I had learned some of the social contexts. As a result, I aimed for a specific and purposeful kiss: a victory kiss. I wanted a kiss in the cafeteria outside the gym as the team exited the locker room after a game. The girls who dated the players waited for the boys there, and this, Lydia had informed me, was where the girls gave their boys a victory kiss or a kiss to comfort them in defeat. It came like lightning: this was the way to get his attention, to make him see me. Then maybe he would choose me.

Where did I get this stuff?

I prepared. I talked to him at rehearsals, worked with him on set, flirted a little as we cleaned paintbrushes. Then I went with Lydia after games and sat or stood off to the side in the cafeteria, trying not to stare but observing closely how it was done: how the girls could take the lead, how you could touch an arm and swing another around a boy's neck and pull him toward you and say, *Great game!* Or, *The ref was terrible.* That was what you said if they lost. And kiss.

There were reactions you had to account for. Sometimes you just kissed the boy's cheek because some boys were embarrassed, and sometimes you had to cover their surprise or consternation. I realized you had to gauge it, and they had to like you enough to be pleased. But if they didn't, you had to pull away and move quickly so there wouldn't be the yuck factor. I realized, watching Lydia kiss her boyfriend, the delicate nature of this particular kiss. You had to take the lead but not look like you were doing that. And I realized, too, there would be no chance to rehearse, no way to practice like I did for 4-H or a play.

Here you are after the toughest football game of the year, a hard-won game against a hard rival, waiting in the cafeteria with the fluorescents pouring down and the dark gathering just beyond the wide doors. The team has climbed off the bus and marched noisily, happily through the cafeteria toward the gym, and the cheerleaders are there for one last cheer for their team. Then the players disappear into the lockers rooms. Here are the girls waiting, making small talk, giggling, murmuring under the hum of lights. A few parents linger, but mostly they wait in cars outside the cafeteria door. Sweet energy. Our boys have won. It is the most important thing in a small town. The doors open; cold air sweeps in. Doors close; air warms. You wait.

You must be casual. You must be forward. At the same time? How does that work? You think you should go now before you make another stupid mistake. You almost do.

Then the boys, the lovely boys, fresh from the shower, hair wet, some still flushed, amble back through the gym into the cafeteria, sometimes in groups, sometimes pairs, sometimes singly, draped with their red-and-white varsity jackets, their emblems and letters bright under the glare. The girls step forward, reach for their boyfriends. They kiss.

And I am there waiting for one boy, one player who is not expecting me, to exit the gym. And he has to exit alone, and he has to see me.

This is the plan?

Lydia leaves with the guy she's dating. They will wait in the car. Others leave; they push the doors open and walk into the October night, walk out to the open fields. He does not come. Did the coach have to speak with him longer than the others? I wait, giving up because somehow I have missed him. But then the gym door swings open. He comes out, looking tired, and I realize he has played hard. I feel a little thrill. He starts to move toward the door, but he sees me. He makes eye contact. A flicker of . . . something appreciative. It is enough. I step forward, a little run, and then I put my arms around him and remember a soft kiss, a quick kiss.

I pull back, laugh, and say, "Congratulations. Wasn't it a great game?"

He looks surprised, lets his hands drop and rest at my waist. He tips his head, quizzical. "I didn't do much."

"But you did. I saw the interception." I have no idea what an interception is, but it's a term I suspect will fit here, and it does. He looks pleased. He looks at me again, pulls away but slowly, as if he would like not to pull away. We have kissed. A small kiss. I have his attention. I have left a message. I have let him know. And he does know, and I can tell he is thinking about it. Nels is the kind of boy who thinks.

But really, how can a cool guy with a Boy Scout heart have much of a chance against someone like me? Such a Lara move.

How many days later until I see him again? Not many. Here is Nels finally coming forward in the hallway, falling into step and walking me to the bus, asking there on the wide sidewalk, just under the awning, "Will you go to homecoming with me?" And here is me saying yes, and we just stare at each other for a moment. It's so corny that it's cool.

But now I have a problem.

"You did what?" Here is my mother, standing in the kitchen, every cell in her body scolding. "You go with the boy who asked you first. That's the rule."

"I'm going with Nels, Mom. I'll figure out something." She shakes her head. Here is me feeling guilty and thrilled about homecoming with Nels.

I set the problem aside entirely, of course, for the gown. While my mother clucked, I selected the pattern. I had seen it on the 4-H runway in Lansing. The gown is a new style, the layered formal, a tight-fitting orange slip—yes, a slip—with spaghetti straps overlaid with an orange tent dress of frosty orange lace. Imagine lace over satin, tent over slip, all in orange.

My mother kept scolding. The slip of slippery nylon slipped. More scolding. She widened the straps so there was no chance they'd break. I shrilled at her about interfering. She insisted the lace patterns match at the seams—at least *you'll do that right*. She said that if yellow had not been my color, how did I think orange was any better? I said orange was in. She said orange was *garish*.

But finally, there was no more avoiding the issue of the other boy.

And here is me, at last seeking out the other boy, telling him clumsily that I had been confused, that I had already been asked before he had asked but had thought it was a joke, that I was so sorry but that I had an obligation to the boy who had asked me first. The lie and the irony stood in front of me, an orange dress lie, but I didn't care. Once more, I had hurt someone else.

Here is the dance. Everything matches: the dress of orange lace, see-through to the orange satin slip; the corsage of yellow carnations with fake maple leaves, just the right contrast against the lace; and the gym, this time the castle decorated with boughs of autumn leaves. I feel like it is all coordinated, all together for the first time.

And so, having begun with the victory kiss, what could we do but continue?

What did I know about how history evolves?

The lesson of the Russians?

Just give me their fur coats and their kisses.

Whereas junior year might have been, should have been, an awakening, I would bury myself in dresses and kisses. I sewed to fill the time until I could see Nels again, sewed to avoid my schoolwork, sewed to make my mother mad, to spend money, to comfort myself when the news on TV and the radio would enter the house like a rush of cold air. That other history.

And I kissed. And the kisses kept coming. Slowly at first, for he was shyer than I imagined and old-fashioned in a way that surprised me. I learned the pleasure of waiting a while, so we moved slowly at first. Perhaps because he knew that small thing about timing, I wanted to kiss him more than I ever imagined. And the guilt for all the kissing? The guilt I had always lived with? The guilt was there, but, holy cow, with Nels I could ignore it.

I was so happy. Me, the moody dreamer, the master wallower, was happy.

Dangerous territory.

I would become the kind of girl I had once despised, the kind of girl who ignores the world so she can make out on the overstuffed chair in the corner with her boyfriend.

CATECHISM

The airwaves launched my first cultural criticism: every sound from the strangely nostalgic "Penny Lane" to the whimsical "Incense and Peppermints." Bob Dylan had rocked the world by turning to rock. And then came "Light My Fire." When it hit the charts, we followed it to the top like a bird rising. It was our anthem. "Come on, baby, light my fire. Time to set the night on fire."

I lived for weekends, for parties, for this new music that was making our adults shake their heads and cringe over the influence these too-explicit lyrics might have on us kids. We stared them down and danced. I turned sixteen that autumn, and my mother allowed me a garage party. My friends brought their records, and we stabilized the skipping needle on our old hi-fi by taping a nickel to the arm to weight it. And we danced. *Light My Fire.*

Cornstalks, bushels of apples, bundles of orange and red maple leaves, homemade ice cream, and a Barbie cake. My mother, unbelievably, made these cakes for her daughters' birthdays. Barbie is stuck inside the round layer cake in such a way that the cake becomes the skirt of her dress. Her too-perfect body is covered with a frosting bodice, the rippling confection like layers of ruffles. *Try and make that dress,* my sister Marijo teased me. I ate the cake directly off the plate, letting the sweet butter frosting spread all over my face. After I wiped it off, Nels confessed he would have liked to kiss it off. The thought sent me spinning. We were all spinning there in that beautiful rural world. We were starting to spin.

What could possibly slow us down?

The church. As it should. Or at least it tried.

But here's the thing: Pope John XXIII had called for the Catholic Church to hold the Second Vatican Council, and the trickle down to even our country parish was nothing short of revolutionary. The church had seen that the "times, they were a changin'" (though perhaps not in Bob Dylan's words) and had set out a better way. Our priest, Father Hoop, a beloved and humble man, had proposed to the parish council that a Catholic catechism would include a Catholic view of sex education in a weekly catechism class. And here was the unbelievable part: my parents supported it.

Maybe it was my sweet sixteen party or the new music, or maybe they had realized that they couldn't, in this changing time, do all this chil-drearing alone. No longer could they depend on do-it-yourself parenting. They had not given up, but they were willing to call in the troops, and if a priest teaching some Catholic version of sex ed would keep me in line by one degree, they were all for it. The wildness that was starting to rise even in their own well-chaperoned children and the wildness that was rising all over the country had to be curtailed. *One thing leads to another,* my mother warned knowingly. What did she know? I was keeping everything a secret. Or so I thought, and I went on kissing. So when this priest, Father Hoop, said he could teach this program about Catholic sexuality for young people, my mother and father, after praying about it, decided that they would sup-port it because clearly the job of keeping us (me) out of trouble was proving too much. That was the greatest fear: trouble. Girls got into trouble. Boys got into it, too, but there were things that could be done. Girls, if they got into trouble, got pregnant. I laughed out loud when my mother said that. Trouble was for people who were doing something else, going all the way. I was just kissing, making out a little. That wasn't really sex. Was it?

Church hall. Brown tables. Drop ceiling. The stale scent of the old kitchen wafted from the back, and the strange odor of cigarettes drifted from the adult study in the far corner. Catechism class met on Wednesday night, and so, with some half dozen other high schoolers, all country kids, we began sex ed as the church saw it.

I, like many girls in the public schools at the time, had seen the *on becoming a woman* films, and the boys had seen the equivalent, but no one was talking about the specifics of intercourse in the context of the church. Those specifics in the context of the church were what my friend Don called a *sorrowful mystery*, vague and full of loss, especially for the women.

"Maybe there will be pictures," someone called out as we herded into the building. We had laughed a little nervously. Some of us remembered the previous films, with the drawings (never photos) of the sex act in awkward positions.

Before we started, we prayed. Father began with discussion of "it." We talked about "it" (sex)—always "it"—but there were no pictures. We were given specific anatomical names but no pictures. What was the purpose of the class? We were to simply hold this knowledge so we would not be swept away when the temptation arrived, as it surely would. Then, as good Catholics and with the help of the Lord, we could be prepared to exercise our good will.

How could we be swept away when there were no pictures?

Of course, Don, the most outspoken of us, began with what we knew best.

"Is French kissing a sin?" he asked.

Yes, French kissing was wrong.

"Why?" Don fingered his fringed jacket, blushing but determined.

"Because," the good priest chose his words patiently, "as I said, it puts you in the way of temptation." He tapped the table.

Again, Don demonstrated the persistence we were all coming to appreciate. Don was now braiding his fringe but asked, not looking up, "How come?"

"Because." Another pause. "The French kiss is temptation for further acts of intimacy."

Acts of intimacy?

I felt myself becoming warmer. Technical vocabulary hadn't done for a second what this sideways vocabulary did almost as well as pictures.

Don, like any good lawyer, continued the line of questioning. "But, Father, it's not sex, so why is it wrong?"

Did Father have the grace to blush? He paused, as though he had to find the words. "If you are overcome with lust, there is no room for God. God must be the third party in all acts of intimacy."

It would be years before I learned the term *ménage à trois*, but it did occur to me that it would be odd to have God present. Three of us? God sure as heck wasn't around when Nels and I were kissing. Nope, zip, nada.

But now Father had his spiel going. "And because God is present, acts of intimacy are sacred acts. They must be sanctified as are all sacred acts, by the sacraments, and this one is sanctified by the sacrament of marriage."

How did we get to marriage? Who said anything . . . we are just talking about the French kiss here, the one kiss most of us knew was the hottest thing on the Earth. A sacrament? Was this part of the *no sex until your wedding night* thing?

Don would not to be distracted. "Yeah, but how does French kissing lead to those acts of intimacy?" Did I detect a trace of mockery in his voice?

"Because . . ." Father was taking a lot of deep breaths, tapping his fingers. "French kissing is . . . suggestive." *Oh baby.*

But he had the courage to continue, perhaps misreading our mock astonishment (was it really mocking, or were we pretending to mock by then?) as attention. "If one loves the Lord, one must make all the acts of life sacred acts, and thus, sex is a sacred act. One must avoid the occasions of sin, of all unsacred behaviors. Therefore, the French kiss would be putting oneself in the place where sin would be occasioned, where the light of the world would be shut off because this act could lead to other much more unsanctified acts."

Somewhere in English class I had learned about metaphor. But it had been all linguistic, not physical metaphor. I was about to encounter the physicality of metaphor. Then good Father said, "The penetration of the tongue in the mouth is like the penetration in the act of sex."

Light my fire, baby. We were getting specifics now.

"It's like sex?" a shaky voice from the back asked for confirmation.

Father nodded. Dead silence.

Sigh. "Thus, it puts you in the way of mortal sin."

By deduction, French kissing was not mortal sin but could put you in the near occasion of mortal sin, which was real sex in the flesh, which was a mortal sin, unless you were married.

Were we all calculating how much French kissing we could do before we were in the sack?

But this good priest knew us, and with his quiet voice, he brought us back. "You do not want to be in the presence of overpowering temptation, do you? To be helpless before the urge to have unsanctified sex, without God's blessing and presence?" He said it sincerely, he said it looking at each of us, and we remembered that he was the priest who had prepared us for confirmation, who had baptized our siblings, who had come to our houses and blessed us. He said this, and, as only a good priest can, took our souls into his hands. Some of the old world held, though our imaginations spiraled in a parallel universe.

We were sober.

We were quiet.

We were hot.

In our young brains, each and every one of us was, perhaps for the first time, imagining a French kiss so overwhelmingly good and deep that it would lead to *penetration*.

He was a good priest. He said we could ask forgiveness. He said this often and kindly. He discussed the feeling of being out of God's grace. But he did not take it back. We were sinners.

Then he got us on our feet and led us out into the cold night. He spent the rest of the class time walking us around the block, cooling us off. He did this every week for weeks on end. He gave us the language, planted the pictures in our brains, and told us we could not do it. Then, knowing full well what he had done, he walked us out to our own country roads and fields, reminding us who we were.

What was the church thinking?

STORE-BOUGHT, 1968

Tet Offensive.

Photo of a man shooting a Vietcong.

Highest casualties in Vietnam.

Sweatheart's Ball.

I was the class representative. My grades were shot. My heart was not. I was going with Nels, and we had been kissing a lot, French kissing.

I was the class representative. I was tickled pink.

In social studies we talked about Vietnam while I dreamed of dress patterns.

The dress, the dress. A dress for the ball.

February is also the season of Lent, my mother would remind me. "What are you giving up?" she asked.

"Oh, probably ice cream. Again." I was flip.

"That's pretty easy for you. You should choose something more thoughtful."

"The dress, Mom. The dress." Could she not stay on task? "How about pink?"

"It will be Lent. Maybe something quieter."

"Well, it's not orange." This by way of perspective.

She was relieved, and knowing better than to push her view any further, she simply asked, "What fabric?"

"Satin brocade." I had seen it, and I loved how the jacquard pattern caught the light. The news blared in the next room; sometimes there were gunshots.

My mother looked skeptical. Then she saw the pattern. Slim-fitting. Sensational—if you were slim. My mother looked at the pattern, looked at my body, and tried to say it as only a mother can: "Perhaps that's not the best cut for you."

Then that's the one I wanted.

I wanted to look like that: slim and sophisticated. Never mind that I had filled out, and not in entirely flattering ways. The softness in my middle had gone straight to what my dad called *plump* that winter, and because I did not play sports, did not exercise significantly now that I wasn't in the fields or the restaurant, the pounds I lost in the summer had reappeared, then multiplied over the holidays. I thought the pattern would slim me down. My mother knew that it would not.

She turned off the TV without looking. That's what we had come to.

I had a week, plenty of time. I bent over the machine, threading the pink. The light was sharp coming in from the dining room window, but the thread frayed and wouldn't enter the eye. I cut the facing off-bias; it didn't lay right. I ripped and restitched and discovered that the jacquard fabric was like ice, cold and slippery, and without mercy. Halfway through the week, I was only half finished. I was depressed more because I was beginning to see what my mother saw than because it wasn't finished. The shining brocade I saw in the store was evolving on the sewing table. On Thursday night I gave up. The dress was a wreck.

Friday morning before school, Lydia and Ted picked me up, which they did when he could get their family car. I waved, climbed into the smoky car. Ted smoked Winstons. I watched and thought it was cool but didn't try it—not yet.

"So'd you get the dress done?" Lydia turned to me in the backseat.

I shook my head. She looked at me. "What you gonna do? You're the rep."

I shrugged. "Wear what I wore to the Christmas dance, I guess."

"It was a nice dress."

"Not a Sweetheart's Ball dress, though."

"My mom says that they have a sale in Ludington. At the Penney's."

"I can't do that."

"Why not?"

"Store-bought."

"Store-bought?" She didn't get it.

"You know, something you bought in a store?" Gosh, did no one else live as we did?

"You can't buy a dress? Why not?" She looked stunned.

Ted caught my eye in the rearview mirror.

"We make all our clothes."

"Underwear?"

"Except underwear."

"For the boys, too?"

"No. Maybe a shirt once in a while." Why hadn't I realized this? The boys did not have homemade clothes. Probably because Mom found their pants and work shirts in the church rummage bin. She was good at remaking things, but sometimes she did buy store-bought Sunday clothes for my brothers. Why not for her girls?

"We always make our dresses. It's the 4-H pledge. 'My hands to better living' and all that."

Lydia stared. "If I can talk my mom into going to Ludington this weekend, you wanna come?"

When I arrived home, the brocade dress hung from the dining room curtain rack, completed by my compassionate mother. It was a beautiful dress for someone slim and without curves. This time the color was not the problem, as it had been with the orange gown. The color was fine. When I put it on, even with a girdle, the softness of my extra five pounds drew the seams tight. She frowned. I frowned. I took it off. She looked at the seams. *I can let it out a little. I tried to tell you about this pattern.* I chewed my nails, took up the seam ripper, tried to pull the seams without marring the brocade. But I knew already that I didn't like the dress because, as my grandma would say, I was too big for the box. Too tight, wrong cut. What I had seen in my mind did not match reality. I was not the girl on the cover of the pattern.

"You've got no choice now." My mother said this firmly, and I nodded quietly, already hatching the plan.

Later I announced to Mom that I was going to Ludington with Lydia on Saturday morning, and I'd have my hair done on the way back in Crystal Valley, where a little side shop had opened and there was a woman who would curl and set it for reasonable money. Mom was upset. I was going to Ludington on the day of the dance? Getting my hair done? And how much would that cost?

Maybe she knew I was about to break an oath.

In Penney's, the racks glowed with red satins and frills so pricey that I couldn't imagine in a million years where I would get that kind of money. A red silk Cinderella skirt with a white patent leather belt flowed like nothing I had ever seen. It was fifty dollars for just a skirt. My entire wardrobe probably cost that much. This was hopeless.

But Lydia knew what to do. She consulted a sales lady who pointed to a sale rack there in the back. We pawed through it, flipping hangers, looking at dress after dress. Nothing.

"Here's one," she said quietly. I didn't look up. I was still flipping.

"What is it?"

"Oh, just something with lace." Her comment was too offhand.

I looked up, and she was holding it out like a church vestment. A ruffle like cream frosting at the neck, pink ribbon at the breast, three-quarter bell sleeves, straight lace skirt to the knee with—*oh how sweet*—lace-edged scallops at the hem.

"You probably don't like it." We grin like hyenas.

A whopping thirty dollars. But it's on sale, down to twenty-five dollars and some change. I had twenty. Lydia loaned me the five and change.

When Lydia dropped me off, smelling of Ludington and hair spray and still flushed from the hair dryer, I carried the Penney's sack into the house boldly; it was the only way. My mother saw it as soon as I entered the kitchen. She put down her coffee, pushed back the scarf covering her hair—she had been outside, feeding rabbits—and her face turned sad, then hard.

"Store-bought?"

I nodded. I could feel her hurt in the kitchen, pouring out of racked dishes, rising from the bread bin, the cooling casserole. I had no choice.

I pulled the dress out, held it to the light. She could see how it was. She could see I liked it. She looked at the finished brocade dress hanging on the broom closet door. She looked at the white lace with pink ribbon in my hand. Again with the lace. She sighed. *Do what you want; you're going to anyway.*

The pink brocade would hang there for days, an empty sentinel of betrayal, before I moved it to the attic storage. I don't know if I ever wore it.

But that night, after Nels's old car putt-putted up our driveway and he entered the kitchen and saw the dress I was wearing, he smiled. The corsage was white and pink. A perfect match. Once in the car he said, "You look beautiful." I felt like a queen.

If there was a prayer I could have prayed, it would have been this: *Oh, let there always be dances. Let there always be the rush of music in the ears and the rustle of a pretty dress and the warmth of a boy next to me. Let there always be the beat. Let there always be the rush of the kiss.* That simple. It would be years before I would pray for boys (and girls) to come home safe from wars, to not kill themselves or anyone else, to be whole.

To dance, to kiss—that was all there was.

We danced the dances without a thought to the future. We lifted our bodies to a beat. We placed ourselves inside those silly songs: "Baby, Now that I've Found You," "Spooky Little Girl," and "Love is Blue." With not a thought of anyone else in that gym, their pain or sorrow or sadness or the existence of brutality or illness or loss, we turned toward each other over and over, and that protected us from all of the above.

Except the near occasion of sin.

Afterward, home again, leaning against the kitchen counter where my mother cooked every day, we Frenched until my mouth hurt. I forgot to ask God to come along for this one. Oh, and did I say that the ruffle framed a lovely scoop neck? I did not. There was skin. I'd have a mark in the morning. My first hickey. This is how the devil marks you.

LENT, 1968

Nels was someone who followed politics, someone who saw the bigger picture. In social studies we argued about the line "We had to destroy the village in order to save it," allegedly said by an army officer about the destruction of Ben Tre, a city in Vietnam. And Nels said, "Golly gee, it's so good we've got a dead city on our hands. No trouble at all now." It was the first time I'd heard that kind of bitter sarcasm, right down to the mock *golly gee*, in relation to this war. When I asked him what he thought the officer meant, he said, "I think that sentence has a logic problem." I laughed, because I saw it, how it was. But I was puzzled because it was the first time anyone close to me had actually questioned our place in the war. It was the first time I had to think deeply about the other side of the world. I had to think deeply because he did.

Still, in our Michigan winter, life was local and Lenten.

It all came down to giving up something.

Catholic Lent meant giving up something that you loved right there in the darkest time of the year. It could be something simple, of course, but we all knew the church wanted you to really feel this thing, to get in touch with your sins and the suffering of Jesus, and so encouraged everything from fasting to flagellation—though this last part had become less popular since Poppa John (as my friends had irreverently started calling Pope John XXIII) said it was better to focus on good works. But good works, in the middle of the winter, were buried under six-foot drifts. And really, Lent was supposed to represent forty days in the desert, but here was the dreary winter dragging its tail through crusty snow to the vernal equinox, which in itself is barely a day of note, everything being equal. A desert would have been a relief. We were pretty sure the old popes invented Lent in Italy, somewhere in an almost eternal summer.

Lent is ashes, dust to dust, forty days.

On Ash Wednesday, the first day of Lent, our foreheads smeared with ash, my family gave up, as we had for years, our favorite desert— ice cream. Our family's famous sweet tooth, mainlined straight through both sides of the Belgian and Dutch ancestral lineage was, during Lent, to be bludgeoned into submission, except my mother, with some sense of understanding of the cravings that ran as our purest bloodline, always relented on Palm Sunday and let us each have a little ice cream to get through that last week, which would include innumerable church services, fastings, and midnight prayer rituals. She knew human nature. She and my father, on the other hand, doubled their prayers.

Nels and I were trying, despite ourselves, to be good Catholics. There was much intense intellectual and spiritual discussion. I believe it was he who began the conversation.

Do you think we should, you know, give up . . .
What we're doing . . .
You know . . .
I know. . . .
It'd be hard.
It'd maybe be good for us. . . .
Nah.
Nah.
We could never do it.
Nah.
Do you think we couldn't?

I underestimated his competition and will. I'm pretty sure this last challenge did it for him only because it certainly didn't for me. I'm pretty sure I was not much concerned with our souls. Still, for all our surreptitious making out in the corners, we were on some kind of trajectory that had less to do with giving up than going down—though not that far down. The necking was progressing. We had heard Father's quiet explanation (or was it my mother's?) that *one thing leads to another* and in fact could trace the progression in our front-seat, in-the-corner, on-the-couch making out. We had felt . . . well . . . elated with each new degree of intimacy. We were on the slippery slope and sliding fast.

But now, Lent. We should give all that up? Once said, I had no choice but to agree. We promised: no more French kissing, no more necking, no more touching of buttons in the dark. We would sit quietly each and every time he brought me home. We would hold hands and kiss chastely a few times and then part.

What did we know about teasing? How once one knows the pure joy of kissing with abandon, how once one knows the frantic feel of someone's hand sliding down your cleavage, the warmth, the escalation to . . . what? Then to cease, not to grope toward the next . . . How could we stop touching for six weeks? Forty days?

We had never been so excited.

I had no idea that certain repressions could tantalize one beyond mind and will, beyond oath, straight to the groin. We sat in his car, stood in the mudroom, leaned against sets in the dark after rehearsals, and held onto each other, vibrating, a tease-induced fantasy dressed in the quiet costume of penitent Lent. You never see the slit up the dress until she's turned away.

On the surface we became social again, reentered the light, gathered with the others, played hearts on Formica tables or Twister in our parents' living rooms with them looking on benevolently.

Distraction, distraction, distraction.

To taunt us further, the Drama Club was producing *A Midsummer Night's Dream*. Anyone who knows the Bard's work knows *Midsummer*. That most lush, love-oriented of the comedies is a sixteenth-century romantic comedy in blank verse. I had earned, again, the smallest role, a lady in waiting, but I was also on the prompt book, cuing lines if some lead lost her mind in the middle of one of those love spats in the dark forest. Another ploy of the devil was learning to read that text. While Nels and I dreamed of and avoided backstage kisses, we distracted ourselves with the play, unpacking the aristocracy in the *Midsummer* forest, thinking this intellectualism would keep our minds off the lovers. Nels was curious about the Duke of Athen's quandary, how to woo the conquered queen and win not only Hippolyta's country but her mind. I was obsessed with Titania, her declarations of will, her humiliation at the hands of Oberon. If I lingered over her descriptions of the donkey lover, Bottom, and felt something beyond the mockery of love as I read the lines, I didn't admit it. We talked back and forth about their decisions and leadership, and when I asked him how Theseus would have made peace in Vietnam, he said with a wicked grin, "Capture the women, and those communists come right in line." I couldn't have been more delighted.

Despite innuendo, we thought we were in the clear until Mrs. B started rehearsing the lovers—all played by experienced kids with full awareness of the roles and a willingness to play them to the hilt. Our intellectual sparring stopped cold. Because really, who cares about Bottom going off in a bray when one of those boys is proclaiming, "O Helena, goddess, nymph, perfect, divine! To what, my love, shall I compare thine eyne? Crystal is muddy. O, how ripe in show Thy lips, those kissing cherries, tempting grow!"

Goddess? Nymph?

I was riveted when Helena whimpered: "Your wrongs do set a scandal on my sex. We cannot fight for love as men may do. We should be woo'd and were not made to woo. I'll follow thee and make a heaven of hell, to die upon the hand I love so well." Woo'd? Oh, the word had a kiss built inside it. *Please, let me be woo'd.* The apostrophe alone was a linguistic taunt.

If the tease of abstinence hadn't been enough, now the devil was prancing around costumed in Elizabethan garb, complete with codpieces, wielding a secret weapon: the way language, not in the form of dirty talk but in the form of subtle metaphor or passionate declaration, lifts lust right off the page, oxygenates it, and puts the face mask of all that hot breathiness right over your mouth, which is hanging open.

As we painted the set and prettied the forest where the lovers tryst, Nels and I looked at each other, lust in our eyes. We stared, hearing and not hearing the declarations of love and despair in the lines. We ached our way through iambic pentameter, through the blank verse of our minds, now gone utterly empty.

Lent was braying like an ass in humiliation.

We might still have made it, but there was Holy Week, the final week before the stone gets pushed away and Christ rises. Think of us, two kids raised in the Catholic Lenten traditions, and our vow, and now it's Good Friday.

Thirty-eight days days down, two to go.

Good Friday services begin at ten or one or three, depending on how much braying . . . er, praying you feel up to.

Catholic kids were excused from school at noon for services. We went to St. Joseph's, the county's majestic cathedral cherished among country people. We said the rosary and Stations of the Cross, me lingering over Veronica wiping the face of Jesus. The Veronica station stood out because the woman who wiped the face of Jesus was heroic; she offered a little comfort. During those services, I had the proper imaginings, the contemplation of His suffering, how He died so that I might live. This was why we had taken the oath, simple as it was. This was why Nels and I gave up what we gave up, so we would form a kinship with Him who gave his life for us.

I kept telling myself we were almost there.

But I remember something else about that day, some restless thing, an awareness that on Easter my vow, my giving up, would be done, and I would no longer be bound by this thing that I shouldn't, according to the rules, according to the oaths, be doing in the first place. What value did that give the vow if what was wrong one time, even if I wasn't doing it, was still wrong the next time? One minute we would be keeping a vow something like chastity, and a minute later it would be a sin, just the same as it was the minute before except that a minute before we hadn't been doing it? There was a logic problem.

All this touching, all this kissing that I loved—why had we given it up? The oaths of church and club intersect right here. My heart to greater loyalty. Loyalty to what? My church, my young body, my naive heart? This fine boy? My nerve endings, every one of them on high alert?

I had fasted all day. No food, just water.

I had dressed in a navy blue skirt I made from a new synthetic knit material, just a yard now to make a skirt, and a blouse with a wide white collar that I had cut from an outdated shirtwaist with a nice collar. Over my outfit I wore a paler blue coat that my mother and I had cut down from one that my aunt Catherine had found in a raid on one of the church collections. I was the perfect Catholic, dressed in Blessed Mary blues, the perfect junior girl, and a 4-H representative.

What was I representing now?

I had stood in line at the front of the church with hundreds of others and kissed the feet of the corpus with the crucifix held by the hands of the altar boys and the priest. After each congregant kissed, they wiped the feet of the corpus with a white handkerchief. I don't know that they ever changed the handkerchief or how seriously they wiped the foot of the cross that a few hundred other people were also kissing. We were not supposed to care. It was that kind of spirituality.

I had not French-kissed in almost six weeks.

The statues of Mary and Joseph were covered with purple until Resurrection Sunday. I had said every prayer there was to say, and I had come home and broken my fast with my mother's terrible salmon patties, her Friday night special, and then I had gone back to church, to the quiet pews for evening meditation. I couldn't think anything by then, and my stomach roiled.

After sitting vigil at his own church at St. Gregory's in town, Nels picked me up after candlelight services, after every last prayer that can be said, and the good Lord lay in the tomb, and Nels could drive me home. *Fine, fine*, my parents said, both tired and aware that I (and my siblings) had practiced about as much faith as one can expect.

Here is Nels's ancient Mercedes putt-putting up the driveway on that chilly April evening. Here we are standing under the yard light, silent for a long time in that spring night. Here we are, almost at the end of our sacrifice, and we are supposed to wait until Sunday before we kiss like that again. Is it the depth of our thinking into the Catholic sacrifice, that deeper thought that drives us to understand? Because we know suddenly, trembling from cold or heat, how odd our vow has been. Those weeks, and now this day of Veronica, candles, and kissing a clay foot has been too long. The services have left us clean and hungry, two very young human beings who, sincere as we have been, are aware that what we hoped for our souls is illusory. We are not saints, and in that true humility, we have no reason not to kiss. We have reached our capacity for being good.

We go into the house to get warm.

What I want to say is about the oath and not that it led to my first orgasm, though it did. I want to say instead that I broke my oath, and, as promised, I was forgiven before I did. For the first time in my rising sexuality, I did not feel guilt because that orgasm happened exactly as it should happen, in the hands of a boy I had come to truly love, after six weeks of abstinence, on my mother and father's blue couch, in a dark living room just on the other side of the wall where, sometimes even still, I listened to my parents kiss.

We didn't have intercourse. Do I need to say that?

Because what's more important is this: we *gave up being good* on Good Friday night. And I didn't know it was going to happen and so felt the true wonder of the body as it comes to the young. Everything I had felt before that—all the unarticulated longing, all the amazement of yearning and the strange burning below the belly, even the terrible running of the previous summer—had been yellow, the piercing wonder of yellow.

This was white light so damned bright that it blinded me.

Perhaps, for a single moment, we felt holy. Maybe there were three of us.

In the breaking of that oath, there was a gratitude I did not know I could feel.

Holy Saturday dawned too clear. I woke shocked and knowing. Resurrection took on a whole new meaning. So this was what all the fuss was about.

DENOUEMENT

Martin Luther King, Jr. was assassinated that April. Most of us knew very little about him. We knew he was the man who preached nonviolence, who led the peaceful civil rights marches but had been present when they turned violent—controversy there. We didn't know much else, and nothing deeply. But the word *assassination* rose like a ghost and spread wings again over the news and into our living rooms. As the seriousness entered even the halls of Hart High, many of us felt surprise, then shame; then came questions, tentative at first, as we discovered him—all this after he was dead. As the American press brought his life and his speeches even to our remote schools, we saw the man at last. Because Nels was enraged, then sad, I learned about King. The world widened. We talked about nonviolence. The concept was hot; our fathers had fought in World War II. My dad said, *You don't know what you'll do when facing death.* For all of maybe five minutes, I thought deeply about it, but it was able to hold my interest only because of Nels's interest. That month, the ridiculous letter arrived and I forgot about King. I hadn't believed the letter would come. Ever.

Nels had gotten a scholarship to Lake Superior State College in Sault Ste. Marie, six hours away in the far north, where the winters were even harder, where the world was even stranger with ice. Soo Locks? What were those? Feats of engineering? I was Goldilocks. I knew feats of engineering. I was trying out as many ways to have orgasms as I could manage. This one too small? This one just right? And though no one would believe this now, it was all *manual labor*. Like so many Catholic girls of the time, not to mention 4-H'ers, we became the Queens of Everything But, which allowed one to learn more about, well, other things. But that ridiculous letter would mean an end to all this *socializing*—my mother's word for running around, Nels's and my code word for making out. I was in despair. After that, I didn't much care who was assassinated. The single thing that finally brought me out of a self-induced funk was prom. What became clear was that I needed to do something sensational for this prom—not just for me but for him. He was not leaving right away but soon. He was leaving and it scared me. I wanted him to remember me. I didn't want him to forget. Ever.

But I was broke. It was that simple. I'd blown my money on the store-bought dress; I couldn't pull that stunt again. The way to earn money was to pick asparagus, but when asparagus season started, I was overcome with loathing for those long hours of bending to the dirt. I found or invented school activities to keep me away from fieldwork. My mother was overworked and fed up with me. I had betrayed her, bought that "fluffy" dress for Sweetheart's Ball. And now more hoopla about prom? She was having none of it.

How could she understand? She had never said good-bye to anyone. Had she?

I ransacked my closet, looking for inspiration among a dozen home-made dresses until she, fearing greater havoc than usual, entered my room and stared over my shoulder into the chaos. After she heard out my high drama, she pointed and said, "That's it. That's what you've got."

I stared at her. How could she be so stupid? She looked back, steady as a stone. I looked back at the dress. The "it" was the yellow gown of my sophomore year, hanging in the plastic, wrinkled and dusty from its beating at Exploration Days at Michigan State. Who on earth wanted to revisit that moment?

She looked straight at me. "You've worn it twice, if you count the modeling, and it's a perfectly nice gown."

How could she expect that I would wear that dress to prom? I had worn it last year, with Earl. Now to wear it with Nels? Why add betrayal to the humiliation of the runway?

But my mother was unmoved. She tipped her head toward the dress, unsympathetic as weather. I threw myself backward onto my bed.

"Really, Mom, this dress? Again?"

"Well, then do *something* with it," she said. She was done talking.

I rolled over and stared out at the fields. Was that what I'd be forced to do—get up early, and, as I had done in middle school, pick asparagus before school and go to classes with *eau de asparagus* on my hands? I had to have a new gown because I'd begun to understand that the dress was not just how you looked on the outside, not simply how you looked with someone, nor how you felt like someone better. No, with Nels, the dress had become a part of the only manual labor I loved—sewing. Long before I knew the word foreplay, I would feel its potential in the way a guy could run his finger just under the slim strap of a dress, the way he could follow that invisible hem above the knee, just touching the inner fabric.

I stared at the dress. It hung, now oddly conservative, tidy, and dull under its plastic, battered from trekking through the gardens. What had I been thinking with those cap sleeves? Someone should just rip those off. And that neckline? And with that, rebellion coupled with fashion and foreplay. I'd show Mom. Long before cheap remnants, before recycling, there was my mother's way: remodel and remake. Do *something* with it, she had said. I may have broken the oaths, but with my 4-H skills, newly retooled on lust, I knew just what to do. I stripped the plastic off and turned the whole thing inside out. Those modest cap sleeves? Despite pretty decent workmanship, probably my mom's, I *could* rip them off—and while I was at it . . . Before the week was out, I cut those shoulders to narrow bands and cut the neckline deep and squared it off, front and back, to reveal as much skin as possible.

My mother, *hoisted on her own petard*, so to speak, frowned as I monopolized the sewing table and spent my evenings remaking the dress. When she came close, I stared her down; she stared back. We stopped speaking. She had, after all, suggested this.

Or something like this.

Okay, not at all *like this.*

Then I tore out the front pleat, sewed the front seam most but not all the way down—oh, sweet clean line, smoothed and pressed, to slim then kick open just above the knee, just where it should.

Sweet Jesus I was good.

Now for the back. Here, a misstep. I wanted to reset that pleat, to get some trail in the back. Did I cut it down, gather it? I sat for an hour, pinning and unpinning. My mother, frying bacon, watched me from the kitchen, saw me fumble. Finally, before I did any irreparable damage, she wiped her hands, moved to the machine, and, without speaking, gave me a little shove with her hip.

She could see this would be beyond my skills.

"Finish frying." She dismissed me to the stove, shooing with her hands. Grudgingly, I retreated to the frying pan. From the kitchen I watched in awe as she opened the seam and reset the pleat in back, inserting it so that the skirt would open just enough to cover my hips and fall in perfect geometry. It was a custom design with all the new lines. And there's no denying it: the dress was sexy.

Then my mother, as though she might know a thing or two about the rites of fashion as foreplay, went one better. Despite the days of silence between us, she knew me, knew my heart. This new thing had no softness, no romance, and she said, tilting her head thoughtfully, "It needs something."

She looked sly, told me to pick up two yards of cheap yellow chiffon on sale. What? Chiffon? After a brief altercation about who should pay for it, we split the difference. By then, I had half forgiven her for . . . oh, everything. I carried chiffon into the house for the first time, swallowing my pride, burning with curiosity, and placed it into her hands. She frowned at it, then sat down at that beloved Singer, stitched one edge of the yardage, gathered and set it, then pinned it to the back of the dress. She had made a *train*, for heaven's sake, that dropped from the low-cut back like a waterfall of sunshine and wisped away behind me. Unbelievable. I added tiny white daisies not in a row but scattered so as not to weigh it down. My mother and I looked at each other, so delighted that we could have giggled, but neither of us could admit how much fun we were having. Still we basked in a momentary light.

The night of prom, I stood in front of the bathroom mirror pulling my hair up, pulling tendrils down. At her insistence, the remaining chiffon draped over my shoulders, a soft shawl to satisfy some rule of modesty that would merely tempt.

That night, I wore a white-and-yellow carnation corsage, a longish spray this time, from Nels. When I caught my reflection at the door of the gym, I knew the word *luminous*. For a moment, for just a moment, I felt great confidence, knew my own beauty. It was a gift for me. For once, I had attained a small perfection.

Titania, thwarted at the bower, becomes Hippolyta, the queen.

And the Duke of Athens was never going away.

Promise. Prom is the first part of the word *promise*.

Prom was also the night that so many couples decided to "go all the way." It was a night fraught with old history or even prehistory, falling as it does near May Day, the day of the mating. So when the promenade was over, I thought we might. After all the dancing and the after-party and the long ride toward the farm, I thought there might come a moment.

We did not.

We pulled away from each other, satin rustling in the crisp spring night. I want to say it was he who did so first, but I cannot be sure. He was a critical year older, and he had a better sense of the future than I did. He would leave for college without that final gesture, and bless his heart, he never asked. And it was that lovely reserve still laced with his hunger that did it. I was determined not to lose him. Right then, I pledged my heart to greater loyalty.

Instead of going *all the way*, we declared our love for each other in words for the first time. We rode out the school year in the knowledge that this was love, and we would not have sex, though truth be told, we were learning all sorts of other things about our bodies. This was our sexuality. It killed me and I thrived.

Shortly after graduation in June, the news came that Robert Kennedy had been assassinated. Unlike Martin Luther King, Jr., about whom we'd had to be educated, we knew who Robert Kennedy was because of John Kennedy. My father didn't like Robert Kennedy, thought he was *even more of a hothead than his brother*. My mother liked Ethel, though never with the same affection she'd had for Jackie. But we knew who Robert Kennedy was, knew that he wanted to run for president. And now, only two months after Martin Luther King, Jr., Robert Kennedy was dead, too.

It shocked us, and we could feel the fabric of the nation tearing again.

And so the declaration we made to each other floated between these terrifying tragedies, these two world-changing assassinations, like a trail of chiffon off the shoulder, a dream, alive and growing against the threat of suitcases snapped shut, the Greyhound bus roaring its way north.

PART III: LOVE

What we've lost hasn't left us bereft;
what we've lost has put us in motion.

Dan Beachy-Quick

86 DAYS, 1968

By then, we had watched so many national tragedies that we weren't sure what tragedy was. In August of 1968, the Democratic convention in Chicago exploded into yet another riot. Chicago became tainted territory, as marred by violence as Detroit had been. Women's Lib evolved into controversy to be argued, denigrated, marched on. I waffled on this; we ought to have rights, I thought, but I loved the idea of being protected and wooed. *Apollo 11* circled the Earth 163 times, dizzying us, spinning around our gravitational center. Would we win the space race after all? We lived in anomaly: alarmed and impressed by our history but relieved that it wasn't happening to us.

It allowed us self-absorption.

Meanwhile, I faced the problem of dating a senior. He left the county, along with his friends, just when I turned into a senior. By then, I could slam a combination lock with the best of them, but down that long hallway was loneliness. He was not there. Through the summer, the impending separation had brought us closer, more certain of each other. Wild berry picking, late night bonfires, the sunset club with a gang of us who gathered after our summer jobs to stare into the spotlight of the sun as it sizzled into Lake Michigan—it all felt tender as new grass.

Now he was not here. He wouldn't be here for 86 days. His leaving had been thunder to the gut—that fierce. Now I waited like a good and loyal girlfriend. I thought I would die before he returned. I missed everything from our sexual play to the politics in our talk. I missed his company as a body misses its lost arm.

Still, I was rarely alone. The remaining Drama Club friends clustered close. We all felt adrift without Nels and those seniors to anchor or lead.

We had depended on them for resourceful fun and setting tradition, and now they were gone, many of them until Thanksgiving. Would we find our footing? Would we come into our own?

First thing, we abandoned the cafeteria for new territory. We claimed the unlikely art room. Because several of us had classes there, the art teacher, Mr. Rand, kindly let us eat lunch there. I loved art class—not just the class itself but the whole subject. I had begun studying art in my Catholic middle school under the tutelage of a woman who taught me to look at paintings, to study images, to enter the work. I loved the sensuality of paint, its tubes and textures. I had some raw if unrefined sense of color but no real talent. I became enamored with how a painting made me feel, how it could say more than what it seemed to say, how it revealed itself as you studied it. My imagery was romantic and sentimental, but I understood that image could suggest not just mood but narrative, entire worlds. Now that Nels was up north, I was supposed to be getting my grades up for college applications, solidifying plans for my future, but I wasn't sure about college. I wasn't sure of anything but my longing. I wrote countdown numbers on the board so everyone would know how long until they returned—though it was really only about him. We brought our peanut butter and jelly, our bologna and carrot sticks and sat at the Pollock-spattered tables and tried to figure out who we were without the class of '68.

"We" were leftovers, crumbs of a once vital core that the Drama Club was unlikely to see for years to come. Gone were Nels, Ted, Don, and four of the best actresses of a four-year stint that Mrs. B had run to the end, culminating in *Midsummer*. Of those remaining: Flip drew exquisite calendar girls, alive in pencil. (I didn't know what to say when I looked at them—voluptuous, amazing, and so forthright that I blushed.) His girlfriend, Gwen, had also graduated, though she commuted home on weekends. There was Little Bear, a plump and friendly girl we all adored for her humor and warmth; Katie, the smartest girl in the class, a willow tree with dark hair and warm eyes; sometimes Ian, a moody Irish boy; and Lydia, my oldest friend, who had gone quiet over the summer. We sat together among the half-finished replicas of the Old Masters and ate sandwiches. Every day I wrote on the board the number of days until Thanksgiving when Nels would come home. It was mid-September. It didn't seem like forever; it was forever.

Part of the boredom of forever was going to classes. Government and econ were as appealing as mud. I could get from writs to rights, but the gross national product was just gross. I had completed the two years of required math and couldn't bear another quadratic anything. I held my own in history and French. I excelled at social studies and English when I bothered to do the homework but found real joy in art. I ate up the Impressionists, Cubists, Modernists—artists who lived a brash courage I envied. And the words—from chiaroscuro to pentimento—were words I loved.

In some state of illusion that I could be the next Monet, I tried one painting, a moody water piece of greens and blues, but I overblended, and the colors turned to swamp. The swan itself was a lone gray blob floating in the middle of a dark pond, a Monet insult. Katie called it the ugly duckling. Flip asked if it was a stone. Finally, Mr. Rand held his hand over my own and brushed. The stone turned back into a swan, albeit a dirty one.

Perhaps because the painting had gone so badly, Mr. Rand came to Katie and me with a project. A woman wanted a hooked rug in the new shag style, and she would pay money to have it made by hand. We would design the pattern, cut the yarn, and hook the rug. She wanted warm oranges, reds, and browns, all overlapping tones in the style of some modern expressionist. We chose autumn quarter moons multiplied in repeated arcs. He and Katie charted the design and labeled the colors. We spent a week cutting yarn, and then we picked up the hooks. The grid of tiny squares would last the entire quarter. For every day we moved through the rows, my chaste friend Katie, tall and smart and headed for a fine college, spoke of her dreams. She asked me every day about my college applications and shared with me what she was working on. Every day I nodded and wished she wouldn't. I was in a state about college. I knew I should at least see if I could get in, but I only wanted one thing: to be with Nels. So we hooked the rug instead of painting and considered it a privilege. I returned to the art room again and again to eat lunch, noting the days on the board. The number began in the eighties, twice the length of Lent, and slowly lowered itself, one by one. Thus the year became less.

Imagine a room where the walls are hung with the art posters of the masters and the exercises of the inept, where there are half-done paintings, odd sketches, the sentimental rose next to Goya. Imagine a hooked rug the color of flame. Imagine an enflamed longing. I pushed the steel hook under the weft of each tiny grid, centered the short length of yarn, pulled it back, tugged it tight. The next and the next, each little square, one after another, filling with bright yarn that contrasted with the mood of the painting. I did not know how bright my life was.

Imagine a girl, alone and pregnant in an age in which it is against the oaths to be pregnant. Imagine that loneliness. I did not. I was not.

Lydia and I had drifted apart at the end of junior year. Even though we continued to share a locker, she stopped gossiping with me, and we no longer attended the same parties. She was running with a different crowd. She had met a new boy from another school who looked like someone out of *Rebel Without a Cause*. Cool, but I couldn't figure out her silence. When we both ended up in the same English class, we sat near each other again. I thought we would be able to talk about *Hamlet*, about Ophelia's dramatic death. When she slid me the note, I unfolded it, looked at her, felt a strange rippling through me. After that, I was even more awkward, not knowing if I should support her or condemn her. It could have been me, but due more to a good boy than to my own will, it wasn't.

I distanced myself.

Lydia stopped coming to lunch in the art room, looked pale in the mornings. She came to an away game with her boyfriend. To the next one, a home game, she came alone. She talked to me about it once, I think, but I had become like the person I once was hurt by, aloof to those unlike me. I had my club, my group, and even if that group had become diluted by absence, I had an identity that would carry me, for good or ill, through senior year. I think she told me the next part in early fall. "I'll need to drop out soon." She squared off her books, lining up the corners.

"Drop out?" My jaw dropped. Were we talking about her? She was pretty and smart. Why drop out?

"I'm starting to show. When I really show, then they want me to take classes at home."

The peasant dresses, popular at the time, covered her belly for now. I had no idea how far along she was or when she was due. I didn't ask. Did we ever talk deeply again? At some point, there was mention of a shower for her. When my mother heard the news at church—Catholics always heard about protestant trouble—she asked me, and I nodded. I expected her to be upset, to parlay it into a warning for me, but my mother looked sad, merely said that it was *really too bad*, shook her head, and stared off into the distance. I didn't understand it. I don't remember the exact sequence, but at some point, one of the more popular town girls in my class asked if I wanted to share a locker with her, because *yours will be empty pretty soon, and mine's further down. This way, you'll be closer to the cafeteria anyway*. I was grateful and didn't think to wonder what had possessed her, didn't think to wonder how moving to that locker would hurt Lydia. I don't know if it did. Though we were both counting days, our worlds were worlds apart.

Mid-October. The turning of the seasons. My favorite time of year. I was absorbed in being as lonely as I could and committed to the full experience of advertising my fate. One day in the art room it came to a head. I had gotten a speaking part in *Lilies of the Field* only to find out that the 4-H conference in Chicago was during the performances. I had to drop physics, though why that surprised me is a mystery. I had wanted to write my English research paper on blank verse, because I assumed I understood rhythm by being on prompt book, but Mrs. B, who by then knew me pretty well, suggested I write on J.R.R. Tolkien instead because perhaps blank verse was too broad a subject. After all, I had read *The Lord of the Rings* once already. My friends would not tolerate my guitar playing. My oldest friend was pregnant, and I was letting her drift out of my life. My boyfriend was at the North Pole as far as I was concerned. I was hooking a rug I hated. But the final straw was the homecoming dance. Gwen was coming home to go with Flip. So that left Katie and Little Bear and me to go together as a threesome. And have a good time.

I burst into tears and wailed, "I just miss him so much."

My friends stared and rolled their eyes. I was going to be no end of trouble. This was beyond sympathy all the way to downright embarrassing. Something must be done. And bless them—they set out to save me from myself.

Imagine feeling alone but going to the homecoming game with a group of friends who are so excited and thrilled about it that you think they are crazy. But you say, *Oh all right*. You have all arranged to sit with the Pep Club, to rah-rah the players, admire the boys, share a hot dog three ways, and smear mustard on each other's noses. There is some talk of sneaking around under the bleachers, just for kicks, but you find yourself invested in the game, which the Pirates seem to be winning, and then lights betray you, lifting you up a little. At halftime, you watch the homecoming court move across the field on those ridiculous floats, and for just a moment you wonder what it was all about, all those dances, corsages, and ambition for those dresses—4-H dresses that became progressively more un-4-H—not to mention ambition for the boys. And you think Nels is *never coming home*, but here is a game, and you are here with friends, who are being so nice and laughing a lot, and joining the cheers. *Gooo, Pirates!* And tomorrow is the dance, and for the first time, you don't much care what you wear. You will be with them, and you will get through this weekend somehow.

Then the halftime show is almost over, and they say again, *Let's go. Let's get off the bleachers. Let's go, let's go.* And you don't know why, but they say, *Come on, come on.* They say, *Follow us, follow us.* And something in their excitement catches you, and you smile and think, *Okay, okay. Let's just run.* You catch their excitement; it spills from them like wine. And you follow them down the rough gray steps, off the bleachers, and around the back. Out there into the dark you run as you have in the past. You're all holding hands now, running into the dark. *Over there, over there,* they say, and you turn and run. And there behind the hot dog stand, behind the stand where the announcers drink from flasks they pull from deep in their parkas, there in the half-spilled shadows, nearly dangerous shadows, someone steps out. A shadow, a silhouette that you know.

They have planned this since the day you cried. They saw that they were not good enough, and they had understood that it wasn't to do with them. They were bigger than that. They took the high road, shaped a plan so good that it puts you in your place. They had entered the dream you had and altered it. They had sent money, and his parents had sent money, and others. He had skipped classes to ride a bus all the way from the Soo. They had cut 86 days in half.

I stood in the dark and recognized the face, the wiry strong body I loved, and they got to watch, and I understood that, too, on some deep level, and I knew I had been shown a different way. They said I ran into his arms. I remember that—none of the sweeping wonder of movies, none of the lift and twirl, but a physical collision. We ran into each other. It felt hard and strange, and that first kiss was hard and strange, too, and I was suddenly afraid of this hardness, this collision course.

I felt that, and all the love poured toward my friends, and all the surprise and uncertainty poured toward him. Then I was crying, and he was laughing, and then we kissed again in front of everyone, and it was better, and my friends applauded and were smug and wonderful. After a while, someone said, *We're going to lose the game.* And I said, all wide-eyed and innocent, *We are?* as if it were news. And for no good reason but plain happiness, that set everyone off again, and then there was more kissing, better and better.

Suddenly my parents were there. And his. As news of the plan had spread among the friends and families who had watched this budding love, they had *tsked* and shaken their heads, but in the end they approved. The women smiled slyly at last, and the men nodded. *A good thing that*, to bring that boy home to his girl, because for some it reminded them of other more serious homecomings. With that faint echo in their hearts, they had said, *Well, maybe now they'll both be in good moods for a while.* And those good men and women looked at each other and said, *All that money for a bus ticket?* But they grinned as they saw us running, Nels and me, running around the edge of the end zone, hand in hand, with our friends surrounding us, our hearts in our mouths, and everyone for a little while just crazy as hell.

And if, off to the side, a dark-haired girl sat alone in a white-and-red Pirate jacket, pregnant and scared, I had forgotten her. If there was an angry boy anywhere among that crowd, if there was a lost child tearful among the rough-booted legs of adults, if there were lies and betrayal, the beginnings of mental illness or divorce or loss or even the death that this war would bring in short order to the town, we were not of that moment. We had broken from a hooked rug existence for this one homecoming. Those people of my club had brought one home for the sake of another one, and they saw, as the Bible says, that it was good, and so we were joyful. We did not know how to live anything else but the fulfillment of this simple dream.

And my mother? Her role was that of the fairy godmother. She had made the dress, the true-blue, waist-hugging, full-skirted, high-twirling, puffed-sleeved dress with a pert stand-up collar, all in secret. Abracadabra. It looked like a midnight dream come true, and I held it to me with a happiness that was almost unbearable, and with my heart in it, I was able to thank her at last.

CHICAGO, NOVEMBER 1968

The art room was still the art room. The rug was still the rug. Was this life—moments of being so high you could fly and then falling back into drudgery? And now I had a debt. I wasn't allowed any more pity nor could I be morose or even plain grumpy. Everyone who had participated in making me happy expected me to remain at least moderately so. I felt a small betrayal. I had been a lover of the dark moments, and though my loneliness had been real, I had counted on its attention-getting drama and on my friends' sympathy in order to remain the center of the universe. Now I was expected to be pleasant or at least grateful. It was galling.

Now when I complained about the numbers on the board stretching down from a mere forty, my friends just hooted. Little Bear asked drily, "You really think we're going through this again?" They fell into hysteria. I was forced to laugh. Their loyalty had made them famous throughout Hart High. As the story passed from gang to clique, they rode the tale of their own generosity to the end. Momentous to begin with, they embellished: the price, the planning, collecting money (quarter by quarter became penny by penny), the secrecy, the surprise, and the reward—*You shoulda seen it!* The story grew exponentially throughout the school, and they gained a certain half-legendary status. So for all that trouble, I could at least keep glowing. It would make them small gods for at least another week.

So loneliness became a half-broken spell mostly because my friends insisted. I learned that the practice of happiness becomes, to some degree, self-fulfilling. After a while, pretending became more persuasive, even for me. As for Nels and me, we had been together again but a little unfamiliarly, a little tentatively. We would grapple with awkwardness, but it did not lessen our longing. I also learned that love flexes, shifts inside its cocoon. It is not stable but dynamic. It was a shock, and it put me on edge, but I could not speak it.

The forty or so days remaining in the desert had but one oasis: the Chicago 4-H conference, where delegates from all fifty states gathered to exchange ideas and decide about their 4-H future. A rented bus routed from the far north picked up scattered representatives all along the west coast of Michigan and drove us the long hours south to the center of the city. We would stay at the Conrad Hilton, only blocks from where the convention riots had been. We would join delegations from every state in the country, all fifty of us. There were to be talks and demonstrations, discussions of the future, trips to the Art Institute, the Adler Planetarium, the Field Museum of Natural History.

I took the most modern, up-to-date, hip clothes I could: a newly made short burgundy dress with a long waist and hip belt; orange knit bell-bottom pants hemmed with wild braid and topped with a navy turtleneck as tight as I could get away with; and a store-bought (yes, again) faux leather jumper that I had found at an after-summer sale, sleeveless but if I added a black turtleneck and black beret from a secondhand shop, the outfit made me look so cool that I almost cried. It also made me sweat, but I didn't care. For the gala banquet, I chose the velvet dress from my first Christmas dance. I had ripped off the lace sleeves and added black-and-silver trim. It was now a chic and daring sheath.

When I climbed off the 4-H bus at Michigan Avenue, I saw for the first time real skyscrapers, but the idea behind them, to *scrape the sky,* hadn't prepared me for the sense of soaring gray concrete making geometry with height. I also hadn't been prepared for the noise. On the farm, daily industry was the steady sound of one tractor putt-putting over a field, a single yellow bus on the road, a handful of cars tooling down the highway, animals making animal sounds. Here even shafts of light banged between the buildings, dissonant with taxi horns. The elevated trains thundered and screamed overhead; I almost ducked. The street, scented with diesel, exhaust, hot dogs, and exotic perfume, paralyzed me. Under a multi-stacked traffic light, I stood still, taking it in. Only when a Muskegon rep pushed me from behind and hissed, *Try not to look like a hillbilly,* could I grab my suitcase and step aside, dumb with curiosity.

People-watching—a practice that would serve me well—rose from some natural spring of nosiness and ran true. I saw long coats in rich autumnal hues: deep red, dark olive, even mustard yellow. Tailored herringbone midis with wide belts. Suits in geometric designs, symmetrically shouldered or asymmetrically curved. Mod.

I looked at the makeup women were wearing, from the ever-darker eyeliner to the iridescent pink lipstick. I stared at go-go boots with short-short skirts. I noticed the wide collars and wide ties, long sideburns on men. I noticed the sheen of sophistication, eyes that knew so much that they could ignore you. Even 4-H kids from other states looked older than our gang of Oceana County kids down from Michigan to visit the Second City. I picked up and dropped price tags, seared by a new economy of money and fashion. My own clothes became nothing notable, but I saw in store windows that I was young, and if I put the right things together and wore them with even the smallest confidence, I would be forgiven almost anything.

At the Conrad Hilton, sweeping stairs, elegant carpet, and gilded banisters were dwarfed by the dazzling ceilings overhead. Of the meetings and the talks I have little memory. What held in memory was height: enormous chandeliers hanging in enormous rooms, sparkling like sun on high water. A dinosaur rib cage big enough to serve as a barn soared over me at the Field Museum, as if that skeleton embodied not the past but some high, unfleshed future. Chicago meant that even the stars, invisible in smog and city light, turned artificially overhead: the cosmos was explained at the Adler Planetarium. In the sudden quiet of the auditorium seats, I fell asleep, woke embarrassed and disoriented, thinking I had slept outside on the farm under my home stars.

A big blonde boy, Paul from Newaygo County, finagled an invitation to the Hawaiian hospitality party on some floor with a number so high that it felt mountainous. Several of us crowded into elevators and felt our ears pop as we soared upward. The Hawaiian 4-H'ers were attending this conference for the first time, to much applause and recognition. The Hawaiians, with their delicate flowers and festive shirts, gave us all-knowing smiles and dropped leis over our shoulders. The girls and even the boys, brown-eyed to a one, all had dark hair full of shining mystery and moved with such grace that I wanted only the privilege of watching. I had never seen such beauty.

Chaperones hovered, then disappeared. A bottle appeared, lights dimmed, loud music rose, and we were miles above the streets. I walked to a window and stared at a city sprawling with lines of traffic beneath us all the way to the dark boundary of Lake Michigan. Paul, holding a cigarette, put his arm around my shoulders. His breath smelled of smoke and a coconut sweetness. I felt the weight of his arm, so awkward compared to Nels, and slipped out from under. The cigarettes put me on edge. Cigarettes were harder to hide should the adults return. Where had the adults gone? I should have known that adults could smell trouble even if they couldn't see it. On cue, two Michigan chaperones appeared at the door and asked all members of the Michigan delegation to leave.

The party died in it tracks.

These adults were friends of my parents, and whether I had or had not smoked or drank would be irrelevant. My parents would hear it this way: your daughter was found on the twentieth floor in a smoky hospitality room with members of the Hawaiian delegation.

I could hear my mother. *Hawaiians? What were you doing with the Hawaiians?* As if they were something foreign.

We left promptly.

The result? A sleepless night. At seven o'clock the next morning, I showered, dressed in my quietest outfit, and found the room of our chaperone. I apologized for being stupid, said I had gone to the party late to ask Paul, the blonde boy, to leave before it got wild. I made myself a story as empty as dinosaur bones and just about as big as those at the Field Museum. Perhaps my fear (and false heroism) was more touching than the lie, because this middle-aged man accepted the apology quickly and shut the door with such haste that I was left to wonder why I had bothered. Over breakfast, I told Paul, who had not an ounce of remorse, about what I'd done and the man's strange behavior. He said, "You think they want our parents to think they were bad chaperones?" It had never occurred to me that my behavior could get a chaperone into trouble. I liked this idea that there were nuances in trouble—not all one-note.

"Besides," Paul said, "you probably woke him up."

But Chicago, more than anything, meant art and the Art Institute. Our chaperones had arranged, out of some perversity, not a tour of the famous paintings of neo-classical battles but of the *finest miniature collection in the world*. Miniatures? Here not enormity but smallness was set against the largeness of the city: one tiny room after another, each with perfectly tiny couches, tables and chairs, and perfectly miniscule replicas of tea with microcosmic crumpets. Here was an interior world, small as thought, inundated with Victorians, Edwardians, and the aristocrats of turn-of-the-century America, in small, glassed-in showcases. Nothing was too small to replicate.

I had never felt claustrophobic, but imagining myself in those tiny rooms trapped my breathing. Where were the soaring heights and the stars now? What was I supposed to do with the tight propriety of the miniatures? I stood among the forty other kids, suddenly dizzy. In a tired flash, I asked for a restroom, making the gesture a girl makes, a small drop of the hand toward the abdomen that says, "It's more than just a quick run. I've got cramps."

I couldn't return to the miniatures. I wandered up and down the marble stairs and along elegant hallways, saw room after room of Egyptian mummies, Ming vases, medieval armor, axes, and swords. A hallway opened suddenly onto a room that felt like a garden, was a garden. The light in the atrium invited me to step down among the sculptures, and there I found myself. My breathing shifted from shallow to deep. Here were bodies in shining white, matte gray, and black marble stilled in motion, poised as though about to explode. Here were not miniatures of affluent rituals, as contained as teatime, but breasts and buttocks stilled in poses of reaching sensuality, contemplation, and near copulation.

Here, in a luminous three-dimensionality, was the thing I knew best: the kiss. Body untrapped, revealed. I stood, filling up with what no one could have anticipated, my own sensuality rising in response to the body held in lovely stone. I circled and circled, and nothing else of that visit to the Art Institute stayed with me except those two things: the tight miniature interiors and the larger-than-life flow of marbled bodies. That contradiction was beginning to speak of my life.

NOVENA

We believed in our right to a white Christmas. In the North, Christmas for good Catholics like our family, and even for some Methodists, must be marked by snow. It was not simply a hoped-for thing. This white blanket of cold made Christmas Christmas. It was required for the holiday to occur at all. The snowier the better. A skimmer would do if the days were crisp and clear, but the best holidays were doused with snow, thundered with it. We believed it right down to Christmas cards showcasing Bethlehem (complete with steeples) among snow-covered hillsides and northern constellations. Jesus, we knew in our heart of hearts, was born somewhere in North America, probably in northern Michigan, and those camels may have been some variation on a cow.

The best Christmas would consist of a good snowstorm starting the day before Christmas but tempered at first so wandering family members could make it home and talk about the roads drifting. *Gosh those north-south roads will be closed by morning! Bet on it.* To have a really good Christmas, there must be some threat that you won't get out to Midnight Mass, that you might turn back at the big curve where the visibility always goes bad, but your dad gasses it through the drifts, and you get to that service of services, though during mass, in the long majestic moment of the child, your siblings fall asleep to the sound of the wind as much as to the hymns.

After the baby is caroled to birth, you drive home from Midnight Mass. Now that northeaster has picked up, drifts threaten, and once or twice in your childhood, you get stuck on that last side road. Your father puts his hat back on and trudges to a familiar farmhouse, knocks, and apologizes. On that night of nights, the farmer and his boys come out with shovels, or they fire up the

John Deere. They step out into the wind, heads covered with plaid caps, and shovels rise and fall to free the tires while the family waits in the car. When it is done, your mom rolls down the window and thanks the snow-covered farmer, who tips his hat, and everyone wishes everyone a Merry Christmas. Then your dad is back in the car, shoulders dusted with snow, and you drive home through the squalls, happy and thrilled with the rightness of the world because there is snow.

My senior year, all through the four weeks of Advent—the burning of the purple-candled wreath down to the pink candle, those weeks of preparing for joy—warm spells eroded into mist and chilly rain. As we approached the sacred twenty-fifth, there was not even a crust of snow. Fogged up, short gray days crowded each other. Mornings and evenings were colored like dust with only a lighter variation at midday. Snow did not come.

Christmas my senior year was the rosary on Christmas Eve, then Midnight Mass honoring the new baby Jesus, a statue of discolored plaster with an oddly rosy face that had been placed into a manger with real hay. It was a church decorated with a dozen scotch pine trees cut from the plantation nearby and placed throughout the front of the church, sheltering a three-quarter-sized manger specially set up with layers of cotton drapery because new snow surely must have graced the desert where Jesus was born. And at the offertory, youngsters, my sisters among them as I had been before, placed gifts of canned food in front of the manger. Nels had driven out from his family's house to St. Joseph's, and we made room for him in the pew. Holding hands, we sang "Silent Night," which we all saw in our minds as a night of heavy snow. Which we had not got. Then my family drove home in their car, and Nels and I drove home through the fog in his car, nuzzling the whole way. We went home to eat a midnight breakfast of sausage, eggs, and cinnamon rolls until we were sated. We laughed and giggled, happy to be with each other.

That year, for the first time, our family had a second tree, not real (unheard of!) in the newly renovated family room, which had been converted from a garage, with its Franklin woodstove and red carpeting. This tree consisted of cellophane-like boughs with a light at the base that alternately shone red, green, or blue. An aluminum stem glittered in the middle like a tinfoil candle. It couldn't hold a candle to the real tree, the one in the proper living room, but it became the party tree.

My grandmother was with us, sitting in her chair, sipping a small cordial glass of Mogen David wine. How did she come to love Mogen David? No one knew. Only one glass and only on holidays. She was plump and white-haired, grinning in her eighties. She asked the question hanging over my future, the one my mother had given up on.

"So, you think you might go to college?"

I still had not applied.

I said, "Most applications don't close until February."

"Well, don't forget," she said sweetly.

As if that could happen. Still, I would try. Nels and I looked at each other, smiling giddily until my brother Tom stuck his finger in his mouth and made the gag gesture. Thoughts of college disappeared into the aluminum lights of the trees.

After a while, Nels and I separated ourselves, leaving my family laughing in the artificial light, and drifted into the living room to sit on the blue couch in front of the real tree for our own Christmas.

Later, he quietly slipped out, and I stayed there, touching my warm mouth with my fingertips.

What he gave me.

I sit alone on the blue couch, a young girl who doesn't quite know what to do. I had hoped, against all odds, for a ring—not an engagement ring but a bejeweled declaration, something to hold me in place. A promise ring. But he has so little money and is paying most of his school expenses, and maybe because he is so far away, he has given me something altogether different. I don't know what to do with it. I have thanked him. We have held hands for a long time, him tracing my fingers. We have been close and sincere and have declared our love again. We have kissed good-night with deep affection. He has gone back to his family who miss him and need him almost as much as I do.

So I am sitting alone when my mother, with some sixth sense, comes into the living room from the family room where she and dad have been listening to carols. She stops, picks up some dishes leftover from early snacks.

"Did Nels leave?" she asks.

"Uh-huh."

The silence extends.

"Is something wrong?" And then, seeing the empty spaces around me, she asked, "Oh, Anne, did he forget a Christmas present?"

"He gave me one." I hold the card up for her to see but don't give it to her.

"He gave you a nice card?"

"Um, something else." Her fears rise in the silence. She expects something else, fears most of all a proposal—but he wouldn't do that, would he? He has better sense. She looks at my hand. If I want a ring, she fears it most of all.

She waits. The lights on the tree burn against the needled green. Outside, a bluster of wind but no snow. I stare at our manger, the baby Jesus in our own simple crèche, draped with cotton, surrounded by pine boughs.

"He gave me a novena."

My mother stands in the dim light. This is a moment for her. This is the kind of thing she wants for her daughter. This is the kind of boy and the kind of relationship she wants for her daughter. She already knows our love is too young and too soon, and she has been unable to stop it. So it has come, this too-young, too-soon love, and she has had to watch. But she knows her daughter, knows the ring of a commitment was her daughter's wish. She knows this novena is the answer to her own prayer, a mother's prayer, a prayer that whatever happens between the boy and her daughter, it wouldn't be a too-young promise or the other kind of trouble.

"That's a beautiful gift. An important gift."

"I know."

I show her the number of rosaries, the days he will pray, the length of the time I am to be redressed from what I would suffer after my death. These are prayers he will say for the safety of my soul. These are prayers that will compensate for the sins I have committed, that will shorten, when I die, my time in purgatory. His prayer will alleviate my suffering in the afterlife.

It's a Catholic insurance policy.

My mother is quiet. "You are so blessed," she says. She doesn't elaborate.

There is a long moment until I say, "Uh-huh."

In a sudden burst, she says, "You really are. Oh, Anne, I hope you appreciate this. I hope you understand . . ." She says this with such conviction that I have to look at her. She is right. I do. This is the best gift, given with utter sincerity. This is a gift that no one could fault. This is a gift that will take his time, his thought, his intention. He will think of me and pray for my soul. And for a moment it all fits, a love so great that grace would be the promise, and all of it to keep me from suffering in eternity.

But it cannot hold; I am who I am. I wish he hadn't. I know I should be honored. I know I should be more than grateful. And I am. I tell myself I am. I nod and smile. My mother leaves, and I sit in the dark on the blue couch, the clunky lights shining on me. And it comes to me: I wonder exactly how many years in purgatory I have actually accumulated. Given the activities of the last year, I figure probably a lot. Probably, I realize with a start, so many that his novena will not even make a dent.

And another thought rises. It's not that the novena isn't a wonderful gift, but there's the assumption that I need his prayers. Yes, we are all sinners; I can certainly attest to that. But am I such a sinner that he has assumed that I really do need his prayers? Because, yes, there is no telling how long my purgatory will be—that is, if I even make it to purgatory. I think, well, it's nice that he at least assumes it will be purgatory. Yes, he was sincere, and to taint that purity with suspicion is sin on sin, but, gosh, what if his soul needs a novena, too? Maybe I should give him one back. Wait. Hadn't he participated in our sin? If I thought what we did was sin, wasn't he in on it, too? So how does that work, trading novenas? Novena for novena? Would we cancel each other out?

I look at the list of prayers, and I know. Shared sin or not, I could never stick with it for a whole novena—not because I'm a sinner, but because I have no interest in that much prayer for someone else, which, I suppose, does make me a sinner. And besides, I see it now: someone who would think to give me a novena probably wouldn't need a novena as badly as I need a novena.

Truth is, I wanted a thing that would stand outside myself for this young and selfish love. I wanted not the interiority of prayer but a circle to wear on my finger. I tell myself that I must teach myself deep appreciation of his gift, for it is clear that I am not mature enough to accept it with a pure heart. But a part of me, maybe most of me, leaps beyond and isn't giving a damn about my soul. I sit in the shadows and notice that some of the lights on the tree, perhaps the golden ones, are flickering like disappointment.

The next day, it snows so hard that the roads close. I don't see Nels until the day he leaves to go back to school. I cry so hard after he gets into his car and putt-putts out the driveway that I give myself a migraine, and then my period starts, and I am sick for a week.

LEARNING TO CURSE, 1969

That winter of 1969 was about a Ford Galaxie 500. White, four-door, red seats. Used but unrusted, unscratched, clean as a new soul, and not a glint of trouble except the gas. That big engine, a guzzler. But gosh, white. Farmers never buy white. And when it was washed, sparkling. Totally cool. A cherry of a car.

My father grinned, as proud as I've seen him of any tractor or plow. My mother pretended disapproval of this pretention but smiled quietly when Dad said, yes, he'd take it home. Secretly pleased, she knew he'd gotten a good deal. This was a car she could drive to church and say, *Well, the kids are growing up. We don't need a station wagon anymore.* For me, those woody wagons faded into the past. The Galaxie graduated the family, stepped us up. A Detroit miracle.

I discovered that the Galaxie cruised at eighty. I was driving, and my mother rode shotgun, and the car slipped up to that speed all on its own. I swerved a little, and she promptly insisted that I pull over. She took over the driving, scolding me all the way home. *For heaven's sake, Anne, I thought you knew how to drive.* I was forbidden driving it at all if I couldn't drive under the speed limit—preferably twenty, maybe twenty-five miles under.

I was forbidden even the excitement of speed.

March, wearing a sporty warm spell, slid back its icy cape—except in the north slopes and swamps where winter rags, sodden and dirty, might linger until May. The ice still pocked Lake Michigan, and though every day the light hung on an iota longer, the days cycled through gray mist. Winter lingered in its worst form.

The swamps kept the snow. The rivers held their rotting ice. I was bored out of my mind. My mother was mortifed. And worried. "What are you going to do?"

To answer her question, I should have said, *Wait for Nels*.

The hit song said it better: "There's something happening here. What it is ain't exactly clear."

A March weekend.

No, I wasn't accepted to Central.

No, Nels isn't coming home for prom.

No, I don't want to go to Michigan State.

Please, just let me have the car.

Let me have the car for one night.

My father was working midnights again, using the swing shift rotation so he could keep farming. So one evening, Mom relented, and I was allowed to take the Galaxie 500 to Hart, to the Pizza Place with Flip and Little Bear and whoever else might be there to hang out with.

Be home by eleven.

Far-out!

Be careful with the car.

She meant, *Do anything to that car, and you'll die.*

I understood.

So I drove to the Pizza Place on the edge of town along the river. The small joint offered pop and pizza, which, until the restaurant opened, we had experienced only through a box and a can. When there was no dance, when there was no date, when there was no play and the games were over, the Pizza Place with its cavelike ceilings drew us in. Here was white gooey crust and canned tomato sauce topped with processed cheese and the red wafers of pepperoni. Herbs, optional.

I picked up my friends, parked in the gravel lot, and we climbed out, happy and loud, slamming those solid doors in that meaningful way that says, *Look, look here: I have the car, this car, this white Galaxie, which is a galaxy unto itself*. I wanted everyone to see that car. What a gas. Me in it. I wished there had been a basketball game so more kids would be hanging out and we could drive around, tooting the horn and waving, and they would be impressed. But we strolled in, sat like we ate there every day at a table with red-and-white checkered tablecloths. We ordered pepperoni with extra cheese. We played with the long strands of mozzarella, laughing at the way it stretched. We greeted kids at other tables, and then, after all the goofiness with those canned mushrooms, and sated with sauce-laden dough and Pepsi, we eavesdropped on some dorky older boys going ape about the trouble with the draft, a lottery that was coming, a way you picked guys to go to Vietnam. They were in trouble, there was trouble, it was all trouble. But gosh, we just giggled. We were boss; they were badasses, but we had a Galaxie. Still, they made us uncomfortable, and we had an hour before I had to have the car back. The right plan would have been to run my friends home and drive back early, proving that I had some sense. That would be my mother's argument twelve hours later. But with that car, that Galaxie 500, that packed V-8, there was only one thing to do with that hour, and I had never done it before: take it out on the highway. Flip and Little Bear and me. *Buncha kids* tooling around. A story to tell on Monday, as though it happened every day. Far-out.

US Route 31: a seventy-mile stretch of gray concrete, a two-lane thoroughfare from Muskegon to Manistee and beyond. That highway was our thoroughfare to anywhere worth going, a channel to the rest of the world. We headed out, headed anywhere but where we were, the place to go changing by the minute. We turned north. North, all the way to . . . where? Nels? He was so far north that he was almost in another country. Still, the thought crossed my mind. And maybe that's why I did what I did.

We laughed, turned on the radio and flipped channels, sang along. *There's something happening here. What it is ain't exactly clear*. I took the Galaxie up to eighty again, and we rolled down the windows, and the air was wild and cold, but I slowed down almost immediately, too scared to push my luck. Little Bear complained that no one knew how to build the set for the one-acts because Nels wasn't there anymore. *Yeah, that's right. None of those freshmen know anything.* Truth be told, none of us were building sets either. Still, complaining felt like our due. We crossed the north branch of the Pentwater River. Just beyond that, Mason County loomed, out of our normal territory, beckoning to the North beyond.

We should turn around, give it up. But here is a two-track road, and isn't this the way to that old cabin? The Future Farmers of America cabin is back here in this pine plantation, isn't it? I turn onto the two-track road, clear of snow, and, yes, let's go find that old cabin. It has a fireplace. Let's drive east into woodland. Maybe it's open. Maybe the Future Farmers won't mind if we explore. It comes back to me, that old house with my mother, watching a mother break an oath. Sure. Just once, because I have the car.

We turn east, drive over the two-track road, which veers south through open field and meadow, parallel with the highway, then into a pine plantation for a couple of acres, then out where the scotch pine grow taller and crowd in a little more. It's darker. Little Bear is off and running with stories of how to trim pine trees, what terrible work it is, one of the few farm jobs I have never done and *don't want to, don't ya know*. We laugh. I realize the road runs perpendicular to the river but high above it, on the floodplain. That's good. We will drive east along the bluff. Then the two-track veers again, begins to descend parallel with the river, sloping down the bluff, down toward the river, not steeply but gradually so that for a while it doesn't seem like the wrong thing to do. Of course, the road would go down to the river, down to the side of the river. That's where the fishermen launch their boats. Halfway down, like a forgotten ghost, the snow-covered banks rise to the left of the car. A skimmer of crystal, nothing deep, appears on the road. I feel the tires slip, then hold with the weight of the car. We ride the brake to the bottom of the bluff where Flip says, in his understated way, "I don't think this is the road to the cabin."

He is right of course, and there is too much snow down here on the floodplain. In summer, the two-track road would run like a ribbon along a broad, sapling-covered, mosquito-infested plain. But now it is simply a field of ice with upright trunks like fence posts. I stop the car; we breathe for a moment. I shove the car in reverse, start to back up, but that slope, that slope. I need to turn around down here, so I can see what I'm doing. Then, on the riverbank, a clearing in the scrub trees, an open place, looks easy enough. In the headlights, *holy smokes*, the river runs out there, high and fast. We stare. Still, this spot looks solid, big enough to turn the Galaxie around.

I remember the rules for a three-point turn. I pull forward, turn the wheels, back slowly into the open place. Now we are nosed toward the two-track. I put the car into drive, begin to inch forward slowly. Certain moments change everything. We all feel the sickening lurch. It drops, not very far down, not a real sinking, which might have been easier to bear in some ways, but because it is a floodplain, we slip through rotten ice a few critical inches, then into the muck of a half-thawed floodplain. I have misjudged the ice as solid; we are stuck.

We try for an hour, rocking the big boat of the Galaxie from drive to reverse. Little Bear and Flip climb out on the ice, haul out some deadwood and prop it under the wheels, but it just slips. I have dug myself in up to the hubcaps. I climb out of the car; my sneakers sink into ruined ice, mucking my feet with river mud. We stand on the two track in the headlights and look at the car. It seems too near the river. What if it *sinks forever* or is swept away? Flip looks at the car, grins at me, says, *Nope, not a chance.* No comfort there. We need help.

How do we get back to the highway? We turn toward the dark. We trudge up the grade. There must have been some light. I remember standing on the high bluff, looking down, leaving the Galaxie, a fallen moon below us. We walk more of the two track in the dark, a long mile back through the plantations to US Route 31. We come to the shoulder, stand at the edge of gray concrete. Nearby a dark farmhouse looms, but none of us wants to do that. That means waking someone who will tell our folks.

Flip hatches a plan. We will go to Ian's house and ask Ian for help. *And how do we get there? It's at least ten miles.*

Flip lifts his thumb and wiggles it.

We are going to hitchhike?

I have never hitchhiked.

I am afraid to hitchhike.

I'm not hitchhiking.

Get over it.

Flip puts out his thumb in the cold air and takes that particular wide-legged stance. I sniffle. From the north headlights rise on the highway, coming fast. They speed past, spewing oily exhaust.

"You need to curse," Flip announces.

Curse? What's cursing got to do with it?

Cursing is forbidden in my family. Beyond my father's rare *damn it* and my mother's often-heard slip up of *oh shit*, no profanity crosses our lips—at least not in my parents' Catholic earshot. But Flip, an uncertain protestant, has hitchhiked. He puts his thumb to the wind and commands, "Curse."

I am silent.

To demonstrate he says, *Goddamn it.*

Damn it.

Not good enough. Goddamnit. He runs the words together.

Goddamnit.

Now slow it down. Say it like you mean it.

Goddamn. Loud and clear.

The next car slows, stops, and the back door swings open. A Ford with beer cans in the back. The couple is greasy but willing. Flip and Little Bear climb in. I halt at the door of the backseat, remembering stories of hitchhikers who were never seen again. Flip leans out and yanks me in.

"Just up the road," Flip says to the driver by way of explanation. "Car in the ditch." Oh, if it were only that simple.

We speed south on US Route 31.

Minutes later, we knock on Ian's redbrick farmhouse door where Ian's family, consisting of his Irish folks and Ian's nine or so siblings, Catholics all, live. When no one answers the knock, Flip lets himself in. We slip into the kitchen. Ian appears, tousled, pulling on his jacket but grinning. A little bit of trouble, and he will play God. Keys will do the trick. Is it really the front end of his dad's semitruck, the one his father uses to haul cherries, that we take that night? It was something big, something that didn't fit the task, but we didn't know that. We walk out to the barns, climb up into this cab, and start the thing with a puff of smoke. Little Bear sits on Flip's lap. In the middle, I squeeze my knees against the gearshifts. Ian takes the wheel, full of himself and the power of a big engine, and so four kids ride this workhorse north on US Route 31 with some rope, thinking this will get us out of trouble.

I tell myself that I'm only a couple of hours late. No need to call.

Back in the plantation, down the sloping two-track to the river, to the floodplain. Ian takes stock, looks at me, asks, "How the hell did you do that?"

Ian is driving bravely forward, laughing like crazy.

His face changes as the ground shifts to snow-covered mud. What is it about a big truck's unwieldy high center of gravity without a load? In about two minutes, we've shifted from average sort of kid trouble into much bigger trouble. By the time the semi is thoroughly embedded and blocking the Galaxie, we know beyond a doubt that this is too much for all of us.

Ian is saying, "We need something bigger."

Something bigger?

We hit the highway for the second time. We don't notice that the lights flicker on in the nearby farmhouse. We are just out there on the road.

Flip looks at me. "Four of us. This will be harder."

Oh.

Half a dozen cars pass us with nary a look. I keep up with the litany of Goddamns, joined by Little Bear who has no problem with profanity. "My dad swears like a sailor."

No one stops. Traffic thins.

Flip looks at me. "You'll have to say the big one."

Ian looks out at the highway, nodding, then looks at me and waits.

I can't do it.

Lights in the distance.

"Say it," Flip says.

"Fuck," Little Bear says softly, again by example. The big profanity. The biggest profanity in the world. The one I cannot say because I cannot do it.

"Louder," Flip says. Headlights pop in the north again. Little Bear says it, but the car passes without slowing.

Ian says, "The hitchhiking gods want a virgin." A virgin? "Come on, Annie. You can do it."

They all three stare at me. Overhead, the night has cleared, salted with cold stars. Headlights appear in the distance.

"Fuck," I say softly as the car nears us. The car slows but does not stop.

"Awwww, come on!" Flip says and frowns at the trailing headlights.

Ian says, "Flip, flip 'em off," and Flip gives them the finger, which startles me, and then I'm doubled over, almost sick with fear and a wild wheezing laughter, and Little Bear bends with me, both of us in high hysteria. I come up for air, and there it is: "Ohfuckohfuckohfuck."

FUCK!

The next vehicle is a beat-up hippie van. Plenty of room. They pull right over, and we run forward, and the door slides open, spilling out that rare scent of the summer. Ian shrugs at me, says, "It's hay."

We climb in. Ian and Flip talk eagerly.

I sit in silence, mouth tingling.

Back at Ian's, Bridget is up—red-haired Bridget, Ian's mother, and mother of their brood. She's standing at the stove, cigarette hanging, a glass of something brown on the table. On the stove in a frying pan sizzles a large steak and onions. She looks up, turning the steak, which smells suddenly thick and peppery. Here is someone no longer surprised by trouble. I am so happy to see her that I could cry. We tell her about the car, and then, yes, about the big truck. Her red eyebrows rise. "Pat's?" she asks, referring to her husband. We all know his reputation for impatience. She sits down and smokes half a cigarette. She looks at me.

"You. Call your mom." She looks at me again. "Call Dodges Towing and tell them they need the big one for this. Phone book's on the table."

She looks at all of us, gets up, and forks over the steak. "You meet the tow out on the highway, and show them where these vehicles are, and you stay there and sort this out."

My mother is sobbing when she picks up the phone, and that's worse than all the things she says later. I offer her a truncated version to assure her that we are all okay. She doesn't believe me. I tell her we're with Bridget. It doesn't help.

I call Dodges. He knows who I am. Yes, they have a truck. Yes, they'll pick us up on the way. *Really, four of you? Really, Pat Donelly's truck? Really, that white Galaxie your dad just bought?* It's a small town, and even the townies have noticed my father's choice of vehicle. And everyone knows Pat's farm operation right on the highway there. I realize with a start that this is not just about my family nor two families who happen to be in the same church fold and might, out of respect, keep things between them. Now the whole town is in on the rescue of the truck and the Galaxie.

Back on the highway, the tow picks us up. We are driving back to the plateau, back to the floodplain where everything, everything is stuck. When we turn off US Route 31, I notice the lights are on in that farmhouse. Figures move in the windows. Then we turn into the plantation and down the two-track road.

We are told to walk down to the car, and they will pull the semi out and then come for the car. My hands sweat, despite the cold, through a precarious moment when I think the tow truck, easing down the bluff road, will not be able to pull out the semi. It stalls, puffs; the gears shift, throaty and harsh. It comes to me, and I repeat the words softly, "Oh fuck oh fuck oh fuck," and Ian nods approval. Suddenly, the semi pulls free, then up the road and idling in the clear.

Now the Galaxie.

I slosh through the mud and into the car, turn it on, put it in neutral. The tow backs carefully down, hooks up. Dodges shakes his head at how close the river is, how far the car has dropped through the shelf ice, how the clots of mud have sprayed the chrome and the white finish with dark characters. He puts the tow truck in gear and tugs slowly, and it is like suction letting go, a slow unslurping out into the road, up the bluff. Now I am murmuring, *Thank you thank you thank you*, not to God exactly because I'm quite sure I am on God's shit list but to some force beyond me, powers of chance and fate. The car rests on the two-track road at last, facing the bluff road, and I think, *This will be okay now*. I just need to get it home, face my mother.

I put the car in drive and touch the gas with near reverence. It refuses. That perfect white Galaxie, now mud-covered, refuses to move. I try again, but it will not move in any gear. In and out, in and out the engine revs, but the car will not move. I hear a strange rattle, a gone-wrong sound. I climb out, run toward headlights, flag Dodges, ask him to try. He hurries. It's late, and he has another call. He gets in, repeats the process. In gear, out of gear. He climbs out, sighs, looks at me, and says, "Could be the transmission." I know what *transmission* means. I feel nauseous.

"We'll have to haul it in," he says. For the second time, he hooks up the tow and pulls the Galaxie, lumbering slowly, up the bluff toward the road, where he stops. Is that when the flickering red lights pierce the night, red flashers coming off the highway? The police car tools slowly up to the three vehicles. An officer gets out, nods at Dodges familiarly, who nods toward me and says, "She's the driver."

"All of you, back in the car." The officer says this with quiet authority. "All of you." Despite the angle of the tow, front end lifted, the boys climb in, and what this officer sees are two girls and two boys. He says by way of explanation, "Neighbor saw all the lights. Says you're disturbing the peace."

I try to explain. *No, no, no, nothing like that*. We were just stuck.

"You been drinking?" He interrupts.

I insist, *No, no, never*.

"So you were just driving around." He lets his voice make the statement with all the innuendo layered in. We sit in the light of his flashlight, now two boys and two girls, and he does the math. He makes all the assumptions. *Oh God, no. Don't tell my mom and dad that. Don't tell Nels that.* I'm past nausea all the way to fainting. I look across the dirty white hood, out over the bluff where the river runs fast and hard in this unruly spring, where my heart is sinking into the muck.

"What were you doing down there?" he asks, swinging the light toward the bluff and river.

"Just . . . just driving." Certainly not looking for the FFA cabin. We have that much sense. He asks for our driver's licenses, and though Little Bear and I can produce ours, neither boy has his.

He asks Ian who he is, and Ian says, "Flip Peters." And when the officer turns to Flip and asks the same question, Flip looks directly at the officer and says, "Ian Donelly."

I am stunned at their lies. How can they do this? Don't they know how much trouble we are—I am—in? But I look at their deadpan faces in the dash light, and I am awed at the brazenness, at the bold joke they play on each other. Laughter bubbles up again, and I am fighting a green hysteria in my throat. *Keep it together. Keep it together.* The officer says to *get out. Get on home. Behave yourselves.*

We climb out. Dodges pulls the white Galaxie onto the highway. I watch its dirty white finish disappear down the road. We get into the truck. Ian will drive us back to his house. We pack ourselves in, me jostled against the stick, and the words that take shape are not apology to my friends, my mother and father. The words are not even gratitude that we didn't drive ourselves into the river—as my mother will remind me a hundred times—but the huge profane words that I understand now contain wonder and despair at what the world can do to you when you aren't even thinking about it. Silently, I curse and curse and curse. Then, as the miles roll under the semi, I open my mouth, softly, over and over. My friends know, nodding, the depth of trouble, and sometimes they join me in a soft chorus of curses until the words shift from muttering anger to awe, to something sweet, a liturgy holy and broken into and stolen from the church. This liturgy says that the future, the whole world has to deal with wrongheadedness. There is a galaxy of trouble, and it belongs to everyone, and so we shouldn't say these things lightly. We should mean them because trouble is real and hard and needs its words, and you can drown or get hurt, and there must be words saved just for that. I say them until I know, like prayer, like hope, that these, too, are mine.

PSYCHEDELIC, 1969

Grounded for damages to the car, grounded for being irresponsible, grounded until I grew up. Grounded in my heart, too. Nels remained in that misbegotten college in the far north, oddly unsympathetic when I told him in a long and tearful phone call about the car. Grounded in my college plans. Grounded forever.

Mom reminded me that the final 4-H Achievement Day was in May. "You might just consider using this time to plan your project."

She stared into her coffee.

"You just want me to get the ten-year pin. That's all you care about." That would show her.

"Anne, you can't wait for Nels forever." How did she know these things?

"Then let me go out." How could I stop waiting for someone if I couldn't go out?

"And what will you learn from that?"

At that point, I would do almost anything to avoid learning whatever it was she and my dad wanted me to learn.

I'd show her.

I called my friend Gwen, who was in her first year at Grand Valley State College near Grand Rapids, two hours away. It took only minutes to arrange. After the call, I told my mother as she stood in the kitchen, trying for pineapple upside down cake.

"Gwen will be home this weekend."

"That's nice. You're still grounded, but she can come out here."

"I've been talking to her about Grand Valley."

"Grounded. Your dad said."

"He wants me to go to college."

"It's a little late for that."

"I'd like to visit Grand Valley."

"Why on Earth?" Do I sense a flash of relief?

"A lot of kids visit colleges before going." I pretended to be casual.

"I believe they are accepted first."

"I'd know then if I liked it. Then I'm not wasting the application fee."
She thought about this. I came in for the clincher.

"Mom, she's coming home on Friday to see Flip, but she has to go back on Saturday morning to study for a test. She could take me. I could stay over until Monday and talk to admissions. I'd get to see the campus and spend time with the girls who are her roommates."

"She has an apartment?"

"It's on campus. I'd be supervised."

She poured a cup of coffee that had been so long in the percolator that I could smell the burn.

"My grades are up. Maybe they'll take me." I watched her face. Why did I get the feeling that she was smug?

If so, she played it well. "They would have taken you at State." Michigan State had been the one school where my parents could have helped me get in. I had refused.

"Mom, I'm grounded for being immature and stupid. State? Really? You're just making me feel guilty." She was silent for a moment. Did she bite her tongue?

She let me go.

I didn't tell her about the party that Gwen had invited me to. I didn't tell her that I was far less interested in applying than in simply going somewhere, anywhere, away. If I couldn't go all the way to Lake Superior State, then just let me get away.

Grand Valley was located outside of Grand Rapids, one of the most conservative cities in the state. But the college, on the edge of cornfields in the middle of a farming region, was new and progressive. On a Saturday morning, I drove south with Gwen, giggling with freedom all the way to her apartment complex, where I would go to a college party.

I didn't grasp that I would also spend part of the weekend on my own walking the campus because Gwen really did go to the library to study for several hours. Once we'd passed through the wide doors, she explained quickly how to use the stacks, where to find my favorite fiction. She settled into a carrel. Once I realized she really was going to study, the last thing I wanted to do on this first weekend of freedom was to sit and read. I left her, stepped out of the library, and walked down wide steps and out onto the campus—open sky, fields in the distance, deep ravines spanned by foot-bridges. On one bridge, I stopped, looked down through the branches into a tributary creek of the Grand River, then up and out through the canopy of trees. I studied the lay of the land. It was April, and though this campus was just two hours south of Hart, here was an earlier inland spring.

The campus was small but handsome. New buildings with graceful architecture gleamed in the sun and new grass. This campus was not grand and old like State, not agricultural. It did not sponsor programs like 4-H. There were only a few thousand students. I had no history here. I had one friend. I stood on the bridge over the ravine. I felt a small click in the brain, like a photograph you didn't know you would take, but when you get it back, something of how you'd like to see yourself is in the accident of it. An unexpected image. The truth was, I couldn't get into Lake Superior State College. That had been the thing I had never said. No one had. But if I came here, what would it mean? I had cursed my way through trouble. I had been grounded. I had waited and waited.

Could I apply? And if I got in, could I come here and still have Nels in my life?

I went to the party. I saw, for the first time, black light—it's distortion of color. I listened to people only a scant year or two older speak of Students for a Democratic Society, the war going bad, the cool thing called the Summer of Love that, too bad, you kids coming up have missed. LSD. I learned at last the meaning of the word *psychedelic*. I was informed by a girl dressed in a tunic of bright fluorescent colors who smoked long cigarettes that it meant *mind made manifest*.

Before I left, I completed and turned in the application, talked to admissions. Yes, I could still apply. Yes, they were still accepting. No, there was no scholarship money left for fall semester, but if I made good grades in the first semester, I would be eligible for the second. In the meantime, there was the National Defense Education Act.

I could borrow money? The thought was dangerous and monumental.

All the long miles home, I felt oddly hopeful, interested, eager. Something was happening. But when I walked back into the house, I was still grounded. I wouldn't know about my acceptance for weeks. Nels was still gone. I wondered why I had bothered.

But this much had changed: a dress for my last 4-H Achievement Day took shape in my mind. Yes, I would earn the damned ten-year pin. I would do as she asked and enter a final gown. But it wouldn't be what she expected; it would be—I was so excited that I would laugh into my pillow—psychedelic. Psychedelic felt ripe, stripped of the romantic: clashing colors; the Beatles and *Sergeant Pepper's* and the *Magical Mystery Tour*; pink that did not occur in the natural world, orange so vivid that it faded the sunset, and yellow so bright that you had to look away but then could not.

I had one thought: I was going to wake everyone up. My last 4-H project would be psychedelic.

My first gambit: "If you want me to do a project, I need to go to Muskegon," I said with a "so there" attitude.

She drove.

The fabric store fills us with dreams. Wool, gabardine, cotton, velvet, and lace dreams. Bolts piled twenty high in slick new colors dreams. Buttons, zippers, and spools for every palette. Resting on great angled tables, the pattern books opened to dreams not just from McCall's, Butterick, and Simplicity but also Vogue. Vogue dreams. Patterns from France. Dreams spiraled, lined up, stacked so high that clerks climbed ladders to reach the top. Dreams for every occasion for dresses we hadn't yet imagined, but they slipped into our consciousness as we walked the fabric canyons, ran our hands over dreams of ourselves. Here was who we could be. More than boyfriends or college, these sewing dreams would give me a thousand pictures of myself.

Mind made manifest.

And then I touched it. Rainbow. Two layers. One a thin satin rainbow, the other tissue-thin of the same rainbow but swirling like a frosted window. You cut out both layers as one. You had to sew this tissue and this lining as though they were the same. Hard, so hard. But I saw how it could be done. The pattern, an A-line shift to the floor, indicated no trim, just clean-as-a-whistle lines to showcase the fabric. The colors shimmered and moved, a rainbow reshaping with every move. It was expensive because it was essentially two dresses. Double trouble. Mom saw it, tried to lure me away.

"Showcase your skills, not a fabric," she said.

I did not hear her. I wanted to make a dress of every feeling I felt—not just the yellow of my longing for love or the pink or white lace of store-bought girlhood but the whole range of what I was beginning to see and feel. If I was what I was wearing—part of the unwritten oath of 4-H—then this was the fabric. These were layers of being. I bought the minimum amount of the rainbow fabric, rippling psychedelic in my hands. Mind made manifest. We walked out of the store with my psyche in my arms, brown-paper-wrapped dreams.

The concept was right, but the gown was doomed. The stripes had to match, layer over layer. But when I lined them up, I was short on the underlayer. The top, with its carefully fitted neck and shoulders, offered no opportunity for saving fabric. The sacrifice had to be made at the hem. We discovered I was taller than I thought, and that growth, once again, had occurred in my legs. The dress would not touch the floor, would not sweep, would not flow. The skirt stopped at the ankle, turning the dress into a weird high-water gown, spindled by my too-big feet.

I was awarded a red ribbon for workmanship. The hem, which I had pieced for another inch of the length, was not acceptable. My mother stopped speaking to me except to remind me, "You have to model that thing, you know." She was ashamed of the red ribbon and ashamed of this otherworldly too-bright dress. Her mind was made manifest in her silence. I gave up again and called Nels, who laughed and said, "You are a rainbow." I would wait as long as it took.

ACHIEVEMENT DAY, 1969

I haven't heard from Grand Valley yet, but my ally, Gwen, is home, unpacked and settling back in by helping Mrs. Carlson in the home ec room. We are catching up in the art room, moping over the peanut butter sandwiches, surrounded by newly hung freshmen expressionism, terror in acrylic. I am morose about the modeling showcase that will happen that night, the red ribbon, my mother's silence. The dress, I know, looks awful on me. In contrast, Gwen has made a beautifully tailored red suit, a startling success, making her look like an elegant postwar character.

"What are you going to do?" she asks as she picks peanut butter out of her teeth.

"Burn it."

She nods. I sigh.

"Model it I guess. Don't want to."

"The colors are pretty. Maybe they won't notice the hem."

"They'll notice my big feet."

We both look down at my size nines as if by looking hard we might change them to something delicate.

"Even with big feet, you've got great legs, even longer than they were yesterday."

"Nobody will see the legs for the size of these clodhoppers."

"You could wear those black flats. Less obvious."

"Mom said I have to wear the yellow platforms because I spent all that money on them."

"Platforms don't even go with that kind of dress."

"Tell her that."

Gwen is thoughtful. "That length is kind of close to that new midi length. They were showing that cut at mid calf. You could change the narration to say it's showing that, make it seem like it's on purpose."

I have thought about showcasing that length as some new fashion. But no. "Let's face it: the dress looks like a tent perched on pillars either way. It's too short to flow, too long to look sporty. To make it worse, I'll probably grow another quarter inch by tonight."

Gwen giggles. "By tonight, the dress will be a mini on you."

I shoot her a scowl, chew my nails.

We turn to each other slowly.

I say it first: "A miniformal."

"A minisemiformal."

"A minisemi."

She laughs. Then she stops. I can see her planning, and I head her off. "We model in seven hours. There's no chance. Even if I could get the dress, it's a double hem. We'd have to measure and cut, and I'd have to hem two layers."

She grabs my hand. "Can you see it?"

This is the line we use with each other. This is the line that 4-H has taught us through ten years. Can we visualize how it will look? That's the way you think in 4-H. When you choose the raw material, can you see a future? Whether it's the dress, the full-grown steer, the high-stepping horse, or the beautiful rabbit with the rare ears, can you see your rough-hewn dream? Can I see this now-lost sweeping gown as something short, really short?

"How?" Implementation is the trick.

There's a reason Gwen has created an outfit that looks like the power suits two decades ahead of our time. "You have a free period, and you're teacher's aid after that. Go over to that gym right now. It should be open 'cause they're setting up. Bring the dress back to Mrs. Carlson's room. I'll meet you there."

Mrs. Carlson's room, where Gwen is helping out, is the one room guaranteed to have sharp scissors, a sewing machine, needle, thread, and, most important of all, a waist-to-floor hem stand, a rare piece of efficiency for cutting a dress short.

And like that, we're running away from the table, abandoning expressionism to its garish colors, leaving the remains of peanut butter sandwiches for startled friends. We're running, two girls, down the long hall, seeing it all.

After the mad dash to the old gym, after the startling theft of the dress off the exhibit rack, after running the streets with the dress on its hanger trailing like a rainbow over my shoulders, we head back in the home ec room. Dear competent Gwen has persuaded Mrs. C that we are good girls in a bit of a bind who need to use her room, er . . . actually all of her sewing equipment.

I stand on the home ec table for twenty minutes while Gwen measures and pins the skirt at a daring length right at the middle of my thigh. I turn that complete and slow circle. And then it's time for the cut. I slip it off.

We stare at the fabric, pinned and laying on the table.

"I can't do it."

She picks up the sheers and makes the first small cut through the layers of rainbow. "There, now you have to."

"Okay." I nod. I have the skills and the means and the finesse and the love of show and the friend who will help. I have my head and hands and health and heart right there as I have been taught, and I am using them to sever layers of psychedelic rainbow. I cut the fabric, snip with slow care, following the line of pins. At last, the freed strip of skirt and hem slips off the table to the floor, a ring of rainbow crumpled at our feet. We lift the dress, turn the edges, and press and pin again, steady in this endeavor. We each take one layer of the hem and spend the next hour side by side connected by these bright colors in two layers, using the piercing needles as we have been taught, and the 4-H secret hem stitch that hides and binds everything.

Minutes before the bell rings, I slip it on and stand in front of the full-length mirror. We both gasp. It is very short, and my long legs are showing more skin than I thought possible. But the dress is what I never dreamed: fun and sassy and wildly sexy. Dressy, yes, but unexpectedly me, my minisemi, bright with defiance.

At the edge of the light, I hand off the narration card for the mistress of ceremonies to read. I walk into the light, concentrating on not letting the yellow platforms hit the wooden floor too hard. I hear the sharp intake of breath as the audience takes in this dress. I step forward, hear a murmur. The dress is daring. The dress is new. The dress is working and strong. And I am strong in it with my long legs and my big feet in the platforms creating a crazy compliment to the whole outfit.

Only as I listen in the light do I realize I have not rewritten the narration for the dress, and so I am modeling a dress different from the one being described. Suddenly, I am not the girl that 4-H narration is saying I am. I am the girl in the short dress with the long legs and the big feet made for traveling. I am the girl for whom the world will never quite match what is being said.

I am the girl who will embarrass her mother.

After we drive home that night, at that old farmhouse in the beautiful spring evening, after she has scolded me to tears, after we have fought about my arrogance, audacity, oversight, and that *ridiculous dress* (which I am still wearing, though now with dirty sneakers), we both walk into the kitchen. The thin light falls on a scattering of old newspapers and mail.

"Please make yourself useful and clean off the table," she says briskly.

She leaves to empty a load of laundry, muttering her way out the door. Exhausted, I sink into a chair, put my head down on the old oak table. What have I done? After a while, I stand, pick up the newspaper, gather the odd envelopes, and head for the trash.

Does it happen that night? Is that the night I bend to drop them all in, an act I carry out a dozen times a month, but this time, one corner of a wide envelope catches my eye.

When it is open and read, I carry it outside. There, in the early dark, in the spill of light from the house, under the maple tree that has accompanied every childhood fantasy, I read it again and again. My mother, coming from laundry or kitchen or bedrooms, someplace in that rambling house, impatience oozing out of every pore, opens the screen and starts with, "I asked you to . . ." She sees my eyes, the letter, and stops.

"Grand Valley accepted me."

We look at each other, the long question between us. She leans on the frame, faces the orchard to the south that's just now coming into bloom, a spirit light opening on a few branches. She sighs, nods at me, gives me the smallest smile. The screen door closes, and she returns to the kitchen, leaving me in the last light, holding a future I can at last see.

THE MOON

It was about to happen.

Nels and I curled together under a coarse blanket on the floor of Gwen's living room. She and Flip were somewhere else in the house. The low sound of the TV fogged through our kisses. On the gray screen were images of the moon. We knew it was close, knew it was near, this moment. *Apollo* was circling; the *Eagle* had landed.

As the announcers counted off the moments, we shrugged ourselves up and stared at the screen. We saw the *Eagle*, that small strange capsule, and heard the voice saying, "One small step . . ." We sat in the living room of my best friend's house and stared at what was happening on the moon. We were there, one small step away from . . . I leaned forward, hugged my knees, held out my hands, and he took them. We sat amazed, and, because we were young and full of belief in ourselves and the world, not amazed. Of course, this had been done. Of course, we were witness to it. After that decade of despair, our nation had put the first man on the moon. We accepted the unbelievable as we had accepted so many other unbelievable things. We watched for a long time, knowing this was our norm; we were young in the time of the man on the moon. It had been the oath of a dead president. It had been a goal through the years when the country was coming apart. It had been done. The black-and-white images were huge with meaning.

After we had taken it in, we lay down again on the rug with the blanket and held each other and promised not to forget this moment. We spoke that much, and then we didn't speak anymore—though the TV droned on and on. Say what you will, it was a sacred moment for the country. Yet we wanted what we wanted—the feel of each other—so we accepted the unbelievable and returned to those two lunatics, love and sex. The promises made or fulfilled in that moment came and went to history. They were important but small compared to touch, to the heat of our hands and mouths.

A few weeks after the moon landing, I was back at the Drift Inn. I came racing up the steps a little late for the dinner shift, but after the screen door to the kitchen slammed, I entered a quiet kitchen. Cook was not playing the radio; the dishes were not done. I walked to the back room, a narrow area where we wrote up our checks. Alice came out of the dining room, her eyes red, her breathing ragged.

"Are you all right?"

She looked at me, her eyes lost. "You don't know?"

I knew this feeling, this silence before . . .

It was the boy, the sweet dishwasher boy who we tipped nightly, the boy who had taken me with him whenever someone had a car. He was younger than me by two years but a little on the wild side, fun, part of the weave of summer and sunny days. We saw him every day and yet did not see him.

"Out on River Road. That big old tree on the curve. That one just before you drive into the valley, right on the curve."

Missed the curve?

Going really fast.

Him. Three others.

Three? Four?

One might live.

He's . . . ?

The day went white and empty.

They had closed the restaurant over lunch to visit his family, but they would open for dinner; it was still high season. Alice was in no shape to work. Would I take her tables? I walked from room to room, table to table, mouthing empty words, serving food that had no scent, hearing only the roar of cars on the street. I looked at people's faces, smiled automatically, said the right words. Here were beach people, hippies, the polished summer folks, sailors and beats. I watched them sipping coffee, lifting French fries dolloped in ketchup, laughing. I thought about the wreck, about the way he always asked if I wanted to go. I had to stop twice, standing at the line trying to sort out an order I didn't remember taking. From the grill, Cook looked at me, shook his head. "Don't stop," he said. Once he whispered hoarsely, "Keep it together."

No one bussed tables; we cleared our own. Late that night, Alice's mother came in and did dishes for two hours straight, sobbing into the dirty water. I closed out, counted my tips, pulled the 10 percent cut for him, and carried it to the kitchen, holding the bills and change in my hands. Alice's mother said, "You don't have to . . ." then handed me his tip jar, and I dropped his cut in. She set it back on his shelf, over the steaming water.

Through those ten years, through all the national and international events, through riots and assassinations, the oaths and the prayers had protected me even as I wore them down, twisted them, and broke them. Even when I had not felt safe, even when I had run, I had been quietly protected by what they taught me and by my love for Nels.

I had not gone in the cars with them all summer though I had wanted to.

I had worked blindly, saving for college. I had been too tired and more interested in Nels and . . .

What were the chances?

That day, stepping from kitchen to dining room and back, I looked at all the people. Did they know death this way? Though it was supposed to be winding down, the war was still rocking the world. Had it touched them? We had seen riots and marches gone violent. Assassinations. Deaths of talented people to drugs and darker things. Who among them had felt that? If this happened here, to me, then we could not trust the world to protect us. And all this was happening while I was playing dress-up in dozens of colors, in lace and rainbows. It was gone at last, the sweetness. I was about to live my life.

That summer, Nels transferred to Grand Valley. In the fall we would both attend the same college, and we would both try and then not try and then try again to date other people. We would be the kind of couple who came back to each other over and over for nearly two more years—sometimes so in love that we could not bear it, sometimes so uncertain that we cried over this casualty of change. And then it would happen, a slow ending as we both entered different forms of activism, as we both became involved in ways to protest the injustices of our time—he through science and medicine, me through art. It would be me who would end it for good and all, answering the call of some dream that could not bear the continuation of love in the form of the daily ordinary. I got involved with the theater, with its glitz and wonder, and with the boys of the theater, their glitz and wonder. No turning back from that.

The old oaths lost their hold, but what was left? The real skills—the knowledge of how a thing could be made, shaped from a past, recreated to make something new—would hold. I would always know how to make something from little to nothing, would always know how to look at a pattern, to take whole cloth and shape it into an actual thing to be worn with grace. The possibilities in the act of *making* would always excite me no matter how inadequate the materials. I would become a being who made things. As I turned the corner into the seventies, I would rely on that and the deep corollaries of what it meant to give my hands over to some work and to have my healthy ordinary life. I would eventually learn to use my head—though that part would be hard won. I would know how to love because once I had truly pledged my heart.

ACKNOWLEDGMENTS

Deep and sincere thanks to all of the following:

- Annie Martin, acquisitions editor at WSUP, who took on the initial editing of this project, kept me from wandering, and told me what I was trying to say in plain words. Also, to Carrie Teefey, Emily Nowak, Kristina Stonehill, and all the staff at WSUP who make it easier to be a writer, and sincerest thanks to Tracy Schoenle for the difficult task of copyediting.
- Early readers Katey Schultz and Teresa Scollon.
- My writers' groups:
  - Powerfingers: Mardi Link, Heather Shumaker, Cari Noga.
  - The Swans: Fleda Brown, Teresa Scollon (again), Jennifer Stienorth.
- Michigan Writers, Inc. and the many members who shape our writing community.
- Doug Stanton and the National Writers Series for further elevating the literary culture that permeates our region.
- My beloved friends in the Beach Bards, twenty-five plus years and still saying poems of the heart: Norm Wheeler, Bronwyn Jones, Joe Vander-Muelen, as well as Bobby Sutherland and "Fuzz."
- Mimi Wheeler for the good chocolate and the good talk.
- The sauna family (you know who you are) for the lively camaraderie of artists.

- Interlochen Arts Academy colleagues who have supported this book in untold ways: David Griffith, Mika Perrine, Lesley Tye, francine harris, and Vice-President of Education Ted Farraday.
- My Interlochen students, recent and past, for seventeen years modeling over and over how this must be done.
- The Solstice MFA in Creative Writing at Pine Manor College: all my dear colleagues and particularly Meg Kearney and Tanya Whiton for their support and patience as I balanced deadlines. Much gratitude also to the amazing student body and alumni who inspire me with their courage.
- Michael Delp, Jack Driscoll, and Aaron Stander for all kinds of writerly support.
- The Oomen family: my parents, Ruth and the late John Oomen, Tom Oomen, Rick Oomen, Marijo Bakker, and Pat Harpe for tolerating my version of our shared lives.
- The community of Hart: though you are altered in words, you are not altered in my heart.
- S. Theo Early and Caitlin Stanley for being family.
- Finally, but most important of all, to David Early, my beloved husband and partner in all things. Without you pen does not touch paper.